CASENOTE LEGAL BRIEFS

WILLS & TRUSTS

Adaptable to courses utilizing **Dukeminier** and **Johanson's**
casebook on Wills, Trusts and Estates

NORMAN S. GOLDENBERG, SENIOR EDITOR
PETER TENEN, MANAGING EDITOR

STAFF WRITERS

TERRY MOLLOY
ROBERT SWITZER
RICHARD LOVICH
JAMES ROSENTHAL
SUZAN YUDELSON
TED PETERSON
SALLY MOLLOY
PATRICIA LAIACONA
STEVEN McGINTY
INGE VAN HERLE

ALSO AVAILABLE!
WILLS, TRUSTS & ESTATES
OUTLINE
This Casenote Legal Briefs volume
is now cross-referenced to the new
Casenote Law Outline
on Wills, Trusts & Estates
by Prof. William M. McGovern

PUBLISHED BY **CASENOTES PUBLISHING CO., INC.** 1640 5th ST., SUITE 208, SANTA MONICA, CA 90401

ISBN 0-87457-068-9

FORMAT FOR THE CASENOTE LEGAL BRIEF

PARTY ID: Quick identification of the relationship between the parties.

NATURE OF CASE: This section identifies the form of action (e.g., breach of contract, negligence, battery), the type of proceeding (e.g., demurrer, appeal from trial court's jury instructions) or the relief sought (e.g., damages, injunction, criminal sanctions).

FACT SUMMARY: This is included to refresh the student's memory and can be used as a quick reminder of the facts.

CONCISE RULE OF LAW: Summarizes the general principle of law that the case illustrates. It may be used for instant recall of the court's holding and for classroom discussion or home review.

FACTS: This section contains all relevant facts of the case, including the contentions of the parties and the lower court holdings. It is written in a logical order to give the student a clear understanding of the case. The plaintiff and defendant are identified by their proper names throughout and are always labeled with a (P) or (D).

ISSUE: The issue is a concise question that brings out the essence of the opinion as it relates to the section of the casebook in which the case appears. Both substantive and procedural issues are included if relevant to the decision.

HOLDING AND DECISION: This section offers a clear and in-depth discussion of the rule of the case and the court's rationale. It is written in easy-to-understand language and answers the issue(s) presented by applying the law to the facts of the case. When relevant, it includes a thorough discussion of the exceptions to the case as listed by the court, any major cites to other cases on point, and the names of the judges who wrote the decisions.

CONCURRENCE / DISSENT: All concurrences and dissents are briefed whenever they are included by the casebook editor.

EDITOR'S ANALYSIS: This last paragraph gives the student a broad understanding of where the case "fits in" with other cases in the section of the book and with the entire course. It is a hornbook-style discussion indicating whether the case is a majority or minority opinion and comparing the principal case with other cases in the casebook. It may also provide analysis from restatements, uniform codes, and law review articles. The editor's analysis will prove to be invaluable to classroom discussion.

CROSS-REFERENCE TO OUTLINE: Wherever possible, following each case is a cross-reference linking the subject matter of the issue to the appropriate place in the *Casenote Law Outline*, which provides further information on the subject.

QUICKNOTES: Conveniently defines legal terms found in the case and summarizes the nature of any statutes, codes, or rules referred to in the text.

PALSGRAF v. LONG ISLAND R.R. CO.

Injured bystander (P) v. Railroad company (D)

N.Y. Ct. App., 248 N.Y. 339, 162 N.E. 99 (1928).

NATURE OF CASE: Appeal from judgment affirming verdict for plaintiff seeking damages for personal injury.

FACT SUMMARY: Helen Palsgraf (P) was injured on R.R.'s (D) train platform when R.R.'s (D) guard helped a passenger aboard a moving train, causing his package to fall on the tracks. The package contained fireworks which exploded, creating a shock that tipped a scale onto Palsgraf (P).

CONCISE RULE OF LAW: The risk reasonably to be perceived defines the duty to be obeyed.

FACTS: Helen Palsgraf (P) purchased a ticket to Rockaway Beach from R.R. (D) and was waiting on the train platform. As she waited, two men ran to catch a train that was pulling out from the platform. The first man jumped aboard, but the second man, who appeared as if he might fall, was helped aboard by the guard on the train who had kept the door open so they could jump aboard. A guard on the platform also helped by pushing him onto the train. The man was carrying a package wrapped in newspaper. In the process, the man dropped his package, which fell on the tracks. The package contained fireworks and exploded. The shock of the explosion was apparently of great enough strength to tip over some scales at the other end of the platform, which fell on Palsgraf (P) and injured her. A jury awarded her damages, and R.R. (D) appealed.

ISSUE: Does the risk reasonably to be perceived define the duty to be obeyed?

HOLDING AND DECISION: (Cardozo, C.J.) Yes. The risk reasonably to be perceived defines the duty to be obeyed. If there is no foreseeable hazard to the injured party as the result of a seemingly innocent act, the act does not become a tort because it happened to be a wrong as to another. If the wrong was not willful, the plaintiff must show that the act as to her had such great and apparent possibilities of danger as to entitle her to protection. Negligence in the abstract is not enough upon which to base liability. Negligence is a relative concept, evolving out of the common law doctrine of trespass on the case. To establish liability, the defendant must owe a legal duty of reasonable care to the injured party. A cause of action in tort will lie where harm, though unintended, could have been averted or avoided by observance of such a duty. The scope of the duty is limited by the range of danger that a reasonable person could foresee. In this case, there was nothing to suggest from the appearance of the parcel or otherwise that the parcel contained fireworks. The guard could not reasonably have had any warning of a threat to Palsgraf (P), and R.R. (D) therefore cannot be held liable. Judgment is reversed in favor of R.R. (D).

DISSENT: (Andrews, J.) The concept that there is no negligence unless R.R. (D) owes a legal duty to take care as to Palsgraf (P) herself is too narrow. Everyone owes to the world at large the duty of refraining from those acts that may unreasonably threaten the safety of others. If the guard's action was negligent as to those nearby, it was also negligent as to those outside what might be termed the "danger zone." For Palsgraf (P) to recover, R.R.'s (D) negligence must have been the proximate cause of her injury, a question of fact for the jury.

EDITOR'S ANALYSIS: The majority defined the limit of the defendant's liability in terms of the danger that a reasonable person in defendant's situation would have perceived. The dissent argued that the limitation should not be placed on liability, but rather on damages. Judge Andrews suggested that only injuries that would not have happened but for R.R.'s (D) negligence should be compensable. Both the majority and dissent recognized the policy-driven need to limit liability for negligent acts, seeking, in the words of Judge Andrews, to define a framework "that will be practical and in keeping with the general understanding of mankind." The Restatement (Second) of Torts has accepted Judge Cardozo's view..

[For more information on foreseeability, see Casenote Law Outline on Torts, Chapter 8, § II. 2., Proximate Cause.]

QUICKNOTES

FORESEEABILITY - The reasonable anticipation that damage is a likely result from certain acts or omissions.

NEGLIGENCE - Failure to exercise that degree of care which a person of ordinary prudence would exercise under similiar circumstances.

PROXIMATE CAUSE - Something which in natural and continuous sequence, unbroken by any new intervening cause, produces an event, and without which the injury would not have occurred.

NOTE TO STUDENT

OUR GOAL. It is the goal of Casenotes Publishing Company, Inc. to create and distribute the finest, clearest and most accurate legal briefs available. To this end, we are constantly seeking new ideas, comments and constructive criticism. As a user of *Casenote Legal Briefs,* your suggestions will be highly valued. With all correspondence, please include your complete name, address, and telephone number, including area code and zip code.

THE TOTAL STUDY SYSTEM. Casenote Legal Briefs are just one part of the Casenotes TOTAL STUDY SYSTEM. Most briefs are (wherever possible) cross-referenced to the appropriate *Casenote Law Outline,* which will elaborate on the issue at hand. By purchasing a Law Outline together with your Legal Brief, you will have both parts of the Casenotes TOTAL STUDY SYSTEM. (See the advertising in the front of this book for a list of Law Outlines currently available.)

A NOTE ABOUT LANGUAGE. Please note that the language used in *Casenote Legal Briefs* in reference to minority groups and women reflects terminology used within the historical context of the time in which the respective courts wrote the opinions. We at Casenotes Publishing Co., Inc. are well aware of and very sensitive to the desires of all people to be treated with dignity and to be referred to as they prefer. Because such preferences change from time to time, and because the language of the courts reflects the time period in which opinions were written, our case briefs will not necessarily reflect contemporary references. We appreciate your understanding and invite your comments.

A NOTE REGARDING NEW EDITIONS. As of our press date, this Casenote Legal Brief is current and includes briefs of all cases in the current version of the casebook, divided into chapters that correspond to that edition of the casebook. However, occasionally a new edition of the casebook comes out in the interim, and sometimes the casebook author will make changes in the sequence of the cases in the chapters, add or delete cases, or change the chapter titles. Should you be using this Legal Brief in conjuction with a casebook that was issued later than this book, you can receive all of the newer cases, which are available free from us, by sending in the "Supplement Request Form" in this section of the book (please follow all instructions on that form). The Supplement(s) will contain all the missing cases, and will bring your Casenote Legal Brief up to date.

EDITOR'S NOTE. Casenote Legal Briefs are intended to supplement the student's casebook, not replace it. There is no substitute for the student's own mastery of this important learning and study technique. If used properly, *Casenote Legal Briefs* are an effective law study aid that will serve to reinforce the student's understanding of the cases.

Totally free access to briefs online!

Download the cases you want to include in your notes or outlines with full cut and paste abilities. Please fill out this form to be given access. No photocopies of this form will be accepted.

①   **Name:** _____   **Phone:** (____) _____

     Address: _____   **Apt.:**_____

     City: _____   **State:**_____   **Zip Code:** _____

     Law School: _____   **Year (circle one):**   1st   2nd   3rd

②   **Cut out the UPC found on the lower left hand corner on the back cover of this book. Staple the UPC inside this box. Only the original UPC from this book will be accepted. (No photocopies are allowed.)**

③   **E-mail address:** _____

④   **Title (course subject) of this book:** _____

     Adaptable to which casebook author: _____

⑤   **Mail the completed form to:**   Casenote Online Access
                                          1640 Fifth Street, Suite 208
                                          Santa Monica, CA 90401

⑥   I understand that online access is granted solely to the purchaser of this book for the academic year in which it was purchased. Any other usage is not authorized and will result in immediate termination of access. Sharing of codes is strictly prohibited.

_____
                        Signature

Upon receipt of this completed form, you will be e-mailed codes so that you may access the briefs found in this book at www.casenotes.com.

SUPPLEMENT REQUEST FORM

At the time this book was printed, a brief was included for every major case in the casebook and for every existing supplement to the casebook. However, if a new supplement to the casebook (or a new edition of the casebook) has been published since this publication was printed and if that casebook supplement (or new edition of the casebook) was available for sale at the time you purchased this Casenote Legal Briefs book, we will be pleased to provide you the new cases contained therein AT NO CHARGE when you send us a stamped, self-addressed envelope.

TO OBTAIN YOUR FREE SUPPLEMENT MATERIAL, **YOU MUST FOLLOW THE INSTRUCTIONS BELOW PRECISELY** OR YOUR REQUEST WILL NOT BE ACKNOWLEDGED!

1. Please check if there is in fact an existing supplement and, if so, that the cases are not already included in your Casenote Legal Briefs. Check the main table of cases as well as the supplement table of cases, if any.

2. **REMOVE THIS ENTIRE PAGE FROM THE BOOK.** You MUST send this ORIGINAL page to receive your supplement. This page acts as your proof of purchase and contains the reference number necessary to fill your supplement request properly. No photocopy of this page or written request will be honored or answered. Any request from which the reference number has been removed, altered or obliterated will not be honored.

3. Prepare a STAMPED self-addressed envelope for return mailing. Be sure to use a FULL SIZE (9 X 12) ENVELOPE (MANILA TYPE) so that the supplement will fit and AFFIX ENOUGH POSTAGE TO COVER 3 OZ. **ANY SUPPLEMENT REQUEST NOT ACCOMPANIED BY A STAMPED SELF-ADDRESSED ENVELOPE WILL ABSOLUTELY NOT BE FILLED OR ACKNOWLEDGED.**

4. MULTIPLE SUPPLEMENT REQUESTS: If you are ordering more than one supplement, we suggest that you enclose a stamped, self-addressed envelope for each supplement requested. If you enclose only one envelope for a multiple request, your order may not be filled immediately should any supplement which you requested still be in production. In other words, your order will be held by us until it can be filled completely.

5. Casenotes prints two kinds of supplements. A "New Edition" supplement is issued when a new edition of your casebook is published. A "New Edition" supplement gives you all major cases found in the new edition of the casebook which did not appear in the previous edition. A regular "supplement" is issued when a paperback supplement to your casebook is published. If the box at the lower right is stamped, then the "New Edition" supplement was provided to your bookstore and is *not* available from Casenotes; however, Casenotes will still send you any regular "supplements" which have been printed either before or after the new edition of your casebook appeared and which, according to the reference number at the top of this page, have not been included in this book. If the box is not stamped, Casenotes will send you any supplements, "New Edition" and/or regular, needed to completely update your Casenote Legal Briefs.

NOTE: **REQUESTS FOR SUPPLEMENTS WILL NOT BE FILLED UNLESS THESE INSTRUCTIONS ARE COMPLIED WITH!**

6. Fill in the following information:

Full title of CASEBOOK _____ **WILLS & TRUSTS** _____

CASEBOOK author's name _**Dukeminier and Johnson**_

Copyright year of new edition or new paperback supplement

Name and location of bookstore where this Casenote Legal Brief was purchased _____

Name and location of law school you attend _____

Any comments regarding Casenote Legal Briefs _____

NOTE: IF THIS BOX IS STAMPED, NO NEW EDITION SUPPLEMENT CAN BE OBTAINED BY MAIL.

PUBLISHED BY CASENOTES PUBLISHING CO., INC. 1640 5th ST, SUITE 208 SANTA MONICA, CA 90401

PLEASE PRINT
NAME _____ PHONE _____ DATE _____
ADDRESS/CITY/STATE/ZIP _____

Announcing the First *Totally Integrated* Law Study System

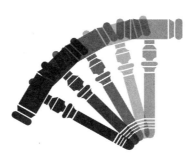

the Ultimate Outl[ine]

CASENOTE LEGAL BRIEFS™

PRICE LIST EFFECTIVE JULY 1, 1999 • PRICES SUBJECT TO CHANGE WITHOUT NOTICE

No.	Course	Adaptable to Courses Utilizing	Retail Price
	ADMINISTRATIVE LAW	ASIMOW, BONFIELD & LAVIN	20.00
	ADMINISTRATIVE LAW	BREYER, STEWART & SUNSTEIN	21.00
	ADMINISTRATIVE LAW	CASS, DIVER & BEERMAN	19.00
	ADMINISTRATIVE LAW	GELLHORN, B., S., R. & F.	19.00
	ADMINISTRATIVE LAW	MASHAW, MERRILL & SHANE	20.50
	ADMINISTRATIVE LAW	REESE	19.00
	ADMINISTRATIVE LAW	SCHWARTZ	20.00
	AGENCY & PARTNERSHIP (ENT.ORG)	CONARD, KNAUSS & SIEGEL	23.00
	AGENCY & PARTNERSHIP	HYNES	23.00
	ANTITRUST (TRADE REGULATION)	HANDLER, P., G. & W.	19.50
	ANTITRUST	SULLIVAN & HOVENKAMP	20.00
	BANKING LAW	MACEY & MILLER	19.00
	BANKRUPTCY	JORDAN, WARREN & BUSSELL	19.00
	BUSINESS ASSOCIATIONS (CORPORATIONS)	KLEIN & RAMSEYER	21.00
	BUSINESS ORGANIZATIONS (CORPORATIONS)	SODERQUIST, S., C., & S.	23.00
	CIVIL PROCEDURE	COUND, F., M. & S	21.00
	CIVIL PROCEDURE	FIELD, KAPLAN & CLERMONT	22.00
	CIVIL PROCEDURE	FREER & PERDUE	18.00
	CIVIL PROCEDURE	HAZARD, TAIT & FLETCHER	21.00
	CIVIL PROCEDURE	MARCUS, REDISH & SHERMAN	21.00
	CIVIL PROCEDURE	ROSENBERG, S. & D.	22.00
	CIVIL PROCEDURE	YEAZELL	19.00
	COMM'L LAW	FARNSWORTH, H., R., H. & M.	21.00
	COMM'L LAW	JORDAN & WARREN	21.00
	COMM'L LAW (SALES/SEC.TR./PAY.LAW [Sys.])	SPEIDEL, SUMMERS & WHITE	24.00
	COMM'L LAW (SALES/SEC.TR./PAY.LAW)	WHALEY	22.00
	COMMERCIAL TRANSACTIONS	LOPUKI, W., K. & M.	21.00
	COMMUNITY PROPERTY	BIRD	19.50
	COMPARATIVE LAW	SCHLESINGER, B., D., H.& W.	18.00
	COMPLEX LITIGATION	MARCUS & SHERMAN	19.00
	CONFLICTS	BRILMAYER	19.00
	CONFLICTS	CRAMTON, C. K., & K.	19.00
	CONFLICTS	ROSENBERG, HAY & W.	22.00
	CONFLICTS	SYMEONIDES, P., & M.	22.00
	CONSTITUTIONAL LAW	BREST & LEVINSON	20.00
	CONSTITUTIONAL LAW	COHEN & VARAT	23.00
	CONSTITUTIONAL LAW	FARBER, ESKRIDGE & FRICKEY	20.00
	CONSTITUTIONAL LAW	GUNTHER & SULLIVAN	21.00
	CONSTITUTIONAL LAW	LOCKHART, K., C., S. & F.	20.00
	CONSTITUTIONAL LAW	ROTUNDA	22.00
	CONSTITUTIONAL LAW (FIRST AMENDMENT)	SHIFFRIN & CHOPER	17.00
	CONSTITUTIONAL LAW	STONE, S., S. & T.	21.00
	CONTRACTS	BARNETT	23.00
	CONTRACTS	BURTON	22.00
	CONTRACTS	CALAMARI, PERILLO & BENDER	25.00
	CONTRACTS	CRANDALL & WHALEY	22.00
	CONTRACTS	DAWSON, HARVEY & H.	21.00
	CONTRACTS	FARNSWORTH & YOUNG	20.00
	CONTRACTS	FULLER & EISENBERG	23.00
	CONTRACTS	KESSLER, GILMORE & KRONMAN	25.00
	CONTRACTS	KNAPP & CRYSTAL	22.50
	CONTRACTS	MURPHY & SPEIDEL	24.00
	CONTRACTS	ROSETT	23.00
	CONTRACTS	VERNON	22.00
	COPYRIGHT	GOLDSTEIN	20.00
	COPYRIGHT	NIMMER, M., M. & N.	21.50
	CORPORATE TAXATION	LIND, S. L. & R	16.00
	CORPORATIONS	CARY & EISENBERG	21.00
	CORPORATIONS	CHOPER, COFFEE, & GILSON	23.50
	CORPORATIONS (ENTERPRISE ORG.)	CONARD, KNAUSS & SIEGEL	23.00
	CORPORATIONS	HAMILTON	21.00
	CORPORATIONS (BUSINESS ASSOCIATIONS	KLEIN & RAMSEYER	21.00
	CORPORATIONS	O'KELLEY & THOMPSON	20.00
	CORPORATIONS (BUSINESS ORG.)	SODERQUIST, S., C. & S.	23.00
	CORPORATIONS	SOLOMON, S., B. & W.	21.00
	CORPORATIONS	VAGTS	20.00
	CREDITOR'S RIGHTS (DEBTOR-CREDITOR)	RIESENFELD	23.00
	CRIMINAL JUSTICE	WEINREB	20.00
	CRIMINAL LAW	BONNIE, C., J. & L.	19.00
	CRIMINAL LAW	BOYCE & PERKINS	24.00
	CRIMINAL LAW	DRESSLER	23.00
	CRIMINAL LAW	JOHNSON	22.00
	CRIMINAL LAW	KADISH & SCHULHOFER	21.00
	CRIMINAL LAW	KAPLAN, WEISBERG & BINDER	20.00
	CRIMINAL PROCEDURE	ALLEN, KUHNS & STUNTZ	19.00
	CRIMINAL PROCEDURE	DRESSLER & THOMAS	24.00
	CRIMINAL PROCEDURE	HADDAD, Z., S. & B.	22.00
	CRIMINAL PROCEDURE	KAMISAR, LAFAVE & ISRAEL	21.00
	CRIMINAL PROCEDURE	SALTZBURG & CAPRA	19.00
	DEBTOR-CREDITOR (CREDITORS RIGHTS)	RIESENFELD	23.00
	DEBTOR-CREDITOR	WARREN & WESTBROOK	21.00
	DECEDENTS ESTATES (TRUSTS)	RITCHIE, A, & E.(DOBRIS & STERK)	23.00
	DECEDENTS ESTATES	SCOLES & HALBACH	23.50
ESTIC RELATIONS (*see* FAMILY LAW)			
	EDUCATION LAW (COURSE OUTLINE)	AQUILA & PETZKE	27.50
	EMPLOYMENT DISCRIMINATION	FRIEDMAN & STRICKLER	19.00
	EMPLOYMENT DISCRIMINATION	ZIMMER, SULLIVAN, R. & C.	20.00
	EMPLOYMENT LAW	ROTHSTEIN, KNAPP & LIEBMAN	21.50
	ENTERPRISE ORGANIZATION	CONARD, KNAUSS & SIEGEL	23.00
	ENVIRONMENTAL LAW	ANDERSON, MANDELKER & T.	18.00
	ENVIRONMENTAL LAW	FINDLEY & FARBER	20.00
	ENVIRONMENTAL LAW	MENELL & STEWART	19.00
	ENVIRONMENTAL LAW	PERCIVAL, MILLER, S. & L.	20.00
	ENVIRONMENTAL LAW	PLATER, A., G. & G.	19.00
	ESTATE & GIFT TAXATION	BITTKER, CLARK & McCOUCH	17.00

Ref. No.	Course	Adaptable to Courses Utilizing	Retail Price
	ETHICS (*see* PROFESSIONAL RESPONSIBILITY)		
1065	EVIDENCE	GREEN & NESSON	22.00
1066	EVIDENCE	MUELLER & KIRKPATRICK	19.00
1064	EVIDENCE	STRONG, BROUN & M.	24.50
1062	EVIDENCE	SUTTON & WELLBORN	24.00
1061	EVIDENCE	WALTZ & PARK	21.00
1060	EVIDENCE	WEINSTEIN, M., A. & B.	24.50
1244	FAMILY LAW (DOMESTIC RELATIONS)	AREEN	24.00
1242	FAMILY LAW (DOMESTIC RELATIONS)	CLARK & GLOWINSKY	21.00
1245	FAMILY LAW (DOMESTIC RELATIONS)	ELLMAN, KURTZ & BARTLETT	22.00
1246	FAMILY LAW (DOMESTIC RELATIONS)	HARRIS, T. & W.	21.00
1243	FAMILY LAW (DOMESTIC RELATIONS)	KRAUSE, O., E. & G.	26.00
1240	FAMILY LAW (DOMESTIC RELATIONS)	WADLINGTON	22.00
1231	FAMILY PROPERTY LAW (WILLS/TRUSTS)	WAGGONER, A. & F.	22.00
1360	FEDERAL COURTS	FALLON, M. & S. (HART & W.)	21.00
1360	FEDERAL COURTS	HART & WECHSLER (FALLON)	21.00
1363	FEDERAL COURTS	LOW & JEFFRIES	18.00
1361	FEDERAL COURTS	McCORMICK, C. & W.	22.00
1364	FEDERAL COURTS	REDISH & SHERRY	19.00
1690	FEDERAL INDIAN LAW	GETCHES, W. & W.	22.00
1089	FIRST AMENDMENT (CONSTITUTIONAL LAW)	SHIFFRIN & CHOPER	17.00
1700	GENDER AND LAW (SEX DISCRIMINATION)	BARTLETT & HARRIS	21.00
1510	GRATUITOUS TRANSFERS	CLARK, L., M., A., & M.	20.00
1651	HEALTH CARE LAW	CURRAN, H., B. & O.	23.00
1650	HEALTH LAW	FURROW, J., J. & S.	19.50
1640	IMMIGRATION LAW	ALEINIKOFF, MARTIN & M.	18.00
1641	IMMIGRATION LAW	LEGOMSKY	21.00
1690	INDIAN LAW	GETCHES, W. & W.	22.00
1371	INSURANCE LAW	KEETON	23.00
1370	INSURANCE LAW	YOUNG & HOLMES	19.00
1503	INTELLECTUAL PROPERTY	MERGES, M., L. & J.	21.00
1394	INTERNATIONAL BUSINESS TRANSACTIONS	FOLSOM, GORDON & SPANOGLE	17.00
1393	INTERNATIONAL LAW	CARTER & TRIMBLE	18.00
1392	INTERNATIONAL LAW	HENKIN, P., S. & S.	19.00
1390	INTERNATIONAL LAW	OLIVER, F., B., S. & W.	24.00
1331	LABOR LAW	COX, BOK, GORMAN & FINKIN	21.00
1471	LAND FINANCE (REAL ESTATE TRANS.)	BERGER & JOHNSTONE	20.00
1620	LAND FINANCE (REAL ESTATE TRANS.)	NELSON & WHITMAN	21.00
1452	LAND USE	CALLIES, FREILICH & ROBERTS	19.00
1421	LEGISLATION	ESKRIDGE & FRICKEY	17.00
1480	MASS MEDIA	FRANKLIN & ANDERSON	17.00
1312	NEGOTIABLE INSTRUMENTS (COMM. LAW)	JORDAN & WARREN	21.00
1541	OIL & GAS	KUNTZ., L., A., S. & P.	20.00
1540	OIL & GAS	MAXWELL, WILLIAMS, M. & K.	20.00
1561	PATENT LAW	ADELMAN, R., T. & W.	24.00
1560	PATENT LAW	FRANCIS & COLLINS	25.00
1310	PAYMENT LAW [SYST.][COMM. LAW]	SPEIDEL, SUMMERS & WHITE	24.00
1313	PAYMENT LAW (COMM.LAW / NEG. INST.)	WHALEY	22.00
1431	PRODUCTS LIABILITY	OWEN, MONTGOMERY & K.	24.00
1091	PROF. RESPONSIBILITY (ETHICS)	GILLERS	15.00
1093	PROF. RESPONSIBILITY (ETHICS)	HAZARD, KONIAK, & CRAMTON	20.00
1092	PROF. RESPONSIBILITY (ETHICS)	MORGAN & ROTUNDA	15.00
1030	PROPERTY	CASNER & LEACH	23.00
1031	PROPERTY	CRIBBET, J., F. & S.	23.50
1037	PROPERTY	DONAHUE, KAUPER & MARTIN	20.00
1035	PROPERTY	DUKEMINIER & KRIER	20.00
1034	PROPERTY	HAAR & LIEBMAN	22.50
1036	PROPERTY	KURTZ & HOVENKAMP	21.00
1033	PROPERTY	NELSON, STOEBUCK, & W.	22.50
1032	PROPERTY	RABIN & KWALL	22.00
1038	PROPERTY	SINGER	20.50
1621	REAL ESTATE TRANSACTIONS	GOLDSTEIN & KORNGOLD	20.00
1471	REAL ESTATE TRANS. & FIN. (LAND FINANCE)	BERGER & JOHNSTONE	20.00
1620	REAL ESTATE TRANSFER & FINANCE	NELSON & WHITMAN	20.00
1254	REMEDIES (EQUITY)	LAYCOCK	22.00
1253	REMEDIES (EQUITY)	LEAVELL, L., N. & K-F.	23.00
1252	REMEDIES (EQUITY)	RE & RE	25.00
1255	REMEDIES (EQUITY)	SHOBEN & TABB	24.50
1250	REMEDIES (EQUITY)	RENDLEMAN	27.00
1310	SALES (COMM. LAW)	SPEIDEL, SUMMERS & WHITE	24.00
1313	SALES (COMM. LAW)	WHALEY	22.00
1312	SECURED TRANS. (COMMERICIAL LAW)	JORDAN & WARREN	21.00
1310	SECURED TRANS.	SPEIDEL, SUMMERS & WHITE	24.00
1313	SECURED TRANS. (COMMERCIAL LAW)	WHALEY	22.00
1272	SECURITIES REGULATION	COX, HILLMAN, LANGEVOORT	20.00
1270	SECURITIES REGULATION	JENNINGS, M., C. & S.	20.00
1680	SPORTS LAW	WEILER & ROBERTS	19.50
1217	TAXATION (ESTATE & GIFT)	BITTKER, CLARK & McCOUCH	17.00
1219	TAXATION (INDIV. INCOME)	BURKE & FRIEL	21.00
1212	TAXATION (FEDERAL INCOME)	FREELAND, LIND & STEPHENS	20.00
1211	TAXATION (FEDERAL INCOME)	GRAETZ & SCHENK	19.00
1210	TAXATION (FEDERAL INCOME)	KLEIN & BANKMAN	20.00
1218	TAXATION (CORPORATE)	LIND, S., L. & R.	16.00
1006	TORTS	DOBBS	21.00
1003	TORTS	EPSTEIN	22.50
1004	TORTS	FRANKLIN & RABIN	19.50
1001	TORTS	HENDERSON, P. & S.	22.50
1000	TORTS	PROSSER, W., S., K. & P.	25.00
1005	TORTS	SHULMAN, JAMES & GRAY	24.00
1281	TRADE REGULATION (ANTITRUST)	HANDLER, P., G. & W.	19.50
1410	U.C.C.	EPSTEIN, MARTIN, H. & N.	17.00
1510	WILLS/TRUSTS (GRATUITOUS TRANSFER)	CLARK, L., M., A., & M.	20.00
1223	WILLS, TRUSTS & ESTATES	DUKEMINIER & JOHANSON	21.00
1220	WILLS	MECHEM & ATKINSON	22.00
1231	WILLS/TRUSTS (FAMILY PROPERTY LAW)	WAGGONER, A. & F.	22.00

ASENOTES PUBLISHING CO., INC. ● 1640 FIFTH STREET, SUITE 208 ● SANTA MONICA, CA 90401 ● (310) 395-6500

E-Mail Address- casenote@westworld.com • Website- www: http://www.casenotes.com

PLEASE PURCHASE FROM YOUR LOCAL BOOKSTORE. IF UNAVAILABLE, YOU MAY PURCHASE DIRECT.*
4TH CLASS POSTAGE (ALLOW TWO WEEKS) $1.00 PER ORDER; 1ST CLSS POSTAGE $3.00 (ONE BOOK), $2.00 EACH (TWO OR MORE BOOKS)
*CALIF. RESIDENTS PLEASE ADD 8¼% SALES TAX

GLOSSARY

A FORTIORI: Because one fact exists or has been proven, therefore a second fact that is related to the first fact must also exist.

A PRIORI: From the cause to the effect. A term of logic used to denote that when one generally accepted truth is shown to be a cause, another particular effect must necessarily follow.

AB INITIO: From the beginning; a condition which has existed throughout, as in a marriage which was void ab initio.

ACTUS REUS: The wrongful act; in criminal law, such action sufficient to trigger criminal liability.

AD VALOREM: According to value; an ad valorem tax is imposed upon an item located within the taxing jurisdiction calculated by the value of such item.

AMICUS CURIAE: Friend of the court. Its most common usage takes the form of an amicus curiae brief, filed by a person who is not a party to an action but is nonetheless allowed to offer an argument supporting his legal interests.

ARGUENDO: In arguing. A statement, possibly hypothetical, made for the purpose of argument, is one made arguendo.

BILL QUIA TIMET: A bill to quiet title (establish ownership) to real property.

BONA FIDE: True, honest, or genuine. May refer to a person's legal position based on good faith or lacking notice of fraud (such as a bona fide purchaser for value) or to the authenticity of a particular document (such as a bona fide last will and testament).

CAUSA MORTIS: With approaching death in mind. A gift causa mortis is a gift given by a party who feels certain that death is imminent.

CAVEAT EMPTOR: Let the buyer beware. This maxim is reflected in the rule of law that a buyer purchases at his own risk because it is his responsibility to examine, judge, test, and otherwise inspect what he is buying.

CERTIORARI: A writ of review. Petitions for review of a case by the United States Supreme Court are most often done by means of a writ of certiorari.

CONTRA: On the other hand. Opposite. Contrary to.

CORAM NOBIS: Before us; writs of error directed to the court that originally rendered the judgment.

CORAM VOBIS: Before you; writs of error directed by an appellate court to a lower court to correct a factual error.

CORPUS DELICTI: The body of the crime; the requisite elements of a crime amounting to objective proof that a crime has been committed.

CUM TESTAMENTO ANNEXO, ADMINISTRATOR (ADMINISTRATOR C.T.A.): With will annexed; an administrator c.t.a. settles an estate pursuant to a will in which he is not appointed.

DE BONIS NON, ADMINISTRATOR (ADMINISTRATOR D.B.N.): Of goods not administered; an administrator d.b.n. settles a partially settled estate.

DE FACTO: In fact; in reality; actually. Existing in fact but not officially approved or engendered.

DE JURE: By right; lawful. Describes a condition that is legitimate "as a matter of law," in contrast to the term "de facto," which connotes something existing in fact but not legally sanctioned or authorized. For example, de facto segregation refers to segregation brought about by housing patterns, etc., whereas de jure segregation refers to segregation created by law.

DE MINIMUS: Of minimal importance; insignificant; a trifle; not worth bothering about.

DE NOVO: Anew; a second time; afresh. A trial de novo is a new trial held at the appellate level as if the case originated there and the trial at a lower level had not taken place.

DICTA: Generally used as an abbreviated form of obiter dicta, a term describing those portions of a judicial opinion incidental or not necessary to resolution of the specific question before the court. Such nonessential statements and remarks are not considered to be binding precedent.

DUCES TECUM: Refers to a particular type of writ or subpoena requesting a party or organization to produce certain documents in their possession.

EN BANC: Full bench. Where a court sits with all justices present rather than the usual quorum.

EX PARTE: For one side or one party only. An ex parte proceeding is one undertaken for the benefit of only one party, without notice to, or an appearance by, an adverse party.

EX POST FACTO: After the fact. An ex post facto law is a law that retroactively changes the consequences of a prior act.

EX REL.: Abbreviated form of the term ex relatione, meaning, upon relation or information. When the state brings an action in which it has no interest against an individual at the instigation of one who has a private interest in the matter.

FORUM NON CONVENIENS: Inconvenient forum. Although a court may have jurisdiction over the case, the action should be tried in a more conveniently located court, one to which parties and witnesses may more easily travel, for example.

GUARDIAN AD LITEM: A guardian of an infant as to litigation, appointed to represent the infant and pursue his/her rights.

HABEAS CORPUS: You have the body. The modern writ of habeas corpus is a writ directing that a person (body) being detained (such as a prisoner) be brought before the court so that the legality of his detention can be judicially ascertained.

IN CAMERA: In private, in chambers. When a hearing is held before a judge in his chambers or when all spectators are excluded from the courtroom.

IN FORMA PAUPERIS: In the manner of a pauper. A party who proceeds in forma pauperis because of his poverty is one who is allowed to bring suit without liability for costs.

INFRA: Below, under. A word referring the reader to a later part of a book. (The opposite of supra.)

IN LOCO PARENTIS: In the place of a parent.

IN PARI DELICTO: Equally wrong; a court of equity will not grant requested relief to an applicant who is in pari delicto, or as much at fault in the transactions giving rise to the controversy as is the opponent of the applicant.

IN PARI MATERIA: On like subject matter or upon the same matter. Statutes relating to the same person or things are said to be in pari materia. It is a general rule of statutory construction that such statutes should be construed together, i.e., looked at as if they together constituted one law.

IN PERSONAM: Against the person. Jurisdiction over the person of an individual.

IN RE: In the matter of. Used to designate a proceeding involving an estate or other property.

IN REM: A term that signifies an action against the res, or thing. An action in rem is basically one that is taken directly against property, as distinguished from an action in personam, i.e., against the person.

INTER ALIA: Among other things. Used to show that the whole of a statement, pleading, list, statute, etc., has not been set forth in its entirety.

INTER PARTES: Between the parties. May refer to contracts, conveyances or other transactions having legal significance.

INTER VIVOS: Between the living. An inter vivos gift is a gift made by a living grantor, as distinguished from bequests contained in a will, which pass upon the death of the testator.

IPSO FACTO: By the mere fact itself.

JUS: Law or the entire body of law.

LEX LOCI: The law of the place; the notion that the rights of parties to a legal proceeding are governed by the law of the place where those rights arose.

MALUM IN SE: Evil or wrong in and of itself; inherently wrong. This term describes an act that is wrong by its very nature, as opposed to one which would not be wrong but for the fact that there is a specific legal prohibition against it (malum prohibitum).

MALUM PROHIBITUM: Wrong because prohibited, but not inherently evil. Used to describe something that is wrong because it is expressly forbidden by law but that is not in and of itself evil, e.g., speeding.

MANDAMUS: We command. A writ directing an official to take a certain action.

MENS REA: A guilty mind; a criminal intent. A term used to signify the mental state that accompanies a crime or other prohibited act. Some crimes require only a general mens rea (general intent to do the prohibited act), but others, like assault with intent to murder, require the existence of a specific mens rea.

MODUS OPERANDI: Method of operating; generally refers to the manner or style of a criminal in committing crimes, admissible in appropriate cases as evidence of the identity of a defendant.

NEXUS: A connection to.

NISI PRIUS: A court of first impression. A nisi prius court is one where issues of fact are tried before a judge or jury.

N.O.V. (NON OBSTANTE VEREDICTO): Notwithstanding the verdict. A judgment n.o.v. is a judgment given in favor of one party despite the fact that a verdict was returned in favor of the other party, the justification being that the verdict either had no reasonable support in fact or was contrary to law.

NUNC PRO TUNC: Now for then. This phrase refers to actions that may be taken and will then have full retroactive effect.

PENDENTE LITE: Pending the suit; pending litigation underway.

PER CAPITA: By head; beneficiaries of an estate, if they take in equal shares, take per capita.

PER CURIAM: By the court; signifies an opinion ostensibly written "by the whole court" and with no identified author.

PER SE: By itself, in itself; inherently.

PER STIRPES: By representation. Used primarily in the law of wills to describe the method of distribution where a person, generally because of death, is unable to take that which is left to him by the will of another, and therefore his heirs divide such property between them rather than take under the will individually.

PRIMA FACIE: On its face, at first sight. A prima facie case is one that is sufficient on its face, meaning that the evidence supporting it is adequate to establish the case until contradicted or overcome by other evidence.

PRO TANTO: For so much; as far as it goes. Often used in eminent domain cases when a property owner receives partial payment for his land without prejudice to his right to bring suit for the full amount he claims his land to be worth.

QUANTUM MERUIT: As much as he deserves. Refers to recovery based on the doctrine of unjust enrichment in those cases in which a party has rendered valuable services or furnished materials that were accepted and enjoyed by another under circumstances that would reasonably notify the recipient that the rendering party expected to be paid. In essence, the law implies a contract to pay the reasonable value of the services or materials furnished.

QUASI: Almost like; as if; nearly. This term is essentially used to signify that one subject or thing is almost analogous to another but that material differences between them do exist. For example, a quasi-criminal proceeding is one that is not strictly criminal but shares enough of the same characteristics to require some of the same safeguards (e.g., procedural due process must be followed in a parol hearing).

QUID PRO QUO: Something for something. In contract law, the consideration, something of value, passed between the parties to render the contract binding.

RES GESTAE: Things done; in evidence law, this principle justifies the admission of a statement that would otherwise be hearsay when it is made so closely to the event in question as to be said to be a part of it, or with such spontaneity as not to have the possibility of falsehood.

RES IPSA LOQUITUR: The thing speaks for itself. This doctrine gives rise to a rebuttable presumption of negligence when the instrumentality causing the injury was within the exclusive control of the defendant, and the injury was one that does not normally occur unless a person has been negligent.

RES JUDICATA: A matter adjudged. Doctrine which provides that once a court of competent jurisdiction has rendered a final judgment or decree on the merits, that judgment or decree is conclusive upon the parties to the case and prevents them from engaging in any other litigation on the points and issues determined therein.

RESPONDEAT SUPERIOR: Let the master reply. This doctrine holds the master liable for the wrongful acts of his servant (or the principal for his agent) in those cases in which the servant (or agent) was acting within the scope of his authority at the time of the injury.

STARE DECISIS: To stand by or adhere to that which has been decided. The common law doctrine of stare decisis attempts to give security and certainty to the law by following the policy that once a principle of law as applicable to a certain set of facts has been set forth in a decision, it forms a precedent which will subsequently be followed, even though a different decision might be made were it the first time the question had arisen. Of course, stare decisis is not an inviolable principle and is departed from in instances where there is good cause (e.g., considerations of public policy led the Supreme Court to disregard prior decisions sanctioning segregation).

SUPRA: Above. A word referring a reader to an earlier part of a book.

ULTRA VIRES: Beyond the power. This phrase is most commonly used to refer to actions taken by a corporation that are beyond the power or legal authority of the corporation.

ADDENDUM OF FRENCH DERIVATIVES

IN PAIS: Not pursuant to legal proceedings.

CHATTEL: Tangible personal property.

CY PRES: Doctrine permitting courts to apply trust funds to purposes not expressed in the trust but necessary to carry out the settlor's intent.

PER AUTRE VIE: For another's life; in property law, an estate may be granted that will terminate upon the death of someone other than the grantee.

PROFIT A PRENDRE: A license to remove minerals or other produce from land.

VOIR DIRE: Process of questioning jurors as to their predispositions about the case or parties to a proceeding in order to identify those jurors displaying bias or prejudice.

NOTES

TABLE OF CASES

Continued on next page.

NOTES

TABLE OF CASES (Continued)

CHAPTER 1
INTRODUCTION TO ESTATE PLANNING

QUICK REFERENCE RULES OF LAW

1. **The Power to Transmit Property at Death: Its Justification and Limitations.** The complete abolition of the rights of an owner to dispose of property rights is a taking without just compensation, violating the owner's rights guaranteed under the Fifth Amendment. (Hodel v. Irving)

2. **The Power to Transmit Property at Death: Its Justification and Limitations.** Mortmain statutes that restrict charitable gifts are unconstitutional. (Shriners Hospitals for Crippled Children v. Zrillac)

   [For more information on mortmain statutes, see Casenote Law Outline on Wills, Trusts, and Estates, Chapter 3, § VII, Waiver.]

3. **The Power to Transmit Property at Death: Its Justification and Limitations.** A testator may validly impose a restraint on the religion of the spouse of a beneficiary as a condition precedent to inheriting under the will. (Shapira v. Union National Bank)

   [For more information on the intent to disinherit, see Casenote Law Outline on Wills, Trusts & Estates, Chapter 3, § I, Protection of Children.]

4. **An Estate Planning Problem.** An attorney is liable to intended beneficiaries who have been damaged by the attorney's negligent drafting of his client's will. (Ogle v. Fuiten)

   [For more information on attorney liability for mistake in will, see Casenote Law Outline on Wills, Trusts & Estates, Chapter 6, § V, Malpractice.]

NOTES

HODEL v. IRVING
Secretary of the Interior (D) v. Sioux Indian (P)
481 U.S. 704 (1987).

NATURE OF CASE: Appeal from judgment finding a statute unconstitutional as a taking without just compensation.

FACT SUMMARY: Congress enacted the Indian Land Consolidation Act, which contained a provision that certain fractional interests owned by tribe members would escheat to the tribe.

CONCISE RULE OF LAW: The complete abolition of the rights of an owner to dispose of property rights is a taking without just compensation, violating the owner's rights guaranteed under the Fifth Amendment.

FACTS: The Indian Land Acts enacted at the end of the nineteenth century provided that each Sioux Indian was allotted reservation land which was held in trust by the United States. Eventually the lands were splintered into multiple undivided interests, with some parcels having hundreds of fractional owners. In 1983, Congress passed the Indian Land Consolidation Act. Section 207 of the Act provided that certain fractional interests could not be transferred by intestacy or devise but would escheat to the tribe. No provision was made for the payment of compensation to the owners of the escheated fractional interests. Irving (P), a member of the Sioux tribe and a prospective recipient of one of the fractional interests affected by the statute, filed suit, claiming that § 207 was a taking without just compensation in violation of the Fifth Amendment. The district court found that the statute was constitutional. The court of appeals reversed and declared the statute unconstitutional. Hodel (D), the Secretary of the Interior, appealed.

ISSUE: Is the complete abolition of the rights of an owner to dispose of property rights a taking without just compensation, violating rights guaranteed under the Fifth Amendment?

HOLDING AND DECISION: (O'Connor, J.) Yes. Section 207 amounts to a virtual abrogation of the right to pass a certain type of property — the small undivided interest to one's heirs. A right to pass property to one's family has been part of the Anglo-Saxon legal system since feudal times. The escheatable interests are not necessarily de minimis. Even though the fractional owners have the right to make inter vivos transfers of the interests, such a retained right does not obviate the total abrogation of the owner's rights to devise the property. Affirmed.

EDITOR'S ANALYSIS: In an analogous case, the Supreme Court upheld the constitutionality of a provision of the Bald Eagle Protection Act, which prohibits the right to sell or trade artifacts made from eagle feathers and eagle parts. Andrus v. Allard, 444 U.S. 31 (1979). The Court held that "where an owner possesses a full 'bundle' of property rights, the destruction of one 'strand' of the bundle is not a taking, because the aggregate must be viewed in its entirety." The Court pointed out that the artifact owners could still donate or devise the artifacts.

QUICKNOTES

TAKING - A governmental action that substantially deprives an owner of the use and enjoyment of his or her property, requiring compensation.

JUST COMPENSATION - The right guaranteed by the Fifth Amendment to the United States Constitution of a person, when his property is taken for public use by the state, to receive adequate compensation in order to restore him to the position he enjoyed prior to the appropriation.

INTER VIVOS TRANSFER - A transfer of property that is effectuated between living persons.

NOTES:

SHRINERS HOSPITALS FOR CRIPPLED CHILDREN v. ZRILLIC

Fla. Sup. Ct., 563 So. 2d 64 (1990).

NATURE OF CASE: Judgment finding statute constitutional in action to avoid a charitable devise.

FACT SUMMARY: The testator left the bulk of her estate to Shriners Hospitals (D), a charity, rather than to her daughter, Zrillic (P). Zrillic (P) claimed that this violated a state law restricting charitable bequests.

CONCISE RULE OF LAW: Mortmain statutes that restrict charitable gifts are unconstitutional.

FACTS: Testator died from a long illness two months after executing her will. In her will she left some small family heirlooms to her daughter, Zrillic (P), with the residue of the estate going to the Shriners Hospitals (D). Testator stated that she limited the bequest to Zrillic (P) because of Zrillic's (P) failure to support her during her illness and her overall disapproval of Zrillic's (P) lifestyle. Zrillic (P) contested the will under a Florida mortmain statute nullifying wills that disinherit descendants in favor of charities and that were drafted less than six months before the testator's death. The circuit court held the statute unconstitutional. The court of appeals reversed. Shriners (D) appealed.

ISSUE: Are mortmain statutes that restrict charitable gifts unconstitutional?

HOLDING AND DECISION: (Barkett, J.) Yes. Mortmain statutes that restrict charitable gifts are unconstitutional. The right to devise property is constitutionally protected and may not be interfered with unless it is reasonably necessary to do so. Dead hand statutes, such as this one, originated in feudal England to prevent the church from amassing property. The rationale no longer supports this type of statute. Moreover, while states have an interest in protecting dependent family members from becoming a burden of the state, this statute does not serve that function since it has no requirement that the protesting heir be dependent on the testator. Furthermore, the statute violates the Equal Protection Clause because its classifications are both too broad and too narrow to achieve its goal of protecting testators from undue influence. It is under inclusive as applied to charitable institutions since it leaves out the unscrupulous and greedy relative, friends, and acquaintances who are more likely to have a great deal of influence over the testator. It is also overinclusive because it voids bequests by testators who were not impermissibly influenced. The statute is not reasonably necessary to effect the state's goal. Thus, the right to dispose of property must prevail. Reversed and remanded.

DISSENT: (McDonald, J.) The legislature has a right to put conditions on devises of property.

EDITOR'S ANALYSIS: At the time this case was decided, only three states besides Florida had mortmain statutes still in effect. Such statutes constitute one of the few limitations on testamentary freedom that can be asserted by any heir, not just by a spouse or child of the testator. Over time, society's attitude has changed to the point where charitable gifts, devises, and trusts are now favored and will be held valid whenever possible.

[For more information on mortmain statutes, see Casenote Law Outline on Wills, Trusts, and Estates, Chapter 3, § VII, Waiver.]

QUICKNOTES

TESTATOR - One who executes a will.

NOTES:

SHAPIRA v. UNION NATIONAL BANK
Beneficiary (P) v. Bank (D)
39 Ohio Misc. 28 (1974).

NATURE OF CASE: Declaratory judgment action.

FACT SUMMARY: Daniel's (P) interest under his father's will was conditioned on the requirement that he marry a Jew whose parents were both Jewish within seven years of his father's death.

CONCISE RULE OF LAW: A testator may validly impose a restraint on the religion of the spouse of a beneficiary as a condition precedent to inheriting under the will.

FACTS: Under Shapira's will, his son Daniel (P) could only inherit if he was married to a Jewish woman whose parents were both Jewish at the date of Shapira's death or within seven years thereafter. Daniel (P) sought a declaration that the will was unconstitutional since it restricted his right to marry or that such a clause violated public policy.

ISSUE: May a testator attempt to restrict the right of a beneficiary to marry within a certain religion?

HOLDING AND DECISION: (Henderson, J.) Yes. The right to receive property by will is a matter of statutory law. A testator may either disinherit his children or condition their taking in any manner without offending the Constitution. While the right to marry is a constitutionally protected right, there is no state action present herein which would trigger the Due Process or Equal Protection Clause. The courts are not being asked to enforce covenants. The only official action involves the probate of the will, and this is, in itself, insufficient to be deemed state action. Therefore, a testator may restrict a beneficiary's right to marriage without offending the Constitution. Public policy does not prohibit a limited restriction on the right to marriage restricted to members of one religion. A partial restraint of marriage which imposes only reasonable restrictions is not void as violative of public policy. Gifts conditioned on marrying within a certain religious grouping are deemed reasonable restrictions in a majority of jurisdictions. We find that it is not violative of public policy to condition a bequest on the marriage to one of a particular religion. The clause is valid, and Daniel (P) is bound by its terms.

EDITOR'S ANALYSIS: A condition requiring the beneficiary not to marry a member of a specific religion is also deemed valid. In re Clayton's Estate, 13 Pa. 413. Where the restriction based on religion unreasonably limits the beneficiary's right to marriage, it will be deemed void, e.g., Maddox v. Maddox, 52 Va. 11 (1854), where there were only 4 or 5 unmarried members of the particular sect.

[For more information on the intent to disinherit, see Casenote Law Outline on Wills, Trusts & Estates, Chapter 3, § I, Protection of Children.]

QUICKNOTES

TESTATOR - One who executes a will.

BENEFICIARY - A third party who is the recipient of the benefit of a transaction undertaken by another.

DUE PROCESS - The constitutional mandate requiring the courts to protect and enforce individuals' rights and liberties consistent with prevailing principals of fairness and justice and prohibiting the federal and state governments from such activities that deprive its citizens of a life, liberty or property interest.

EQUAL PROTECTION - A constitutional guarantee that no person shall be denied the same protection of the laws enjoyed by other persons in life circumstances.

NOTES:

OGLE v. FUITEN

Beneficiary (P) v. Attorney (D)

102 Ill. 2d 356, 466 N.E.2d 224 (1984).

NATURE OF CASE: Appeal from judgment finding attorney malpractice.

FACT SUMMARY: Fuiten (D), an attorney, negligently drafted a will for Ogle's (P) aunt and uncle, causing their property to pass in intestacy, rather than to Ogle (P), the intended beneficiary.

CONCISE RULE OF LAW: An attorney is liable to intended beneficiaries who have been damaged by the attorney's negligent drafting of his client's will.

FACTS: Fuiten (D), an attorney, was hired by Ogle's (P) aunt and uncle to draft the aunt and uncle's joint wills. Ogle's (P) relatives intended to leave their property to Ogle (P) if either relative failed to survive the other by thirty days. Fuiten (D) drafted the wills with the following provision: "I give . . . my estate . . . to my wife (my husband) . . . if she (he) shall survive me within thirty days." Thus, Fuiten (D) negligently omitted to include Ogle (P) as beneficiary. Ogle's (P) aunt and uncle died within thirty-nine days of each other, and their estates passed in intestacy. Ogle (P) sued Fuiten (D) for malpractice for negligently drafting the wills and frustrating the relatives' intention to pass their property to Ogle (P). Fuiten's (D) motion to dismiss was granted on the basis that in order to recover from an attorney, a nonclient must allege and prove that the primary purpose and intent of the attorney-client relationship was to benefit the third party. The appellate court reversed on the basis that the testators intended to directly benefit Ogle (P) and that, therefore, Ogle (P) had standing as third-party beneficiary of the wills. Fuiten (D) appealed.

ISSUE: Is an attorney liable to intended beneficiaries who have been damaged by the attorney's negligent drafting of his client's will?

HOLDING AND DECISION: (Goldenhersh, J.) Yes. An attorney is liable to intended beneficiaries who have been damaged by the attorney's negligent drafting of his client's will. Even though the testator's intent to benefit Ogle (P) was not expressly shown by the wills, this fact will not bar Ogle (P) from bringing a cause of action. Ogle's (P) complaint sufficiently states the traditional elements of negligence in tort and third-party breach of contract theory. Affirmed.

EDITOR'S ANALYSIS: This case follows the modern trend to hold an attorney liable to intended will beneficiaries even though there is no privity of contract between the attorney and the beneficiaries. Even though the privity requirement still exists in a few jurisdictions, most recent cases have rejected it completely. Similarly, in England, will beneficiaries are permitted to sue the drafting attorney for negligence.

[For more information on attorney liability for mistake in will, see Casenote Law Outline on Wills, Trusts & Estates, Chapter 6, § V, Malpractice.]

QUICKNOTES

BENEFICIARY - A third party who is the recipient of the benefit of a transaction undertaken by another.

TESTATOR - One who executes a will.

NEGLIGENCE - Conduct falling below the standard of care that a reasonable person would demonstrate under similar conditions.

NOTES:

CHAPTER 2
INTESTACY: AN ESTATE PLAN BY DEFAULT

QUICK REFERENCE RULES OF LAW

1. **The Basic Scheme.** The determination of legal death must be made in accordance with the usual and customary standards of medical practice. (Janus v. Tarasewicz)

   [For more information on simultaneous death, see Casenote Law Outline on Wills, Trusts & Estates, Chapter 2, § II, Lapse.]

2. **Transfers to Children.** An adopted child is no longer considered a child of either natural parent and loses on adoption all rights of inheritance from his natural parents. (Hall v. Vallandingham)

   [For more information on adoption and inheritance from relatives, see Casenote Law Outline on Wills, Trusts & Estates, Chapter 2, § V, Adoption.]

3. **Transfers to Children.** A contract to adopt may not be specifically enforced unless the contract was entered into by a person with the legal authority to consent to the adoption. (O'Neal v. Wilkes)

   [For more information on equitable adoption, see Casenote Law Outline on Wills, Trusts, and Estates, Chapter 2, § V, Adoption.]

4. **Transfers to Children.** For purposes of intestate succession, paternity may not be established for a child conceived after an individual's death. (Hecht v. Superior Court)

5. **Bars to Succession.** A conviction of voluntary manslaughter disables the party from taking under decedent's will or through intestate succession. (In re Estate of Mahoney)

   [For more information on bars to inheritance, see Casenote Law Outline on Wills, Trusts & Estates, Chapter 2, § VII, Misconduct.]

JANUS v. TARASEWICZ

Contingent beneficiary (P) v. Primary beneficiary (D)

135 Ill. App. 3d 93, 482 N.E.2d 418 (1985).

NATURE OF CASE: Appeal from declaratory judgment.

FACT SUMMARY: Stanley and Theresa Janus died after ingesting cyanide-laced Tylenol capsules.

CONCISE RULE OF LAW: The determination of legal death must be made in accordance with the usual and customary standards of medical practice.

FACTS: Stanley and Theresa Janus, a married couple, unknowingly took Tylenol capsules laced with cyanide. Soon afterward, Stanley collapsed. Within minutes, Theresa started experiencing seizures. They were both taken to the hospital. Stanley had no blood pressure, pulse, or signs of respiration. Therefore, the medical director at the hospital pronounced him dead on September 29, 1982. Like Stanley, Theresa at first exhibited no visible vital signs when she was admitted to the hospital. However, hospital personnel were able to get her heart beating on its own again and could detect a measurable, though unsatisfactory, blood pressure. Theresa was judged to be in a deep coma with very unstable vital signs and placed in the intensive care ward. One entry in her records indicated that a nurse detected a minimal reaction to light in Theresa's right pupil. On September 30, 1982, various tests were conducted to determine her brain function. As a result of these tests, Theresa was diagnosed as having sustained total brain death and was pronounced dead on October 1, 1982. The proceeds of a life insurance policy on Stanley's life was paid to the administrator of Theresa's estate. Eventually, Theresa's father, Jan Tarasewicz (D) received the life insurance proceeds as Theresa's heir. Alojza Janus (P), Stanley's mother and the contingent beneficiary on Stanley's life insurance policy, sued Tarasewicz (D) for the proceeds. The court concluded from the evidence that Theresa survived Stanley. Janus (P) appealed, contending that there was not sufficient evidence to prove that both victims did not suffer brain death prior to their arrival to the hospital.

ISSUE: Must the determination of legal death be made in accordance with the usual and customary standards of medical practice?

HOLDING AND DECISION: (O'Connor, J.) Yes. The determination of legal death must be made in accordance with the usual and customary standards of medical practice. Both victims arrived at the hospital with artificial respirators and no obvious vital signs. There is no dispute that Stanley Janus died in both a cardiopulmonary sense and a brain death sense when his vital signs disappeared on route to the hospital and were never reestablished. In contrast, hospital personnel were able to reestablish a spontaneous blood pressure and pulse. Efforts to preserve Theresa's life continued after more intensive efforts on Stanley's behalf had failed. In the medical director's opinion, Theresa's condition did not warrant a diagnosis of brain death, and she did not suffer irreversible brain death until much later. The record clearly establishes that the treating physician's diagnoses of death with respect to Stanley and Theresa Janus were made within the usual and customary standards of medical practice. Affirmed.

EDITOR'S ANALYSIS: The Uniform Probate Code provides that an heir or devisee who fails to survive by 120 hours is deemed to have predeceased the decedent. Attorneys provide for the "no sufficient evidence" problem by providing in a will the following language: "if any person dies with me in a common disaster, any property given to such person by this will shall pass as if such person predeceased me."

[For more information on simultaneous death, see Casenote Law Outline on Wills, Trusts & Estates, Chapter 2, § II, Lapse.]

QUICKNOTES

PRIMARY BENEFICIARY - The individual specified in a life insurance policy to receive the proceeds upon the insured's death.

CONTINGENT BENEFICIARY - A third party who is the recipient of the benefit of a transaction undertaken by another, the receipt of which is based on the uncertain happening of another event.

SURVIVORSHIP - Between two or more persons, such as in a joint tenancy relationship, the right to the property of a deceased passes to the survivor.

NOTES:

HALL v. VALLANDINGHAM
Parties not identified
75 Md. App. 187, 540 A.2d 1162 (1986).

NATURE OF CASE: Appeal from judgment disinheriting relatives.

FACT SUMMARY: After Earl Vallandingham died, Vallandingham (P), his children, were adopted by Kilgore, his wife's new husband.

CONCISE RULE OF LAW: An adopted child is no longer considered a child of either natural parent and loses on adoption all rights of inheritance from his natural parents.

FACTS: Earl Vallandingham died, survived by his wife Elizabeth and their four children, Vallandingham (P). Elizabeth married Jim Kilgore. Kilgore adopted Vallandingham's children. Earl's brother William died childless, unmarried, and intestate. His sole heirs were his surviving brothers and the children of brothers (like Earl) and sisters who predeceased him. Earl's children alleged that they were entitled to their distributive share. The court held that they were not entitled to inherit from William because they had been adopted by Kilgore.. They appealed.

ISSUE: Is an adopted child no longer considered a child of either natural parent, and does he lose on adoption all rights of inheritance from his natural parents?

HOLDING AND DECISION: (Gilbert, J.) Yes. An adopted child is no longer considered a child of either natural parent and loses on adoption all rights of inheritance from his natural parents. The Maryland Estates and Trust Code provides that on adoption, "a child no longer shall be considered a child of either natural parent." To construe this statute so as to allow dual inheritance would bestow upon an adopted child a superior status. Because an adopted child has no right to inherit from the estate of a natural parent who dies intestate, it follows that the same child may not inherit through the natural parent by way of representation. Affirmed.

EDITOR'S ANALYSIS: The states disagree whether or not a child continues to have inheritance rights from both natural parents when the child is adopted by a step-parent. Only a few states draw a distinction between adoption of a minor and adoption of an adult. Adult adoption has been used increasingly more frequently to prevent will contests.

[For more information on adoption and inheritance from relatives, see Casenote Law Outline on Wills, Trusts & Estates, Chapter 2, § V, Adoption.]

QUICKNOTES

MARYLAND ESTATES AND TRUSTS CODE ANN. § 1-207(a) - An adopted child shall be treated as a natural child of his adopted parent or parents. On adoption, a child no longer shall be considered a child of either natural parent, except that upon adoption by the spouse of a natural parent. The child shall be considered the child of that natural parent.

NOTES:

O'NEAL v. WILKES

Virtual adoptee (P) v. Estate executor (D)

263 Ga. 850, 439 S.E.490 (1994).

NATURE OF CASE: Appeal from judgment n.o.v. denying equitable adoption claim.

FACT SUMMARY: O'Neal (P), who had been raised by testator but never formally adopted, petitioned the court for a declaration of virtual (equitable) adoption.

CONCISE RULE OF LAW: A contract to adopt may not be specifically enforced unless the contract was entered into by a person with the legal authority to consent to the adoption.

FACTS: Hattie O'Neal's (P) mother died in 1957, when O'Neal (P) was eight years old. O'Neal's (P) father never recognized her as his daughter. After O'Neal (P) had lived with a maternal aunt for four years, she was taken to live with her paternal aunt, Page. Page ultimately sent O'Neal (P) to live with the testator. She lived with the testator for more than ten years, until she was married. The testator referred to O'Neal (P) as his daughter and her children as his grandchildren. After he died intestate, O'Neal (P) claimed she was entitled to inherit, under the theory of equitable adoption, the property she would have been entitled to had she been the testator's statutorily adopted daughter. Wilkes (D), the executor of the estate, contested O'Neal's (P) claim. The court granted a judgment n.o.v. in favor of Wilkes (D) on the grounds that Page, the paternal aunt who sent O'Neal (D) to live with the testator, had no legal authority to enter into an adoption contract with the testator. O'Neal (P) appealed.

ISSUE: May a contract to adopt be specifically enforced if it is entered into by a person without authority to consent to the adoption?

HOLDING AND DECISION: (Fletcher, J) No. A contract to adopt cannot be specifically enforced if it is entered into by a person without authority to consent to the adoption. Consent to an adoption may only be given by a child's parent or legal guardian. O'Neal's (P) Aunt Page was not O'Neal's (P) legal guardian; she was merely taking over a familial obligation in caring for the child. Because Page had no legal relationship with O'Neal (P), she could not consent to her adoption by the testator. The adoption contract was, therefore, invalid, and thus, O'Neal's (P) claim for an equitable adoption is defeated. Affirmed.

DISSENT: (Sears-Collins, J.) Equity treats as done that which ought to be done. By insisting that a person be appointed as a legal guardian before agreeing to a contract to adopt, the majority is harming the very person the requirement is designed to protect — the child.

EDITOR'S ANALYSIS: The majority does not grant the adoption in this case because the aunt was not the proper party to consent. The opinion, however, recognizes that O'Neal's (P) biological father also had no right to consent since he had abandoned her. The question the court fails to address is whether the child should be punished when there is no proper party to consent through no fault of her own. The result is anything but equitable toward the child.

[For more information on equitable adoption, see Casenote Law Outline on Wills, Trusts, and Estates, Chapter 2, § V, Adoption.]

QUICKNOTES

EQUITABLE ADOPTION - An oral contract to adopt a child, not executed in accordance with statutory requirements, giving rise to rights of inheritance in the child upon the death of the promisor.

INTESTATE - To die without leaving a valid testamentary instrument.

LEGAL CUSTODIAN - Person having responsibility for a person or his property pursuant to law.

NOTES:

HECHT v. SUPERIOR COURT
Beneficiary of will (P) v. Court (D)
Cal. Ct. App., 16 Cal. App. 4th 836 (1993).

NATURE OF CASE: Appeal from an order to destroy a decedent's sperm.

FACT SUMMARY: After Kane deposited his sperm specimens in a sperm bank, bequeathing them to Hecht (P) should she wish to become impregnated with his sperm after his death, Kane's children obtained a court order to have the sperm destroyed on public policy grounds.

CONCISE RULE OF LAW: For purposes of intestate succession, paternity may not be established for a child conceived after an individual's death.

FACTS: Kane, a divorced father of two college-aged children, lived with Hecht (P) for about five years prior to committing suicide. Before taking his own life, Kane deposited fifteen vials of his sperm in a sperm bank. He authorized the sperm bank to release the specimens to Hecht (P), or to her physician, should Hecht (P) desire to become impregnated with his sperm after his death. Kane also left a will, bequeathing all right and title to the sperm specimens to Hecht (P), along with other property. Kane's children contested the will, alleging lack of mental capacity and undue influence by Hecht (P). The administrator of Kane's estate petitioned the court (D) for destruction of the sperm on public policy grounds. The court (D) ordered that the sperm be destroyed. Hecht (P) appealed.

ISSUE: Does artificial insemination with the sperm of a decedent violate public policy?

HOLDING AND DECISION: (Lillie, J.) No. Artificial insemination with the sperm of a decedent does not violate public policy. Because Kane had an ownership interest in his sperm sufficient to constitute "property" within the meaning of Probate Code § 62, the probate court had jurisdiction with respect to the vials of sperm. The public policy of California does not prohibit the artificial insemination of Hecht (P) because of her status as an unmarried woman. Furthermore, nothing indicates that artificial insemination with the sperm of a decedent violates public policy. While any child produced under such circumstances could not inherit under the state's laws of intestate succession, individuals may explicitly provide for such children in their wills. Because the state legislature has not inhibited the use of reproductive technology, any effort by the judiciary to do so would raise serious questions in light of the fundamental nature of the rights of procreation and privacy. Thus, the trial court (D) abused its discretion in ordering Kane's sperm destroyed. The order is set aside.

EDITOR'S ANALYSIS: The court of appeals referred to the Tennessee Supreme Court's ruling in Davis v. Davis, 842 S.W.2d 588, involving the disposition of frozen preembryos of a married couple who had attempted to bear a child through in vitro fertilization but divorced before they could do so. In that case, the court held that a preembryo has a status greater than human tissue but does not deserve the respect accorded to actual persons. It also concluded that decision-making authority regarding preembryos should reside with the persons who provided the gametes.

QUICKNOTES
PERSONAL PROPERTY - Any property that does not fall under the category of real property.

INTESTATE SUCCESSION - The scheme pursuant to which property is distributed in the absence of a valid will or of a disposition of particular property.

NOTES:

ESTATE OF MAHONEY
Widow (P) v. Decedents parents (D)
126 Vt. 31 (1966).

NATURE OF CASE: Appeal from an estate distribution order.

FACT SUMMARY: Mrs. Mahoney (P) was convicted of manslaughter for killing her husband.

CONCISE RULE OF LAW: A conviction of voluntary manslaughter disables the party from taking under decedent's will or through intestate succession.

FACTS: Mrs. Mahoney (P) was convicted of voluntary manslaughter for shooting her husband. Mr. Mahoney died intestate. His estate was ordered distributed to his mother (D) and father (D) since the probate court found that a conviction of voluntary manslaughter disabled Mrs. Mahoney (P) from taking any part of her husband's estate.

ISSUE: May a party convicted of the intentional killing of another inherit property from the decedent?

HOLDING AND DECISION: (Smith, J.) No. Conviction of murder or voluntary manslaughter disables the party convicted from inheriting any property from the decedent. Any inheritance in his favor is held as a constructive trust in favor of the other heirs or next of kin. While decisions in other jurisdictions vary with respect to voluntary manslaughter, the rule imposing a constructive trust appears to be the best solution. Although in this case there was no special finding concerning the voluntariness of Mrs. Mahoney's (P) actions, the court obviously concluded that she had been convicted of the felonious killing of her husband. While a constructive trust could be imposed on the bequest, the probate court could only apply the laws of distribution and descent and incorrectly awarded the property directly to Mahoney's parents. We must remand for a constructive trust action to be brought in a proper court of chancery.

EDITOR'S ANALYSIS: In a majority of states, a killer is barred by statute from inheriting any interest in the estate of his victim. In jurisdictions where no such statute has been enacted, courts have shown a reluctance to impose any restraints on the killer's right to inherit. Sometimes, however, a court of equity will adopt the constructive trust approach favored by the Mahoney court, although the trust device seems to unduly complicate the nature of the relief granted. Note that at earliest common law, the commission of any felony, not only murder, deprived the wrongdoer of his right to inherit property.

[For more information on bars to inheritance, see Casenote Law Outline on Wills, Trusts & Estates, Chapter 2, § VII, Misconduct.]

QUICKNOTES

RESIDUE - That property which remains following the distribution of the assets of the testator's estate.

CONSTRUCTIVE TRUST - A trust that arises by operation of law whereby the court imposes a trust upon property lawfully held by one party for the benefit of another, as a result of some wrongdoing by the party in possession so as to avoid unjust enrichment

NOTES:

NOTES

CHAPTER 3
WILLS: CAPACITY AND CONTESTS

QUICK REFERENCE RULES OF LAW

1. **Mental Capacity.** If a will is a product of an insane delusion, it will not be probated. (In re Strittmater)

   [For more information on incapacity, see Casenote Law Outline on Wills, Trusts, and Estates, Chapter 7, § I, Incapacity.]

2. **Mental Capacity.** A person suffering from an insane delusion as to one of his heirs has no capacity to make a will with respect to that person. (In re Honigman)

   [For more information on insane delusions, see Casenote Law Outline on Wills, Trusts & Estates, Chapter 7, § I, Incapacity.]

3. **Undue Influence.** Undue influence is shown when such control was exercised over the mind of the testator so as to overcome his free agency and free will and to substitute the will of another so as to cause the testator to do what he would not otherwise have done but for such control. (Lipper v. Weslow)

   [For more information on proof of undue influence, see Casenote Law Outline on Wills, Trusts & Estates, Chapter 7, § II, Undue Influence.]

4. **Undue Influence.** A presumption of undue influence arises when an attorney with whom the testator had a continuing fiduciary relationship is a beneficiary under the will, which is not necessarily overcome simply because the will was actually drawn up by an independent attorney with whom the testator consulted on his or her own. (In re Will of Moses)

   [For more information on the presumption of undue influence, see Casenote Law Outline on Wills, Trusts & Estates, Chapter 7, § II, Undue Influence.]

5. **Fraud.** Where a testator is prevented from executing a new will in favor of an intended beneficiary by the fraud, duress, or undue influence of a present beneficiary or heir, the property intended to go to the new beneficiary will pass to the present beneficiary subject to a constructive trust in favor of the intended beneficiary. (Latham v. Father Divine)

   [For more information on the imposition of a constructive trust, see Casenote Law Outline on Wills, Trusts & Estates, Chapter 6, § V, Constructive Trusts.]

IN RE STRITTMATER
Cousins of decedent (P) v. Court (D)
N.J. Ct. Err. & App. 140 N.J. Eq. 94, 53 A.2d 205 (1947).

NATURE OF CASE: Appeal from decree admitting will to probate.

FACT SUMMARY: Srittmater left her estate to the National Women's Party out of an extreme hatred for men.

CONCISE RULE OF LAW: If a will is a product of an insane delusion, it will not be probated.

FACTS: Strittmater, upon her death, bequeathed her estate to the National Women's Party rather than to her cousins with whom she had very little to do. The cousins contested the will. Strittmater's personal physician testified that she felt Strittmater had suffered from schizophrenia all her adult life. Strittmater's mental illness was manifested by her angry comments about her deceased parents, her vocal, intense hatred of men, and her fervent support of the women's movement. However, her relationships with her bankers and lawyer were entirely normal. The orphans court admitted the will to probate, and the cousins appealed.

ISSUE: Will a will that is the product of an insane delusion be probated?

HOLDING AND DECISION: [Per curiam.] No. A will that is the product of an insane delusion will not be probated. The testator must have been sane at the time of the will's execution to enforce the will. Strittmater's extreme hatred of men and "feminism to a neurotic extreme" demonstrated her obvious mental illness. This is true even though she had the capacity to transact ordinary business. While Strittmater gave her money to this organization, to which she belonged for eleven years, she did not involve herself enough in the party to justify her bequest. Strittmater's will was the result of mental illness and, thus, will not be entered into probate.

EDITOR'S ANALYSIS: There are three historical rationales for the sanity requirement. First of all, wills should carry out a person's intent; if the will is a product of insanity, it cannot represent his wishes. Secondly, an insane person is not a "person" as a recognized legal entity and therefore cannot be allowed to bequeath possessions. Thirdly, mental capacity is required in order to protect the family, which relies on the decedent for economic support.

[For more information on incapacity, see Casenote Law Outline on Wills, Trusts, and Estates, Chapter 7, § I, Incapacity.]

QUICKNOTES

PROBATE - The administration of a decedent's estate.

TESTATRIX - A woman who dies having drafted and executed a will or testament.

NOTES:

MATTER OF HONIGMAN
Wife of decedent (P) v. Court (D)
8 N.Y.2d 244 (1960).

NATURE OF CASE: Appeal from the denial of probate of a will.

FACT SUMMARY: Honigman had an unfounded delusion that his wife was unfaithful to him.

CONCISE RULE OF LAW: A person suffering from an insane delusion as to one of his heirs has no capacity to make a will with respect to that person.

FACTS: After forty years of a reasonably happy marriage, Honigman, after a serious operation, began to believe that his wife was unfaithful to him. Honigman began accusing her of all sorts of unreasonable acts, including hiding men in the cellar and closets, having them climb up bed sheets to reach their apartment, etc. Honigman visited a psychiatrist and several times mentioned to witnesses that he was mentally ill. Honigman died, leaving a small life estate to his wife, the remainder to his relatives. His attorney stated that his decision to make a new will just before his death was based on the belief of his wife's infidelity, her large independent estate, and the need of his other relatives. Mrs. Honigman (P) moved to deny probate of the will, alleging that, as to her, Mr. Honigman was operating under an insane delusion and lacked the mental capacity to make a will. While some testimony was offered to establish some slight grounds for Mr. Honigman's belief, the jury found that he lacked mental capacity to make a will with respect to Mrs. Honigman (P), though he was sane in all other respects.

ISSUE: May a will be denied probate where the testator had an insane delusion concerning one of his heirs, though he was sane in all other respects?

HOLDING AND DECISION: (Dye, J.) Yes. A will may be denied probate if the testator lacked the mental capacity to make a will. Probate may also be denied if testator was acting under an insane delusion with respect to one of the natural objects of his bounty, here his wife (P) of forty years. The jury was warranted in finding that there was no rational or reasonable proof of infidelity and that Honigman was operating under a totally insane delusion as to his wife's (P) conduct. It could have also found that the new will was a product of his delusion. It is immaterial that testator could have had other reasons for his actions. It is sufficient that the dispositive provisions of the will might have been caused by the insane delusion. The Probate Court properly refused to probate the will.

DISSENT: (Fuld, J.) It is not enough to show that suspicions are groundless, unwarranted, or even foolish. Testator must be shown to be insane as to that person. The evidence herein fails to establish insanity.

EDITOR'S ANALYSIS: In Dixon v. Webster, 551 S.W.2d 888 (1977), the court stated that to establish an insane delusion more was required than a showing that testator was operating under a fixed, incorrect belief. It was also necessary to establish that testator retained the belief against all arguments raised to disprove it.

[For more information on insane delusions, see Casenote Law Outline on Wills, Trusts & Estates, Chapter 7, § I, Incapacity.]

QUICKNOTES

PROBATE - The administration of a decedent's estate.

TESTAMENTARY INCAPACITY - Absence of the requisite level of mental capacity required by law, at the time a testator executes a testamentary instrument, in order for the document to be valid.

LEGATEE - A person who is granted a legacy or bequest pursuant to a will.

NOTES:

LIPPER v. WESLOW
Son of decedent (D) v.
Disinherited grandchildren of decedent (P)
Tex. Ct. Civ. App., 369 S.W.2d 698 (1963).

NATURE OF CASE: Appeal from refusal to admit will to probate.

FACT SUMMARY: The will of a testatrix was refused probate on the basis that it had been procured by undue influence of her son, who was also the lawyer who had prepared the document. The challenge was brought by three grandchildren of the testatrix who had been specifically disinherited by the terms of the will.

CONCISE RULE OF LAW: Undue influence is shown when such control was exercised over the mind of the testator so as to overcome his free agency and free will and to substitute the will of another so as to cause the testator to do what he would not otherwise have done but for such control.

FACTS: Shortly before her death, Mrs. Sophie Block executed a will that in large measure left her estate to her two surviving children. The will specifically disinherited three of her grandchildren who were descendants of a son who had died some years before. The will contained a lengthy explanation of her reasons for excluding the grandchildren. The basic theme of this portion of the will was that the grandchildren's mother had been unfriendly toward the testatrix and that the grandchildren themselves had shown no interest in the testatrix and had refrained from any contact with her. The will had been prepared by the testatrix' son, who was also a lawyer and had maintained close ties with his mother. The disinheritance of the grandchildren had the effect of increasing his share of the estate by redistributing that portion that would otherwise have gone to the grandchildren. The grandchildren [Weslow (P)] challenged the admission of the will to probate, contending that it had been procured through the undue influence of Lipper (D), the lawyer-son. The Weslows (P) contended the disinheritance clause had been inserted because Lipper (D) disliked his deceased brother. Further, the Weslows (P) disputed the factual assertions in the will that they had neglected their grandmother and contended that their attempts at contact with her had somehow been thwarted by Lipper (D). A jury returned a verdict that the will had been procured by undue influence, and the will was refused probate. Lipper (D) then brought this appeal, contending the verdict did not have a factual basis.

ISSUE: Is undue influence shown when such control was exercised over the mind of the testator as to overcome his free agency and free will and to substitute the will of another so as to cause the testator to do what he would otherwise have done but for such control?

HOLDING AND DECISION: (McDonald, C.J.) Yes. The evidence produced at trial showed that although the testatrix was 81 years old at the time this will was executed, she was sound both physically and mentally. The Weslows (P) were able to show opportunity and motive for Lipper (D) to exercise influence over the testatrix in the preparation of her will. There was a factual dispute over whether the recitation of neglect by the Weslows (P) was a true picture of what actually occurred. However, a showing of undue influence requires more than circumstantial evidence of opportunity and motive. There must be a positive showing that such control was exercised over the mind of the testator as to overcome his free will and free agency and to substitute the will of another so as to cause the testator to do what he would not otherwise have done but for such control, the groundwork for such confidential relationship and motive in the form of an unilateral disposition of the testator's estate. But thereafter, the party contending that undue influence existed must bear the burden of proof that the will of the testator was replaced by that of another. The Weslows (P) laid the groundwork but failed to carry the burden of proof thereafter required. The absence of the required proof of actual influence is sufficient to warrant a reversal of the judgment below.

EDITOR'S ANALYSIS: A principle ignored by the appellate court was that any bequest to the attorney preparing the will is presumed to have resulted from undue influence. The ABA Model Rules of Professional Conduct strongly recommends that where a client wishes to name his attorney as a beneficiary, the attorney should refer the client to another disinterested attorney for preparation of the will. The clause in the will outlining the reasons for the exclusion of the grandchildren would seem to be entitled to little weight in determining the issue of undue influence. If the will was induced by such influence, then this clause would have been no more valid than any other portion and would become merely a self-serving attempt by the influencer to cover his acts.

[For more information on proof of undue influence, see Casenote Law Outline on Wills, Trusts & Estates, Chapter 7, § II, Undue Influence.]

QUICKNOTES
UNDUE INFLUENCE - Improper influence that deprives the individual freedom of choice or substitutes another's choice for the person's own choice.

TESTATRIX - A woman who dies having drafted and executed a will or testament.

PROBATE - The administration of a decedent's estate.

IN RE WILL OF MOSES

Sister of decedent (P) v. Decedent's beneficiary (D)

Miss. Sup. Ct., 227 So. 2d 829 (1969).

NATURE OF CASE: Appeal from denial of probate.

FACT SUMMARY: The fact that an independent attorney was consulted and drew up the will by which Fannie Taylor Moses left most of her property to her attorney/lover did not overcome the presumption of undue influence, according to the court that denied probate.

CONCISE RULE OF LAW: A presumption of undue influence arises when an attorney with whom the testator had a continuing fiduciary relationship is a beneficiary under the will, which is not necessarily overcome simply because the will was actually drawn up by an independent attorney with whom the testator consulted on his or her own.

FACTS: The thrice-married Fannie Taylor Moses had an ongoing affair with an attorney, Holland, who was fifteen years her junior. She suffered from heart trouble, had a breast removed due to cancer, and was an alcoholic during the term of their affair. Her elder sister attacked Fannie Taylor Moses' will on the grounds of undue influence by Holland. The evidence showed that Moses had sought the advice of an attorney on her own, that he had no knowledge or connection with Holland, and that he drafted a will to accomplish what Moses had said was her wish, i.e., to leave her estate to Holland. The chancellor found undue influence and denied probate. Holland appealed.

ISSUE: Is the presumption of undue influence that arises when an attorney with whom the testator had a fiduciary relationship necessarily overcome by showing that the testator sought the advice of and had an independent attorney actually draw up the will?

HOLDING AND DECISION: (Smith, J.) No. The existence of a continuing fiduciary relationship between a testator and an attorney-beneficiary itself gives rise to a presumption of undue influence. While that presumption can be overcome, the mere fact that an independent attorney acted as a scrivener in properly putting into will form what Mrs. Moses wanted will not overcome the presumption of undue influence that exists in this case. There was no meaningful independent advice or counsel touching upon the proposed testamentary disposition to a nonrelative in exclusion of her blood relatives. Affirmed.

DISSENT: (Robertson, J.) If full knowledge, deliberate and voluntary action, and independent consent and advice have not been proved in this case, then they just cannot be proved.

EDITOR'S ANALYSIS: Disbarment was the price that was paid by John D. Randall, president of the American Bar Association in 1959–60, for naming himself as beneficiary of a client's $4.5-million estate. Another area in which undue influence has played an important role is the challenging of wills bequeathing estates to the surviving partner in a homosexual relationship.

[For more information on the presumption of undue influence, see Casenote Law Outline on Wills, Trusts & Estates, Chapter 7, § II, Undue Influence.]

QUICKNOTES

UNDUE INFLUENCE - Improper influence that deprives the individual freedom of choice or substitutes another's choice for the person's own choice.

PROBATE - The administration of a decedent's estate.

FIDUCIARY RELATIONSHIP - Person holding a legal obligation to act for the benefit of another.

NOTES:

LATHAM v. FATHER DIVINE
Cousins of decedent (P) v. Beneficiary (D)
N.Y. Ct. App., 299 N.Y. 22, 85 N.E.2d 168, 11 A.L.R.2d 802 (1949).

NATURE OF CASE: Suit in equity to impose constructive trust on proceeds from a will.

FACT SUMMARY: The natural heirs of a testatrix sought to gain control of a will distribution made to a religious leader who had been named sole beneficiary. The heirs claimed that the testatrix had been prevented from executing a new will in their favor by the fraud and undue influence of the religious leader.

CONCISE RULE OF LAW: Where a testator is prevented from executing a new will in favor of an intended beneficiary by the fraud, duress, or undue influence of a present beneficiary or heir, the property intended to go to the new beneficiary will pass to the present beneficiary subject to a constructive trust in favor of the intended beneficiary.

FACTS: Mary Lyon died, leaving a will which devised her entire estate to Father Divine (D), the leader of a religious cult, and to two corporations controlled by him. The will was accepted for probate after a contest filed by two first cousins of the testatrix. Thereafter, the cousins (Latham [P]), who were the testatrix' only close relatives, instituted this suit, claiming that the testatrix had expressed an intention to alter her will so as to bequeath to them property in the amount of $350,000. Latham (P) further alleged that the testatrix had been prevented from doing so by the false representations, undue influence, and physical force of Father Divine (D). Latham (P) requested that a constructive trust in their favor be imposed on the proceeds of the will to the extent of the property that would otherwise have gone to them if the testatrix had not been prevented from executing the new will. The suit was dismissed for failure to state a cause of action, and Latham (P) appealed that dismissal.

ISSUE: Where a testator is prevented from executing a new will in favor of an intended beneficiary by the fraud, duress, or undue influence of a present beneficiary or heir, will the property intended to go to the new beneficiary pass to the present beneficiary subject to a constructive trust in favor of the intended beneficiary?

HOLDING AND DECISION: (Desmond, J.) Yes. In reviewing an appeal of a dismissal of a complaint for insufficiency, the allegations of that complaint must be taken as true. If, on that basis, the complaint fails to state a cause of action, then the dismissal must be affirmed. Therefore, we must assume that the allegations of fraud, undue influence, and physical coercion actually occurred. Father Divine (D) states that a showing of the alleged acts cannot empower a court to write a new will for the testatrix. In this contention he is correct. But, where a testator is prevented from executing a new will by the wrongful acts of a present beneficiary or heir to the detriment of an intended beneficiary, and the existing will is otherwise valid, then the existing beneficiary takes his bequest subject to a constructive trust as to that portion that would have gone to the intended beneficiary but for the wrongful acts. A court of equity attempts, to the extent possible, to render complete justice. By imposing a constructive trust to avoid the result of the wrongful prevention of the execution of a new will, the court does not violate the Statute of Frauds or ignore the requirements for a valid will. The will itself is not affected; it is only the property passed under that will. If Latham (P) is able to show that the testatrix intended a different testamentary disposition than is reflected in the probated will, then Father Divine (D) cannot profit by his misconduct. The dismissal is reversed with instructions for a trial on the merits.

EDITOR'S ANALYSIS: The constructive trust remedy has also been applied where an impatient beneficiary has killed the testator in order to advance the date of the inheritance. In one instance, a number of beneficiaries were named in a will. The testatrix expressed a desire to change her will, substantially cutting out the presently named beneficiaries. Some of the present beneficiaries succeeded in physically preventing the testatrix from executing the newly drawn will. The result was a trust imposed on the entire proceeds of the will, even though this disinherited some beneficiaries who did not participate in the wrongful acts. The court reasoned that had the testatrix' intent not been thwarted, even the innocent beneficiaries would have lost their bequests. They should not be allowed to profit unjustly by the wrongful acts of the others.

[For more information on the imposition of a constructive trust, see Casenote Law Outline on Wills, Trusts & Estates, Chapter 6, § V, Constructive Trusts.]

QUICKNOTES
FRAUD - A false representation of facts with the intent that another will rely on the misrepresentation to his detriment.

UNDUE INFLUENCE - Improper influence that deprives the individual freedom of choice or substitutes another's choice for the person's own choice.

CONSTRUCTIVE TRUST - A trust that arises by operation of law whereby the court imposes a trust upon property lawfully held by one party for the benefit of another, as a result of some wrongdoing by the party in possession so as to avoid unjust enrichment.

LEGATEE - A person who is granted a legacy or bequest pursuant to a will.

DURESS - Unlawful threats or other coercive behavior by one person that causes another to commit acts that he would not otherwise do.

UNJUST ENRICHMENT - The unlawful acquisition of money or property of another for which both law and equity require restitution to be made.

NOTES

CHAPTER 4
WILLS: FORMALITIES AND FORMS

QUICK REFERENCE RULES OF LAW

1.   **Execution of Wills.** A will is not properly executed unless signed in the presence of two witnesses. (In re Groffman)

   [For more information on witness acknowledgment, see Casenote Law Outline on Wills, Trusts & Estates, Chapter 4, § I, Wills.]

2.   **Execution of Wills.** A subscribing witness to a will who is named in the will as a beneficiary does not become a "disinterested" subscribing witness by filing a disclaimer of his interest after the testator's death. (Estate of Parsons)

   [For more information on interested witnesses, see Casenote Law Outline on Wills, Trusts & Estates, Chapter 4, § I, Wills.]

3.   **Execution of Wills.** A court may not rewrite a clear and unambiguous will even for the purpose of implementing the obvious intentions of the testator. (In re Pavlinko's Estate)

   [For more information on mistakes in wills, see Casenote Law Outline on Wills, Trusts & Estates, Chapter 6, § II, Mistake as to Contracts.]

4.   **Execution of Wills.** Where witnesses, with the intent to attest a will, sign a self-proving affidavit but do not sign the will or an attestation clause, clear and convincing evidence of their intent should be produced to establish substantial compliance with the statutory requirements. (In re Will of Ranney)

   [For more information on formalities, see Casenote Law Outline on Wills, Trusts and Estates, Chapter 4, § I, Wills.]

5.   **Execution of Wills.** A printed form filled out by hand by the testator constitutes a holographic will only if the printed portion could be eliminated and the handwritten portion would still evidence the testator's testamentary intent. (In re Estate of Johnson)

   [For more information on holographic wills, see Casenote Law Outline on Wills, Trusts & Estates, Chapter 4, § I, Wills.]

6.   **Execution of Wills.** An informal document evidencing intent of a conditional gift and a intent to execute may serve as a testamentary document. (Kimmel's Estate)

   [For more information on holographic wills, see Casenote Law Outline on Wills, Trusts, and Estates, Chapter 4, § I, Wills.]

7.   **Revocation of Wills.** A rebuttable presumption of revocation exists where a will cannot be found among a deceased's personal effects. (Harrison v. Bird)

   [For more information on revocation of wills, see Casenote Law Outline on Wills, Trusts & Estates, Chapter 5, § I, Wills.]

8.   **Revocation of Wills.** Revocation of a will by cancellation is not accomplished unless the written words of

the document are mutilated or otherwise impaired. (Thompson v. Royall)

> *[For more information on revocation by cancellation, see Casenote Law Outline on Wills, Trusts & Estates, Chapter 5, § I, Wills.]*

9.   Revocation of Wills. Where the cancellation and making of a new will are parts of one scheme and the revocation of the old will is so related to the making of the new as to be dependent upon it, then, if the new will is not made or is invalid, the old will, though canceled, should be given effect. (Carter v. First United Methodist Church of Albany)

> *[For more information on dependent relative revocation, see Casenote Law Outline on Wills, Trusts and Estates, Chapter 5, § I, Wills.]*

10.   Revocation of Wills. Where a will is mistakenly revoked in the belief that an earlier revoked will would be revived, the doctrine of dependent relative revocation may be applied to revive the mistakenly revoked will. (Estate of Alburn)

> *[For more information on dependent relative revocation, see Casenote Law Outline on Wills, Trusts & Estates, Chapter 5, § I, Wills.]*

11.   Components of a Will. A properly executed will may incorporate by reference into its provisions any document or paper not so executed and witnessed, if it was in existence at the time of the execution of the will and is identified by clear and satisfactory proof as the paper referred to therein. (Clark v. Greenhalge)

> *[For more information on incorporation by reference, see Casenote Law Outline on Wills, Trusts and Estates, Chapter 6, § VI, Incorporation by Reference and Pour-Over Wills.]*

12.   Components of a Will. A valid, holographic codicil may incorporate and republish a prior will which would have been ineffective because of its failure to comply with formal requisites. (Johnson v. Johnson)

> *[For more information on republication by codicil, see Casenote Law Outline on Wills, Trusts & Estates, Chapter 5, § I, Wills.]*

13.   Contracts Relating to Wills. The rights of beneficiaries under a contract to make a will are limited by the possibility that the survivor might remarry and that the subsequent spouse might elect against the will. (Shimp v. Huff)

> *[For more information on contracts relating to wills, see Casenote Law Outline on Wills, Trusts & Estates, Chapter 8, § II, Remedies.]*

IN RE GROFFMAN
Widow of decedent (P) v. Court (D)
I.W.L.R. 733 (1968).

NATURE OF CASE: Appeal from the denial of probate of a will.

FACT SUMMARY: The witnesses of Groffman's will never saw him sign it.

CONCISE RULE OF LAW: A will is not properly executed unless signed in the presence of two witnesses.

FACTS: Groffman signed his will and then went to the home of some friends and asked them to act as witnesses. Two people signed as witnesses, though not in each other's presence, and neither actually saw Groffman sign the will. Mrs. Groffman (P) challenged the validity of the will, alleging that it was inadmissible to probate since it had been improperly executed. The statute required that the testator sign the will in the presence of two or more witnesses who shall then acknowledge the signature in the presence of the testator. The court found that the will had not been properly acknowledged and denied it probate.

ISSUE: Must there be a literal compliance with the acknowledgment statute to have a valid will?

HOLDING AND DECISION: (Simon, P.) Yes. There is no doubt that the will contained Mr. Groffman's testamentary plan or that he had actually signed it. If I could give it effect, I would. However, the Statute of Wills is to be strictly interpreted, and for a will to be valid, it must be executed in literal compliance with the statute. Here, Groffman did not sign the will in the presence of both witnesses, nor did they acknowledge his signature in each other's presence. This will must, therefore, be denied probate.

EDITOR'S ANALYSIS: Normaly, witnesses must sign in the physical presence of the testator. Failure to sign where he can see them renders the acknowledgment void. I.T. Jarman, Wills 138 (8th ed. 1951). An exception is made for those who are blind. In some jurisdictions, an exemption is made where the witnesses are within the conscious presence of the testator, e.g., on the other side of a screen which has been placed around the testator's bed. Glenn v. Mann, 234 Ga. 194 (1975).

[For more information on witness acknowledgment, see Casenote Law Outline on Wills, Trusts & Estates, Chapter 4, § I, Wills.]

QUICKNOTES
PROBATE - The administration of a decedent's estate.

ATTESTATION CLAUSE - That portion of a will purporting to have testamentary effect on the testator's disposition, as attested to by witnesses.

RES GESTAE - Any statement spoken very closely to the occurrence being expressed that it carries a strong presumption of credibility.

NOTES:

ESTATE OF PARSONS

Parties not identified

Cal. Ct. App., 103 Cal. App. 3d 384 (1980).

NATURE OF CASE: Appeal in a probate proceeding.

FACT SUMMARY: Of primary concern during the probate of Geneve Parsons' will was whether or not a subscribing witness to the will could be considered to have been a "disinterested" witness by reason of her subsequent disclaimer of a bequest made therein to her.

CONCISE RULE OF LAW: A subscribing witness to a will who is named in the will as a beneficiary does not become a "disinterested" subscribing witness by filing a disclaimer of his interest after the testator's death.

FACTS: Two of the three persons who signed Geneve Parsons' will as attesting witnesses were named therein as beneficiaries. After the testator's death, Nielson filed a disclaimer of her $100 bequest. Relatives of Parsons claimed an interest in the estate on the ground that the devise of certain real property to Gower, the other subscribing witness to whom a bequest was made, was invalid. The basis for this claim was a statute which provided that a gift to a subscribing witness is void "unless there are two other and disinterested subscribing witnesses to the will." The relatives insisted that Nielson's subsequent disclaimer of her bequest did not change the fact that she was not a "disinterested" subscribing witness, that only one of the subscribing witnesses could, thus, be considered "disinterested," and that the property bequest to Gower was consequently invalid. The trial court rejected that argument.

ISSUE: Does a subscribing witness to a will who is named as a beneficiary therein become "disinterested" by filing a disclaimer of his interest after the testator's death?

HOLDING AND DECISION: (Grodin, J.) No. While the court might like to substitute a rule more to its liking, the fact is that a subscribing witness to a will who is named as a beneficiary therein does not become a "disinterested" subscribing witness by filing a disclaimer of his interest after the testator's death. The statutory provision regarding subscribing witnesses looks solely to the time of execution and attestation of the will. So, it follows that a subsequent disclaimer will be ineffective to transform an interested witness into a "disinterested" one. If such a transformation were possible, the purpose of the subscribing witness statute, as it was designed, would be undermined, i.e. to protect the testator from fraud and undue influence at the very moment when he executes his will. Reversed.

EDITOR'S ANALYSIS: Uniform Probate Code § 2-505 adopts the following rule: "(a) Any person generally competent to be a witness may act as a witness to a will. (b) A will or any provision thereof is not invalid because the will is signed by an interested witness." Solicitation of business by the attorney-drafter of a will in regard to his being employed as the estate's attorney is a violation of the code of professional responsibility. State v. Gulbankian, 196 N.W.2d 733 (Wis. 1972).

[For more information on interested witnesses, see Casenote Law Outline on Wills, Trusts & Estates, Chapter 4, § I, Wills.]

QUICKNOTES

PROBATE - The administration of a decedent's estate.

FRAUD - A false representation of facts with the intent that another will rely on the misrepresentation to his detriment.

UNDUE INFLUENCE - Improper influence that deprives the individual freedom of choice or substitutes another's choice for the person's own choice.

SUBSCRIBING WITNESS - A person who witnesses the execution of a document and signs his name thereto.

NOTES:

IN RE PAVLINKO'S ESTATE
Residuary (P) v. Register of wills (D)
Pa. Sup. Ct., 394 Pa. 564, 148 A.2d 528 (1959).

NATURE OF CASE: Action to have a will admitted to probate.

FACT SUMMARY: Vasil and Hellen Pavlinko inadvertently signed one another's wills. On Vasil's death, Martin (P), a legatee under Hellen's will, sought to have that will probated as Vasil's.

CONCISE RULE OF LAW: A court may not rewrite a clear and unambiguous will even for the purpose of implementing the obvious intentions of the testator.

FACTS: Vasil and Hellen Pavlinko, neither of whom spoke much English, had wills prepared for them. Each left their property to the other, and each designated Elias Martin (P), Hellen's brother, as residuary. Through inadvertence, Hellen Pavlinko signed the will which had been prepared for her husband, and he signed the will which had been prepared for her. Several years later, Hellen Pavlinko died. Some time afterward, her husband also passed away. Upon Vasil's death, Martin (P) filed Hellen's will, the only one which Vasil had signed, and asked that it be admitted to probate as Vasil's will. The Register of Wills refused to admit the will to probate, and when the Orphans' Court affirmed, Martin (P) appealed.

ISSUE: If a party mistakenly signs another will instead of his own, may the will he signed be modified at his death to include the provisions of the instrument which he had intended to sign?

HOLDING AND DECISION: (Bell, J.) No. A court may not rewrite a clear and unambiguous will even for the purpose of implementing the obvious intentions of the testator. The will which Vasil Pavlinko signed leaves the entire estate to him. In order to award the property to Martin (P) as residuary legatee, it would be necessary to rewrite virtually the entire instrument, and such a procedure cannot be countenanced in the case of a will so totally lacking in ambiguity as this one. Thus, the will which Vasil signed cannot be admitted to probate as his will. The will which was prepared for him cannot, of course, be probated, because he never signed it. Therefore, the regrettable result, which is supported by the holding of a case which presented a fact situation substantially the same as that of this case, is that Elias Martin (P) is entitled to no relief.

DISSENT: (Musmanno, J.) The will signed by Vasil Pavlinko should be admitted to probate. Even if it is not possible to give effect to every provision of that will, there is no reason why the court cannot enforce the residuary clause, which designates Martin (P) as beneficiary.

EDITOR'S ANALYSIS: This case illustrates the reluctance of courts to compromise the prophylactic objects of statutes relating to the formal execution of wills. The court declined to "bend the rules" and, thus, permitted the statute to operate as an intent-defeating device. At least one court, albeit a distant one, granted relief in a case similar to In Re Pavlinko's Estate. In Guardian, Trust, etc. Co. v. Inwood, (1946) N.Z.L.R. 614, wills were prepared for two sisters, each of whom left their estates to the other. Jane then signed Maude's will, but a New Zealand court enforced that will after striking the word "Jane" from the body of the will.

[For more information on mistakes in wills, see Casenote Law Outline on Wills, Trusts & Estates, Chapter 6, § II, Mistake as to Contracts.]

QUICKNOTES
RESIDUARY LEGATEE - The recipient of the residuary estate of a testator.

PROBATE - The administration of a decedent's estate.

NOTES:

IN RE WILL OF RANNEY
Parties not identified
N.J. Sup. Ct., 124 N.J. 1, 589 A.2d 1339 (1991).

NATURE OF CASE: Appeal from reversal of a ruling in a will contest denying admission to probate.

FACT SUMMARY: After Ranney's death, his wife, Betty (P), contested probate of his will on the ground that the signatures of the witnesses on a separate self-proving affidavit failed to satisfy the statutory requirements.

CONCISE RULE OF LAW: Where witnesses, with the intent to attest a will, sign a self-proving affidavit but do not sign the will or an attestation clause, clear and convincing evidence of their intent should be produced to establish substantial compliance with the statutory requirements.

FACTS: Ranney signed his will in his attorney's law office, in the presence of another lawyer and a secretary. The witnesses did not sign the will itself, however. Instead, they signed a self-proving affidavit contained on a separate page. Both witnesses believed that they were signing and attesting the will, and both attorneys believed that the signatures on the affidavit complied with the statutory requirements. After Ranney's death, his wife, Betty (P), contested probate of Ranney's will on the ground that it failed to comply with the statutory formality requirements. The surrogate who ordered probate of the will was reversed by the law division of the superior court, but the appellate division reversed and admitted the will to probate. Betty (P) appealed.

ISSUE: Where witnesses, with the intent to attest a will, sign a self-proving affidavit but do not sign the will or an attestation clause, should clear and convincing evidence of their intent be produced to establish substantial compliance with the statutory requirements?

HOLDING AND DECISION: (Pollock, J.) Yes. Where witnesses, with the intent to attest a will, sign a self-proving affidavit but do not sign the will or an attestation clause, clear and convincing evidence of their intent should be produced to establish substantial compliance with the statutory requirements. Substantial compliance is a functional rule designed to cure the inequity caused by the formalism of the law of wills. The primary purpose of formalities is to ensure that the document reflects the uncoerced intent of the testator. However, rigid insistence on literal compliance often frustrates this purpose. It would be ironic if such literal compliance with formalities invalidated a will that is the deliberate and voluntary act of a testator. Thus, the will should be admitted to probate. Affirmed.

EDITOR'S ANALYSIS: Self-proving affidavits and attestation clauses, although substantially similar in content, serve different functions. Attestation clauses facilitate probate by providing "prima facie evidence" that the testator voluntarily signed the will in the presence of the witnesses. Self-proving affidavits, by comparison, are sworn statements by eyewitnesses that the will has been duly executed. In other words, in the attestation clause, the attestant expresses the present intent to act as a witness, while in the affidavit, the affiant swears the will has already been witnessed.

[For more information on formalities, see Casenote Law Outline on Wills, Trusts and Estates, Chapter 4, § I, Wills.]

QUICKNOTES

ATTESTATION REQUIREMENTS - The required actions to be taken by a witness to the execution of a document in order for that instrument to be subsequently valid.

ATTESTATION CLAUSE - That portion of a will purporting to have testamentary effect on the testator's disposition, as attested to by witnesses.

NOTES:

IN RE ESTATE OF JOHNSON
Parties not identified
Ariz. Ct. App., 129 Ariz. 312, 630 P.2d 1044 (1981).

NATURE OF CASE: Appeal from summary judgment denying admission of a will to probate.

FACT SUMMARY: The personal representative for Johnson's estate objected to having admitted to probate as a holographic will a printed will form that Arnold H. Johnson had filled out in his handwriting.

CONCISE RULE OF LAW: A printed form filled out by hand by the testator constitutes a holographic will only if the printed portion could be eliminated and the handwritten portion would still evidence the testator's testamentary intent.

FACTS: Prior to his death, Arnold H. Johnson obtained a printed will form and proceeded to fill in the blanks in his handwriting. When a petition for probate of that instrument was filed, the personal representative objected on the grounds that it was invalid as a regular will in that it was not attested by any witness and that it did not qualify as a holographic will because material provisions thereof were not in the testator's handwriting. Having adopted the position of the Uniform Probate Code, Arizona law provided that a will is a valid "holographic will, whether or not witnessed, if the signature and the material provisions are in the handwriting of the testator." The trial court granted the personal representative's motion for summary judgment.

ISSUE: In order for a printed form that has been filled out by the testator by hand to constitute a valid holographic will, must the printed portions be such that if they were eliminated the handwritten portions that remain would evidence the testator's testamentary intent?

HOLDING AND DECISION: (Wren, C.J.) Yes. When a testator has taken a printed form and filled in the blanks, the resulting document does not satisfy the statutory requirement that the material provisions of a holographic will be in the testator's own handwriting unless the printed portion could be eliminated and the handwritten portion would nonetheless evidence the testator's testamentary intent. In this case, the only words that established the requisite testamentary intent were found in the printed portion of the form. Affirmed.

CONCURRENCE: (Contreras, J.) Although correct, this result defeats the purposes of effectuating the intent of the decedent and simplifying the execution of wills and, thus, justifies a reappraisal of the statutorily expressed requirements of a holographic will.

EDITOR'S ANALYSIS: Only half of the states recognize holographic wills, and they are mostly in the South and West. Several of them require that the "entire" will be handwritten. The cases are replete with odd objects that have been submitted as holographic wills because of writings thereon, including a nurse's petticoat, an eggshell, a tractor fender (onto which the will was scratched), and a sawed-out section of the plaster wall of a bedroom.

[For more information on holographic wills, see Casenote Law Outline on Wills, Trusts & Estates, Chapter 4, § I, Wills.]

QUICKNOTES
HOLOGRAPHIC WILL - A will that is handwritten by the testator or testatrix.

PROBATE - The administration of a decedent's estate.

TESTAMENTARY INTENT - A determination that the document was intended to be a will and as such, reflects the writer's true wishes.

NOTES:

KIMMEL'S ESTATE

Parties not identified

Pa. Sup. Ct., 278 Pa. 435, 123 A. 405 (1924).

NATURE OF CASE: Appeal from entry of a letter into probate.

FACT SUMMARY: Kimmel, the decedent, wrote a letter to his sons mentioning, among other things, what was to happen to his possessions if anything were to happen to him. His sons attempted to probate the letter.

CONCISE RULE OF LAW: An informal document evidencing intent of a conditional gift and a intent to execute may serve as a testamentary document.

FACTS: Kimmel wrote a letter to his sons which was mailed by him on the day of his death. The letter was very poorly written but contained a discussion of the weather, butchering, and a possible trip to town. It also stated, "if enny thing happens all the scock money in the 3 Bank liberty lones Post office stamps and my home on Horner St goes to George Darl and Irvin Kepp [my two sons] this letter lock it up it may help you out." The letter was dated and signed "Father." The heirs at law (P) protested the entry of the letter into probate.

ISSUE: Can an informal document evidencing intent of a conditional gift and a intent to execute serve as a testamentary document?

HOLDING AND DECISION: (Simpson, J.) Yes. An informal document evidencing intent of a conditional gift and an intent to execute can serve as a testamentary document. In this case, Kimmel's language, however poor, telling his sons what should happen if he were not to survive clearly shows a gift that is conditional upon the occurrence of something, namely Kimmel's death. Most holographic wills are informal in character, and the fact that the weather is discussed in the document does not change its testamentary effect. Also, the fact that Kimmel signed all his letters "Father" shows that he considered this letter a final and executed document. The intent to execute is more important than Kimmel's knowledge of the formal requirements for execution. Affirmed.

EDITOR'S ANALYSIS: Most courts interpret conditional wills as stating the testator's inducement to execute the will rather than an actual condition that must be fulfilled before the will can be probated. For example, in Eaton v. Brown, 193 U.S. 411 (1904), the testator's holographic will stated: "I am going on a journey and may not return. If I do not, I leave everything to my adopted son." The testator did in fact return, only to die several months later. The court held the will entitled to probate on the grounds that her statement about not returning was merely an expression of her thoughts at the time she wrote the will, not an event that must occur in order to make the will effective.

[For more information on holographic wills, see Casenote Law Outline on Wills, Trusts, and Estates, Chapter 4, § I, Wills.]

QUICKNOTES

HOLOGRAPHIC WILL - A will that is handwritten by the testator or testatrix.

TESTAMENTARY INTENT - A determination that the document was intended to be a will and as such, reflects the writer's true wishes.

NOTES:

HARRISON v. BIRD
Beneficiary (P) v. Decedent's cousin (D)
Ala. Sup. Ct., 621 So. 2d 972 (1993).

NATURE OF CASE: Appeal from a judgment of intestacy.

FACT SUMMARY: After Speer died, Harrison (P), sole beneficiary of Speer's will, filed for probate a document purporting to be Speer's last will and testament, despite the fact that Speer's attorney had torn Speer's will into four pieces after she informed him that she wanted to revoke her will.

CONCISE RULE OF LAW: A rebuttable presumption of revocation exists where a will cannot be found among a deceased's personal effects.

FACTS: A year and a half after Speer executed a will naming Harrison (P) as the main beneficiary of her estate, she advised her attorney that she wanted to revoke her will. Her attorney tore the will into four pieces, informing Speer by letter that he had "revoked" her will as instructed and was sending the pieces of the will to her. State law required that, to be lawfully revoked, a will must be destroyed in the testator's presence. When Speer died, the letter was found but not the four pieces of the will. The probate court granted letters of administration to Bird (D), Speer's cousin. Harrison (P) filed for probate a duplicate of the original will. The court ruled that, although Speer's will was not lawfully revoked, there arose a presumption that Speer had revoked the will herself since the destroyed will was not found. The court held that Harrison (P) had not rebutted the presumption of revocation and that the estate should be administered as an intestate estate and confirmed the letters of administration issued to Bird (D). Harrison (P) appealed.

ISSUE: Does a rebuttable presumption of revocation exist where a will cannot be found among a deceased's personal effects?

HOLDING AND DECISION: (Houston, J.) Yes. A rebuttable presumption of revocation exists where a will cannot be found among a deceased's personal effects. Under Alabama state law, Speer's will was not lawfully revoked because her attorney destroyed it at her direction and consent but not in her presence. However, where a testator destroys the copy of the will in her possession, a presumption arises that she has revoked her will and all duplicates, even though a duplicate exists that is not in her possession. The burden of rebutting the presumption is on the proponent of the will. Under the facts of this case, there existed a presumption that Speer destroyed her will, thus revoking it. Harrison (P) did not present sufficient evidence to rebut the presumption, i.e., to convince the trier of fact that the absence of the will was not due to Speer's destroying and thus revoking the will. Affirmed.

EDITOR'S ANALYSIS: A will may be revoked either by executing a subsequent will that revokes the previous one (expressly or by inconsistency) or by physical destruction of the will, known as "performing a revocatory act on the will." Revocatory acts include tearing, burning, or obliterating the will, either completely or partially. If neither of the two steps above are taken, the will, if duly executed, will be admitted to probate.

[For more information on revocation of wills, see Casenote Law Outline on Wills, Trusts & Estates, Chapter 5, § I, Wills.]

QUICKNOTES
EXECUTRIX - A female person designated by a deceased individual to effectuate the disposition of his property pursuant to a testamentary instrument.

INTESTATE ESTATE - The property of an individual who dies without executing a valid will.

NOTES:

THOMPSON v. ROYALL
Parties not identified
Va. Sup. Ct. App., 163 Va. 492, 175 S.E. 748 (1934).

NATURE OF CASE: Action to probate a will.

FACT SUMMARY: Mrs. Kroll attempted to revoke her will and codicil by signing notations on the back of each which purported to render them void.

CONCISE RULE OF LAW: Revocation of a will by cancellation is not accomplished unless the written words of the document are mutilated or otherwise impaired.

FACTS: Mrs. M. Lou Bowen Kroll executed an attested will which she gave to Brittain, her executor, for safekeeping. She then executed a codicil, which she signed in the presence of two attesting witnesses and gave to Judge Coulling, the attorney who prepared both documents. She later instructed Coulling to destroy both documents but was persuaded by Coulling to retain the documents for her use in case she decided to execute a new will. She signed a statement written on the back of the will by Coulling which read, "This will null and void and to be only held by H.P. Brittain, instead of being destroyed, as a memorandum for another will if I decide to make same." An identical statement but substituting Coulling's name for Brittain's was written by Coulling on the back of the codicil and was signed by Mrs. Kroll. Upon her death, Mrs. Kroll left an estate valued at approximately $200,000. The will and codicil were offered for probate and contested by various nieces (P) and nephews (P) who were not mentioned in the instruments. The jury found the documents to be the last will and testament of Mrs. Kroll, and from an order sustaining that verdict and probating the will, contestants (P) brought this writ of error.

ISSUE: May a memorandum written in another's handwriting on the reverse side of a testamentary instrument and signed by the testator, purporting to void the document, effect a revocation by cancellation of the instrument?

HOLDING AND DECISION: (Hudgin, J.) No. In order to effect revocation by cancellation, the testator must actually mutilate, erase, deface, or otherwise mark the written portions of the testamentary instrument. It is true that in Warner v. Warner's Estate, 37 Vt. 356, one court permitted cancellation by a writing which did not actually touch written portions of the will, but that decision has not been followed and has been justly criticized by commentators. Thus, although the testatrix obviously intended to revoke her will, she did not revoke it by cancellation. Furthermore, the contestants (P) agree that the memorandum did not constitute a "valid writing indicating an intention to revoke" under the appropriate statute since it was not in testatrix' own handwriting or attested to by witnesses. Therefore, the will and codicil were not revoked, and the order admitting them to probate must be affirmed.

EDITOR'S ANALYSIS: Thompson v. Royall accords with authorities generally. If words purporting to effect the cancellation of a will are written in the margin or on the reverse side of the instrument, they are ineffective to accomplish their purpose. However, the writing of words such as "void" or "canceled" will effect a revocation of a will if written across material portions of the will. The rule of Warner v. Warner's Estate, disapproved by the court, is in general disrepute.

[For more information on revocation by cancellation, see Casenote Law Outline on Wills, Trusts & Estates, Chapter 5, § I, Wills.]

QUICKNOTES

CODICIL - A supplement to a will.

SUBSCRIBING WITNESS - A person who witnesses the execution of a document and signs his name thereto.

DEVISAVIT VEL NON - A matter transferred from a court of chancery to a court of law in order to determine whether a certain document was intended to be a will.

REVOCATION - The cancellation or withdrawal of some authority conferred or an instrument drafted, such as the withdrawal of a revocable contract offer prior to the offeree's acceptance.

NOTES:

CARTER v. FIRST UNITED METHODIST CHURCH
Parties not identified
Ga. Sup. Ct., 246 Ga. 352, 271 S.E.2d 493 (1980).

NATURE OF CASE: Appeal from judgment admitting a will to probate.

FACT SUMMARY: After Tipton's death, her old will was found with pencil marks through the property disposition clauses and was folded together with a handwritten instrument devising a different scheme of property distribution.

CONCISE RULE OF LAW: Where the cancellation and making of a new will are parts of one scheme and the revocation of the old will is so related to the making of the new as to be dependent upon it, then, if the new will is not made or is invalid, the old will, though canceled, should be given effect.

FACTS: After Tipton's death, the will she had executed in 1963 was found among her other personal papers. That will was folded together with a handwritten instrument dated 1978, captioned as her will but unsigned and unwitnessed, establishing a different scheme of distribution of her property. Pencil marks had also been made diagonally through the property disposition provisions of the 1963 document and through the name of one of the coexecutors. Carter (P) opposed probate of the 1963 will, contending that Tipton would have preferred intestacy. The Church (D) argued that Tipton would have preferred the property disposition clauses of the 1963 will over intestacy. The trial court admitted the 1963 will to probate, and Carter (P) appealed.

ISSUE: Where the cancellation and making of a new will are parts of one scheme and the revocation of the old will is so related to the making of the new as to be dependent upon it, then, if the new will is not made or is invalid, should the old will, though canceled, be given effect?

HOLDING AND DECISION: (Nichols, J.) Yes. Where the cancellation and making of a new will are parts of one scheme and the revocation of the old will is so related to the making of the new as to be dependent upon it, then, if the new will is not made or is invalid, the old will, though canceled, should be given effect. Here, the fact that the 1963 will was found among Tipton's personal papers, folded together with the 1978 writing, is evidence tending to establish that the cancellation and the making of the new will were parts of one scheme, and the revocation of the old will was so related to the making of the new as to be dependent upon it. This evidence was sufficient to give rise to an unrebutted presumption in favor of the Church (D) under the doctrine of dependent relative revocation, also known as conditional revocation. Thus, the trial court did not err in admitting the 1963 will to probate. Affirmed.

EDITOR'S ANALYSIS: The doctrine of dependent relative revocation is a doctrine of presumed intention, resulting from an effort to arrive at the real intention of the testator. The Georgia Supreme Court referred to its decision in McIntyre v. McIntyre, 120 Ga. 67 (1904), as representing a sound application of the doctrine. As a general rule, the burden is on a person attacking a paper offered for probate as a will to sustain the grounds of his attack. Here, Carter (P) failed to rebut the presumption against intestacy.

[For more information on dependent relative revocation, see Casenote Law Outline on Wills, Trusts and Estates, Chapter 5, § I, Wills.]

QUICKNOTES

CAVEATOR - A person or party who files a warning with the court or judge against using certain powers within the court or the judge's authority.

DEPENDENT RELATIVE REVOCATION - The doctrine which states that if the same person executes a will which revokes an earlier will, the earlier will is only revoked if the latter will is effective. Otherwise the earlier will remains in full effect and force.

INTESTACY - To die without leaving a valid testamentary instrument.

NOTES:

ESTATE OF ALBURN
Parties not identified
18 Wis. 2d 340 (1963).

NATURE OF CASE: Appeal from the admission of a will to probate.

FACT SUMMARY: Alburn revoked a will in the mistaken belief that this would reinstate an earlier revoked will.

CONCISE RULE OF LAW: Where a will is mistakenly revoked in the belief that an earlier revoked will would be revived, the doctrine of dependent relative revocation may be applied to revive the mistakenly revoked will.

FACTS: Alburn, while living in Milwaukee, had a will drawn up leaving her estate to her husband's relatives. Alburn subsequently moved to Kankakee and had a new will drawn up specifically revoking the Milwaukee will. There were several changes in bequests, but the bulk of her estate was still left to the relatives of her deceased husband. Alburn then revoked the Kankakee will, based on uncontradicted testimony at the trial to probate this will, in the mistaken belief that revocation of the Kankakee will would revive the Milwaukee will. Alburn subsequently died, and her heirs (D) alleged that she died intestate. Both the Milwaukee and Kankakee wills were offered to the probate court. The court found that the Milwaukee will had been revoked and could not be admitted. The Kankakee will was deemed to be valid under the doctrine of dependent relative revocation on the grounds that Alburn had revoked it by mistake and she had not wanted to die intestate since all of her heirs at law, one a minor, had no bequests under her wills.

ISSUE: Where a will has been revoked on the mistaken belief that this would revive an earlier revoked will, may the doctrine of dependent relative revocation be applied?

HOLDING AND DECISION: (Currie, J.) Yes. The doctrine of dependent relative revocation may also be applied to situations such as the one herein where a will is revoked in the mistaken belief that it would revive any earlier revoked will. The uncontradicted evidence establishes Alburn's mistaken belief. The testamentary scheme under the Kankakee will is closer to Alburn's testamentary plan than distribution through intestate succession would be. There is no showing that Alburn wished to die intestate or that any change in circumstances had occurred. Under this type of situation, the doctrine of dependent relative revocation should be applied. Affirmed.

EDITOR'S ANALYSIS: A few jurisdictions and the English courts hold that the revocation of a subsequently executed will revives the earlier revoked will since the revocation clause in the subsequent will has, itself, been revoked. Since a will is an ambulatory document having no legal effect until the date of the testator's death, the revocation clause is ineffective if revoked before the testator's death. Goodright v. Glazier, 4 Burr. 2512 (1770).

_____

[For more information on dependent relative revocation, see Casenote Law Outline on Wills, Trusts & Estates, Chapter 5, § I, Wills.]

QUICKNOTES
DEPENDENT RELATIVE REVOCATION - The doctrine which states that if the same person executes a will which revokes an earlier will, the earlier will is only revoked if the latter will is effective. Otherwise the earlier will remains in full effect and force.

ESTATE ADMINISTRATOR - A person designated by a court to effectuate the disposition of a decedent's estate.

LEGATEE - A person who is granted a legacy or bequest pursuant to a will.

EXECUTRIX - A female person designated by a deceased individual to effectuate the disposition of his property pursuant to a testamentary instrument.

RESIDUARY CLAUSE (OF WILL) - A clause contained in a will disposing of the assets remaining following distribution of the estate.

NOTES:

CLARK v. GREENHALGE

Beneficiary (P) v. Primary beneficiary and executor

Mass. Sup. Ct., 411 Mass. 410, 582 N.E.2d 949 (1991).

NATURE OF CASE: Appeal from a judgment incorporating a notebook by reference into the terms of a will.

FACT SUMMARY: Although Nesmith reserved the right in her will to make a further disposition of personal property by a memorandum, Greenhalge (D), the executor, refused to comply with one of Nesmith's bequests written in a notebook.

CONCISE RULE OF LAW: A properly executed will may incorporate by reference into its provisions any document or paper not so executed and witnessed, if it was in existence at the time of the execution of the will and is identified by clear and satisfactory proof as the paper referred to therein.

FACTS: Nesmith executed a will, naming Greenhalge (D) as executor of her estate and also the principal beneficiary, but reserved the right to make further disposition of tangible personal property as designated by a memorandum. In addition to a memorandum list of items to be distributed, Nesmith periodically made entries into a notebook, designating bequests of personal property. One of those bequests gave Clark (P) an oil painting of a farm scene. After Nesmith's death, Greenhalge (D) complied with all her bequests, except the one for the painting. Clark (P) commenced this action to compel Greenhalge (D) to deliver the painting to her. The probate judge awarded the painting to Clark (P), and Greenhalge (D) appealed.

ISSUE: May a properly executed will incorporate by reference into its provisions any document or paper not so executed and witnessed, if it was in existence at the time of the execution of the will and is identified by clear and satisfactory proof as the paper referred to therein?

HOLDING AND DECISION: (Nolan, J.) Yes. A properly executed will may incorporate by reference into its provisions any document or paper not so executed and witnessed, if it was in existence at the time of the execution of the will and is identified by clear and satisfactory proof as the paper referred to therein. Here, the parties agree that the memorandum document was incorporated into the will, but Greenhalge (D) contends that the notebook was not incorporated. However, the statements in the notebook unquestionably reflect Nesmith's exercise of her right to restructure the distribution of her tangible personal property upon her death. That the notebook is not entitled "memorandum" is of no consequence. The evidence supports the conclusion that Nesmith intended that the bequests in her notebook be accorded the same power and effect as those contained in the memorandum referenced in her will. Affirmed.

EDITOR'S ANALYSIS: The cardinal rule in the interpretation of wills is that the intention of the testator shall prevail, provided it is consistent with the rules of law. To narrowly construe the will to exclude the notebook contents as "a memorandum" would undermine that long-standing policy. The most recent (1991) version of the Uniform Probate Code requires that a will may refer to a separate memo or list disposing of personal property, but such a list must be signed by the testator in order to be given effect.

[For more information on incorporation by reference, see Casenote Law Outline on Wills, Trusts and Estates, Chapter 6, § VI, Incorporation by Reference and Pour-over Wills.]

QUICKNOTES

TESTATRIX - A woman who dies having drafted and executed a will or testament.

SPECIFIC BEQUEST - A transfer of property that is accomplished by means of a testamentary instrument.

CODICIL - A supplement to a will.

NOTES:

JOHNSON v. JOHNSON
Parties not identified
Okla. Sup. Ct., 279 P.2d 928 (1954).

NATURE OF CASE: Appeal from a judgment denying probate to a purported will.

FACT SUMMARY: Johnson typed a three-paragraph "will" but did not sign it or have it witnessed. Later, at the bottom of the same page, he wrote, signed, and dated a short dispositive passage.

CONCISE RULE OF LAW: A valid, holographic codicil may incorporate and republish a prior will which would have been ineffective because of its failure to comply with formal requisites.

FACTS: Johnson, an experienced attorney who had drafted many valid wills for his clients, typed a three-paragraph document by which he purported to make a final disposition of his property. Although the document was apparently intended to serve as his will, he neither signed nor dated it and never had the instrument attested to. Sometime later, he added a paragraph at the bottom of the page. That paragraph, which was signed and dated, was written in Johnson's own hand. It provided in part, "To my brother James I give ten dollars only. This will shall be complete unless hereafter altered, changed or rewritten." Upon Johnson's death, the entire page, consisting of both the typed and handwritten portions, was offered for probate. The opponent (D) of the instrument charged that the entire document constituted a single integrated will which, since it was partially typewritten, failed for want of valid execution and attestation. Its proponents (P) claimed that the paper consisted of an invalid typewritten will and a valid holographic codicil and that the codicil republished and validated the ineffective will. The trial court denied the petition for probate, and an appellate tribunal affirmed. The proponents (P) of the instrument then appealed to the state supreme court.

ISSUE: Can a valid, holographic codicil republish and validate a prior ineffective will?

HOLDING AND DECISION: [Per curiam.] Yes. A valid, holographic codicil may incorporate and republish a prior will which would have been ineffective because of its failure to comply with formal requisites. Any writing which is properly executed may constitute a codicil if it is so intended by the testator. In this case, Johnson's handwritten paragraph qualifies as a valid codicil, and, by the weight of authority, that codicil incorporates and validates the three-paragraph will, which, but for the codicil, would have failed for want of execution and attestation. The judgments of the courts below must, therefore, be reversed and the will ordered admitted to probate.

CONCURRENCE: (Corn, J.) The majority's opinion is a commendable one since it implements the obvious intentions of the testator.

DISSENT: (Halley, C.J.) The language of the handwritten paragraph indicates that it was intended as an addition to the typed will and was not designed to serve as a codicil thereto. The entire page should, therefore, be deemed to constitute one will, which, because it does not comply with the statutory formalities, is ineffective and not appropriate for admission to probate.

EDITOR'S ANALYSIS: Most courts recognize that any will, including an invalid one, is republished and, if necessary, validated by the execution of an effective codicil. Thus, the result of the Johnson case depended on whether or not the handwritten passage added by the testator qualified as a codicil. Ordinarily, a codicil must comply with the same formal requisites as are necessary to create a valid will. Thus, a holographic codicil must be entirely handwritten, it must be signed and dated, it must be intended to serve as a testamentary instrument, and it must dispose of at least some property of the testator.

[For more information on republication by codicil, see Casenote Law Outline on Wills, Trusts & Estates, Chapter 5, § I, Wills.]

QUICKNOTES

CODICIL - A supplement to a will.

HOLOGRAPHIC CODICIL - A handwritten provision added to a testamentary instrument.

UNDUE INFLUENCE - Improper influence that deprives the individual freedom of choice or substitutes another's choice for the person's own choice.

REVOCATION - The cancellation or withdrawal of some authority conferred or an instrument drafted, such as the withdrawal of a revocable contract offer prior to the offeree's acceptance.

NOTES:

SHIMP v. HUFF
Widow (P) v. Beneficiary (D)
Md. Ct. App., 315 Md. 624, 556 A.2d 252 (1989).

NATURE OF CASE: Appeal from judgment denying a widow's right of election in an action for declaratory judgment against a will's contract beneficiaries.

FACT SUMMARY: After her husband died, Lisa Mae Shimp (P) contended that she was entitled to an elective share, despite Mr. Shimp's previous contract contained in a joint will with his first wife that devised his entire estate to Huff (D) and others.

CONCISE RULE OF LAW: The rights of beneficiaries under a contract to make a will are limited by the possibility that the survivor might remarry and that the subsequent spouse might elect against the will.

FACTS: Lester Shimp and his first wife executed an irrevocable joint will, leaving their entire estate to whichever one survived the other, with the estate remaining at the death of the survivor to be divided among certain named beneficiaries, including Huff (D). Lester survived his first wife, later marrying Lisa Mae (P). Upon Lester's death, Lisa Mae (P) filed an election for her statutory share of his estate. Huff (D) and her husband, appointed as personal representatives of the estate, declined to pay Lisa Mae (P) her elective share. She filed suit for declaratory judgment. In a prior suit, the court of appeals had found that a valid contract existed and was the basis for the making of the joint will. Here, the circuit court held that the rights of the contract beneficiaries had priority over the claims of the second wife. Lisa Mae (P) appealed.

ISSUE: Are the rights of beneficiaries under a contract to make a will limited by the possibility that the survivor might remarry and that the subsequent spouse might elect against the will?

HOLDING AND DECISION: (Murphy, C.J.) Yes. The rights of beneficiaries under a contract to make a will are limited by the possibility that the survivor might remarry and that the subsequent spouse might elect against the will. There is a strong public policy in favor of protecting the surviving spouse's elective share from the unilateral acts of a deceased spouse. For example, in a number of cases, transfers in fraud of marital rights have been declared to be void. This doctrine also applies to transfers made prior to the marriage. Thus, the claims of Huff (D) and the other contract beneficiaries are subordinate to Lisa Mae's (P) superior right to receive her elective share. Judgment vacated.

EDITOR'S ANALYSIS: Where a decedent has breached a contract to devise property, the claimants under the contract generally proceed on a theory of specific performance. Where a will conforming to the contract has been executed, as here, some courts have characterized the competing claimants as either

creditors or legatees and evaluated their claims under the applicable priority rules. The remaining courts have relied upon public policy favoring the marriage relationship as the basis for upholding the surviving spouse's claim to an elective share over the claims of contract beneficiaries.

[For more information on contracts relating to wills, see Casenote Law Outline on Wills, Trusts & Estates, Chapter 8, § II, Remedies.]

QUICKNOTES

SURVIVING SPOUSE - The spouse who remains living after the death of the other spouse.

JOINT WILLS - A jointly signed single instrument that is made the will or two or more persons.

ELECTIVE SHARE - Election by the surviving spouse to take either what the deceased spouse gave under the will or a share of the deceased spouse's estate as set forth by statute.

NOTES:

NOTES

CHAPTER 5
WILL SUBSTITUTES: NONPROBATE TRANSFERS

QUICK REFERENCE RULES OF LAW

1. **Contracts with Payable-on-Death Provisions.** A party who establishes a trust consisting of the proceeds of a life insurance policy may, by will, designate a trust beneficiary other than the one named in the trust instrument. (Wilhoit v. Peoples Life Insurance Co.)

    [For more information on the designation of trust beneficiary, see Casenote Law Outline on Wills, Trusts & Estates, Chapter 4, § III, Trusts.]

2. **Contracts with Payable-on-Death Provisions.** The beneficiary of a life insurance policy may not be changed by a will. (Cook v. Equitable Life Assurance Society)

    [For more information on life insurance beneficiary designation, see Casenote Law Outline on Wills, Trusts & Estates, Chapter 5, § IV, Insurance.]

3. **Contracts with Payable-on-Death Provisions.** A partnership agreement clause which provides that each partner's interest, upon his death, shall pass to his spouse, is valid and enforceable. (Estate of Hillowitz)

4. **Multiple-Party Bank Accounts.** One claiming adversely to an agreement creating a joint tenancy has the burden of establishing the donor's lack of intent by clear and convincing evidence. (Franklin v. Anna National Bank of Anna)

    [For more information on the creation of joint tenancies, see Casenote Law Outline on Wills, Trusts & Estates, Chapter 4, § IV, Joint Tenancy.]

5. **Revocable Deeds of Land.** When a grantor reserves a life estate with unlimited power to sell, he retains the fee (so that no interest in praesenti passes to the grantee), and the instrument is not a deed but is testamentary in character. (Wright v. Husky)

    [For more information on life estate trusts, see Casenote Law Outline on Wills, Trusts & Estates, Chapter 10, § III, Tax Advantages of Irrevocable Trusts.]

6. **Revocable Trusts.** Even though the settlor retains the power to revoke the trust and appoints himself as trustee, if the beneficiary obtains any interest in the trust before the settlor dies, a valid inter vivos trust may have been formed. (Farkas v. Williams)

    [For more information on living trusts, see Casenote Law Outline on Wills, Trusts & Estates, Chapter 4, § III, Trusts.]

7. **Revocable Trusts.** When a settlor reserves a power to revoke his trust in a particular manner or under particular circumstances, he can revoke it only in that manner or under those circumstances. (In re Estate and Trust of Pilafas)

    [For more information on revocation of trusts, see Casenote Law Outline on Wills, Trusts & Estates, Chapter 5, § III, Trusts.]

8. **Revocable Trusts.** Where a person places property in trust and reserves the right to amend and revoke or to direct disposition of principal and income, the settlor's creditors may, following the death of the settlor, reach in satisfaction of the settlor's debts to them, to the extent not satisfied by the settlor's estate, those assets owned

by the trust over which the settlor had such control at the time of his death as would have enabled him to use the trust assets for his own benefit. (State Street Bank & Trust Co. v. Reiser)

[For more information on creditors of the settlor, see Casenote Law Outline on Wills, Trusts & Estates, Chapter 11, § IV, Trusts.]

9. **Revocable Trusts.** In the absence of a contrary intent, a divorce will revoke provisions of a spouse's pourover trust that favor the former spouse. (Clymer v. Mayo)

[For more information on revocation by divorce, see Casenote Law Outline on Wills, Trusts & Estates, Chapter 5, § VI, Change of Circumstances.]

10. **Planning for Incapacity.** A state may constitutionally require clear and convincing evidence of an incompetent's desire to have food and water withheld if he or she is in a persistent vegetative state. (Cruzan v. Director, Missouri Department of Health)

WILHOIT v. PEOPLES LIFE INSURANCE COMPANY
Beneficiary (P) v. Insurance company (D)
218 F.2d 887 (7th Cir. 1955).

NATURE OF CASE: Action to recover money held in trust.

FACT SUMMARY: Sarah Wilhoit arranged for Peoples Life Insurance Company (D) to hold the proceeds of her husband's life insurance policy in trust. She then bequeathed the trust corpus to the son (P) of her stepson.

CONCISE RULE OF LAW: A party who establishes a trust consisting of the proceeds of a life insurance policy may, by will, designate a trust beneficiary other than the one named in the trust instrument.

FACTS: As designated beneficiary, Sarah Wilhoit was entitled to receive the proceeds of her husband's Peoples Life Insurance Company (D) policy. She rejected an option which would have involved leaving the proceeds with Peoples (D) in exchange for interest payments at the minimum rate of 3% per annum. Instead, she elected to have Peoples (D) pay the proceeds, amounting to nearly $5,000, directly to her. Twenty-three days after acknowledging receipt of the money, she returned it to the company with instructions to hold it in trust, subject to withdrawal upon demand, at a minimum annual interest rate of 3½%. The trust arrangement, which was expressly accepted by Peoples (D), provided for distribution of the corpus to Robert G. Owens, Sarah's brother, in the event of her death. Robert G. Owens died in 1932; Sarah Wilhoit lived until 1951, then died, leaving a will in which she bequeathed the money in the trust to Robert Wilhoit (P), son of her stepson. At Sarah's death, the estate of Robert G. Owens was reopened, and his son, Thomas (D), legatee under his father's will, joined a newly appointed administrator (D) of the estate of Robert G. Owens in seeking the trust corpus for Thomas (D). Peoples (D) paid the money into court, leaving Robert Wilhoit (P) and Thomas Owens (D) to litigate the issue of who should receive the money. Owens (D) argued that the trust instrument constituted an insurance rather than the provisions of the statute of wills. Accordingly, Owens (D) contended, Sarah Wilhoit had had no right to remove Robert G. Owens as beneficiary of the trust. Robert Wilhoit (P) disputed these contentions, claiming that the trust arrangement constituted nothing more than a contract of deposit, that the provision in favor of Robert G. Owens was invalid as an attempted testamentary disposition, and that any interest created in favor of Robert G. Owens had been extinguished upon his death prior to the demise of Sarah Wilhoit. The trial court granted Robert Wilhoit's (P) motion for summary judgment and awarded the trust corpus to Wilhoit (P). Thomas Owens (D), together with the administrator (D) of his father's estate, then appealed.

ISSUE: May a party who has established a trust consisting of the proceeds of her spouse's life insurance policy include a provision in her will which has the effect of changing the beneficiary designated in the trust agreement?

HOLDING AND DECISION: (Major, J.) Yes. A party who establishes a trust consisting of the proceeds of a life insurance policy may, by will, designate a trust beneficiary other than the one named in the trust instrument. The agreement between Sarah Wilhoit and the company (D) appears to have been a separate and independent contract and was neither an insurance contract nor supplemental thereto in the sense that Thomas Owens (P) has argued. Mrs. Wilhoit had the option of leaving the policy proceeds on deposit with Peoples (D) but instead entered into a different arrangement of her own creation. By the terms of this arrangement, she designated Robert G. Owens to receive the trust corpus in the event of her death. But, she obviously did not intend his estate to receive the money if he predeceased her because after his death, she bequeathed the money to someone else. Therefore, the trial court committed no error in awarding the trust corpus to Robert Wilhoit (P).

EDITOR'S ANALYSIS: The contract entered into by Mrs. Wilhoit is an illustration of a valid type of will substitute. She created an interest in her own favor but included a provision by which her interest would have passed to Robert G. Owens had he not predeceased her. Will substitutes which incorporate or direct the distribution of an insurance policy or its proceeds are usually recognized as valid, although similar instruments which do not involve insurance policies or proceeds may be unenforceable by reason of their failure to comply with the appropriate wills statute. In this connection, note that the court observes that the Indiana wills statute would have invalidated Sarah Wilhoit's contract had it been entered into with a bank rather than an insurance company.

[For more information on the designation of trust beneficiary, see Casenote Law Outline on Wills, Trusts & Estates, Chapter 4, § III, Trusts.]

QUICKNOTES

SUCCESSOR BENEFICIARY - A beneficiary who succeeds to the interest of an earlier beneficiary whose interest in the property has terminated.

TRUST - The holding of property by one party for the benefit of another.

COOK v. EQUITABLE LIFE ASSURANCE SOCIETY
Widow (P) v. Insurance company (D)
428 N.E.2d 110 (1981).

NATURE OF CASE: Appeal from summary judgment awarding life insurance proceeds.

FACT SUMMARY: Douglas Cook divorced Doris Cook (P) and remarried without changing beneficiaries on his life insurance policy.

CONCISE RULE OF LAW: The beneficiary of a life insurance policy may not be changed by a will.

FACTS: Mr. Cook purchased a life insurance policy from Equitable (D) in which he named Cook (P), his wife at the time, as the beneficiary. Douglas and his wife were divorced. Douglas remarried and executed a holographic will in which he left his insurance policy to his new wife, Margaret, and his son Daniel. Douglas died, and his will was admitted to probate. Margaret filed a claim with Equitable (D) for the proceeds. Margaret and Daniel appealed on the theory that Douglas' will showed his intent to change the beneficiary of the policy to Margaret and Daniel.

ISSUE: May the beneficiary of a life insurance policy be changed by a will?

HOLDING AND DECISION: (Ratliff, J.) No. The beneficiary of a life insurance policy may not be changed by a will. Less than strict compliance with policy change requirements may be adequate to change a beneficiary where circumstances show the insured has done everything within his power to effect the change. Here, there is no indication that Douglas took any action in the fourteen years between his divorce from Cook (P) and his death, other than the making of his will to change the beneficiary. Surely, if Douglas had wanted to change the beneficiary, he had ample time and opportunity to comply with the policy requirements. Affirmed.

EDITOR'S ANALYSIS: The instant case follows the majority rule. However, there are several instances where the courts have permitted a will to change a life insurance beneficiary. See, e.g., Kane v. Union Mutual Life Ins. Co, 84 A.D.2d 148, 445 N.Y.S. 2d 549 (1981). The Uniform Probate Code does not contain any provision permitting or forbidding revocation of a payable-on-death designation by will.

[For more information on life insurance beneficiary designation, see Casenote Law Outline on Wills, Trusts & Estates, Chapter 5, § IV, Insurance.]

QUICKNOTES

HOLOGRAPHIC WILL - A will that is handwritten by the testator or testatrix.

BENEFICIARY - A third party who is the recipient of the benefit of a transaction undertaken by another.

NOTES:

ESTATE OF HILLOWITZ
Executors (P) v. Widow (D)
N.Y. Ct. App., 22 N.Y.2d 107, 238 N.E.2d 723 (1968).

NATURE OF CASE: Action to recover the interest of a decedent in a partnership.

FACT SUMMARY: Pursuant to a partnership agreement, Hillowitz' share of an investment club passed to his widow (D). His executors (P) claimed that this asset should have passed to his estate.

CONCISE RULE OF LAW: A partnership agreement clause which provides that each partner's interest, upon his death, shall pass to his spouse, is valid and enforceable.

FACTS: Hillowitz was a partner in an investment club. A clause in the club's partnership agreement recited that, in the event of the death of any partner, his interest would pass to his wife, without any termination of the partnership arrangement. When Hillowitz died, the club, in compliance with the terms of the partnership agreement, paid to his widow (D) the sum of $2800, which amount represented Hillowitz' share of the partnership. The executors (P) of Hillowitz' estate then brought an action against Mrs. Hillowitz (D). The executors (D) contended that the provision of the partnership agreement was invalid because it constituted an attempted testamentary disposition, but did not comply with the requisites of the statute of wills. Hillowitz' interest in the partnership, the executors (P) argued, should therefore have been included as an asset of his estate. Mrs. Hillowitz (D), by way of defense, maintained that the provision of the partnership agreement constituted a valid and enforceable contract. The trial court sustained Mrs. Hillowitz' (D) argument, but the appellate division reversed. Mrs. Hillowitz (D) appealed from the decision of that court.

ISSUE: Is a partnership agreement provision which recites that each partner's interest, upon his death, shall pass to his spouse, invalid as an attempted testamentary disposition?

HOLDING AND DECISION: (Fuld, C.J.) No. A partnership agreement clause which provides that each partner's interest, upon his death, shall pass to his spouse, is valid and enforceable. Such a provision is indistinguishable in form from an ordinary third party beneficiary contract. Like the typical provision which recites that the interest of a deceased partner shall pass to the surviving members of the partnership, the clause involved in this case is not testamentary in nature and need not comply with the formalities of the statute of wills. Therefore, Mrs. Hillowitz (D) is entitled to retain the $2,800 which was received from her husband's investment club.

CONCURRENCE: (Keating, J.) Mrs. Hillowitz (D) is entitled to the $2,800 since her husband presumably intended her to enjoy a right of survivorship in the interest he purchased in the investment club.

EDITOR'S ANALYSIS: Many interests which vest only after the death of the party who controls their disposition are nevertheless deemed not to be testamentary in nature. Examples of interests of this type include the benefits of an insurance policy and the proceeds of an employee pension plan. In many states, legislative enactments exempt certain interests from the status of testamentary dispositions. This enables these interests to vest without the necessity of complying with the formal requisites of a jurisdiction's wills statute.

QUICKNOTES
LIFE ESTATE - An interest in land measured by the life of the tenant or a third party.

INTER VIVOS TRUST - Property that is held by one person for the benefit of another and which is created by an instrument that takes effect during the life of the grantor.

THIRD-PARTY BENEFICIARY - A party who benefits from a promise made pursuant to a contract although he is not a party to the agreement.

NOTES:

FRANKLIN v. ANNA NATIONAL BANK OF ANNA
Executor (P) v. Bank (D)
140 Ill. App. 3d 533, 488 N.E.2d 1117 (1986).

NATURE OF CASE: Appeal from judgment award of proceeds in bank account.

FACT SUMMARY: Prior to Frank Whitehead's death, he opened a joint bank account with Cora Goodard to facilitate access to his funds.

CONCISE RULE OF LAW: One claiming adversely to an agreement creating a joint tenancy has the burden of establishing the donor's lack of intent by clear and convincing evidence.

FACTS: In 1978, two years before his death, Frank Whitehead changed the joint tenant on his bank account from his deceased wife to his roommate, Cora Goodard. Goodard stated that Whitehead put the money in both their names so Goodard could get money when they needed it and that Whitehead wanted her to have the money if she outlived him. Later in 1978, Enola Stevens Franklin (P) began to care for Whitehead. In January 1979, Whitehead sent Franklin (P) to deliver a letter to the bank which stated "I, Frank Whitehead, wish my bank accounts be changed to Enola Stevens joint intendency (sic). Nobody go in my lock box but me." A second letter stated: "I, Frank Whitehead, want Enola Stevens and me only to go in my lock box. . . . In case I can't see she is to take care of my bill or sick." The bank representative said she would take care of it. However, later at trial the bank president testified that he didn't remember receiving the letters and that the bank would not remove a signature from a signature card on the basis of a letter. The trial court found that Goodard was the sole owner of the funds in the joint bank account by right of survivorship. Franklin (P), executor of Whitehead's estate, appealed on the basis that Whitehead never intended to make a gift of the bank account to Goodard.

ISSUE: Does one claiming adversely to an agreement creating a joint tenancy have the burden of establishing by clear and convincing evidence the donor's lack of donative intent?

HOLDING AND DECISION: (Welch, J.) Yes. One claiming adversely to an agreement creating a joint tenancy has the burden of establishing by clear and convincing evidence the donor's lack of donative intent. The form of the agreement is not conclusive regarding the intention of the depositors between themselves. It is proper to consider events occurring after creation of the joint account in determining whether the donor actually intended to transfer his interest in the account at his death to the surviving joint tenant. Here, just nine months after adding Goodard's name to the signature card, Whitehead attempted to remove Goodard's name and substitute Franklin's (P). The second letter showed Whitehead's concern that he might lose his sight and be unable to transact his own banking business. These facts show that Whitehead made Goodard and later Franklin (P) a signatory for his own convenience in case he could not get his money, and not with the intent to effect a present gift. Goodard never exercised any authority or control over the joint account. Reversed and remanded.

EDITOR'S ANALYSIS: The Uniform Probate Code 6-103(a) provides: "A joint account belongs, during the lifetime of all parties, to the parties in proportion to the net contributions by each to the sums on deposit, unless there is a clear and convincing evidence of a different intent." Therefore, the depositor of funds to a joint tenancy account can revoke the joint tenancy by withdrawing the funds and naming a new joint tenant.

[For more information on the creation of joint tenancies, see Casenote Law Outline on Wills, Trusts & Estates, Chapter 4, § IV, Joint Tenancy.]

QUICKNOTES

JOINT TENANCY - An interest in property whereby a single interest is owned by two or more persons and created by a single instrument; joint tenants possess equal interests in the use of the entire property and the last survivor is entitled to absolute ownership.

DONOR - A person who gives real or personal property or value with expectation of compensation or other consideration.

DONATIVE INTENT - Donor's intent to make a gift.

NOTES:

WRIGHT v. HUSKEY

Property owner (P) v. Potential beneficiary (D)

Tenn. Ct. App., 592 S.W.2d 899 (1979).

NATURE OF CASE: Action to clear title and cancel a Notice of Lis Pendens.

FACT SUMMARY: As grantor, Mrs. Wright (P) insisted that the instrument by which she conveyed certain land to her daughter and son-in-law (who was Huskey's (D) father) was not a deed but was a testamentary document that did not meet the statutory requirements necessary to constitute a valid will.

CONCISE RULE OF LAW: When a grantor reserves a life estate with unlimited power to sell, he retains the fee (so that no interest in praesenti passes to the grantee), and the instrument is not a deed but is testamentary in character.

FACTS: Mrs. Wright (P) desired to defeat any claim her husband might assert against a particular piece of real property by divorce proceeding or as her survivor, but she wanted to still reserve in herself the use of the property with the unlimited right to sell. Thus, she executed a grant deed in favor of her daughter and son-in-law but reserved a life estate and the unlimited power to sell. Huskey (D), as the only child and sole heir at law of the son-in-law, subsequently learned that Wright (P) was planning to sell the property, so she filed a Notice of Lis Pendens. Wright (P) brought suit to clear title and cancel the Notice of Lis Pendens, claiming the deed was, in fact, a testamentary instrument and that it was void because it failed to meet the statutory requirements necessary to constitute a valid will. The chancellor held it was a deed which reserved to the grantor a life estate with the absolute power to sell the property.

ISSUE: Is an instrument by which a grantor reserved a life estate with unlimited power to sell testamentary in character?

HOLDING AND DECISION: (Matherne, J.) Yes. An instrument, although couched in terms normally associated with deeds, is testamentary in character if it purports to convey realty to named grantees but reserves in the grantor a life estate and the unlimited power to sell the property. In order to operate as a deed, an instrument must convey an interest to take effect in praesenti, though the enjoyment may rest in futuro. When the grantor, as in this case, reserves a life estate with unlimited power to sell, he retains the fee, and no interest in praesenti passes to the grantee. The instrument at issue was not a deed but a testamentary document that was void for its failure to comply with the requirements of a valid will. Reversed.

EDITOR'S ANALYSIS: People of modest means have typically been those who have tried to use deeds on condition and revocable deeds as will substitutes in an attempt to avoid probate attorney fees. As this case illustrates, it is a dangerous practice. The great weight of authority looks at a delivery deed as being absolute and sees as void under the Statute of Frauds any oral condition accompanying the delivery.

[For more information on life estate trusts, see Casenote Law Outline on Wills, Trusts & Estates, Chapter 10, § III, Tax Advantages of Irrevocable Trusts.]

QUICKNOTES

GRANTOR - Conveyor of property or settlor of a trust.

LIFE ESTATE - An interest in land measured by the life of the tenant or a third party.

REMAINDER INTEREST - An interest in land that remains after the termination of the immediately preceding estate.

GRANT DEED - A deed conveying an interest in real or personal property.

NOTES:

FARKAS v. WILLIAMS
Administrators of estate (P) v. Beneficiary (D)
Ill. Sup. Ct., 5 Ill. 2d 417, 125 N.E.2d 600 (1955).

NATURE OF CASE: Action to determine who, between the administrators of the estate and the beneficiary of the trust, had a right to four stock certificates.

FACT SUMMARY: The administrators (P) of Farkas' estate claim the right to four stock certificates which Farkas held in trust for Williams (D).

CONCISE RULE OF LAW: Even though the settlor retains the power to revoke the trust and appoints himself as trustee, if the beneficiary obtains any interest in the trust before the settlor dies, a valid inter vivos trust may have been formed.

FACTS: Albert Farkas executed a written declaration of trust for four separate stock certificates and named Williams (D) as beneficiary of all four. Farkas retained the power to revoke the trust and the power to vote, sell, redeem, exchange, or otherwise deal with the stock. He also appointed himself as trustee. If Farkas didn't revoke the trust, Williams (D) was required to be alive when Farkas died or the trust would be automatically revoked. Farkas died without having revoked the trust, and the administrators (P) of his estate brought this action to obtain a declaration of rights to the stock certificates. The administrators (P) claimed that the trust was testamentary and not valid because Farkas had not complied with the Statute of Wills in making his declarations of trust. They claimed that Farkas had retained so much control over the trust that it didn't qualify as an inter vivos trust. The circuit court held that the trust was an invalid testamentary trust, and so the stock was an asset of the Farkas estate.

ISSUE: Must a beneficiary obtain some interest in the trust before the settlor dies to have a valid inter vivos trust?

HOLDING AND DECISION: (Hershey, J.) Yes. It is necessary that a beneficiary obtain some interest in the trust prior to the time the settlor dies or the trust will be considered to be a testamentary trust. This means that the settlor cannot retain absolute control over the trust res in making an inter vivos trust. It is true that Farkas retained a great deal of control over the trust res, but Williams (D) did have an interest in the trust before Farkas died. Farkas had to administer the trust in accordance with the declaration of trust, which limited his control over the stock. Even though Williams (D) was required to be living when Farkas died in order to have any right to the stock, which meant that he didn't have an interest which he could bequeath to anyone, he still had a small right to the which further indicates that a valid inter vivos trust was established. The court, therefore, reversed the circuit court and held that a valid inter vivos trust had been established in Williams' (D) favor.

EDITOR'S ANALYSIS: There is a split of opinion among the different jurisdictions as to the amount of power and control the settlor can retain and still have a valid inter vivos trust. The more recent cases seem to hold as the court in this case did. They allow the settlor to retain a great deal of control over the trust.

[For more information on living trusts, see Casenote Law Outline on Wills, Trusts & Estates, Chapter 4, § III, Trusts.]

QUICKNOTES
REVOCABLE TRUST - The holding of property by one party for the benefit of another pursuant to an instrument in which the creator reserves the right to revoke the trust.

INTER VIVOS TRUST - Property that is held by one person for the benefit of another and which is created by an instrument that takes effect during the life of the grantor.

TESTAMENTARY DISPOSITION - A disposition of property that is effective upon the death of the grantor.

NOTES:

IN RE ESTATE AND TRUST OF PILAFAS

Parties not identified

Ariz. Ct. App., 172 Ariz. 207, 836 P.2d 420 (1992).

NATURE OF CASE: Appeal from a judgment finding revocation of a will and a trust in a petition for adjudication of intestacy and determination of heirs.

FACT SUMMARY: When the signed copies of Pilafas' will and revocable trust could not be found after his death, the court held that he had revoked them both, dying intestate, and thus his five adult children were his heirs.

CONCISE RULE OF LAW: When a settlor reserves a power to revoke his trust in a particular manner or under particular circumstances, he can revoke it only in that manner or under those circumstances.

FACTS: Pilafas executed a trust agreement which required that revocation of the trust be in writing. At his death, the trust estate was to be distributed in part to eight nonprofit organizations, with the remaining portion to be held in various trusts for his wife, brother, two of his sons, and a granddaughter. Pilafas specifically omitted his other three children. After divorcing his wife, he amended the trust, deleting her name and simultaneously executing a will. He later revised his estate plan to include all his children. After his death, the signed originals of the documents could not be found. One of his children petitioned for adjudication of intestacy and determination of heirs. The court found that Pilafas had revoked both his trust agreement and will, thus dying intestate and leaving his five adult children as heirs. The nonprofit beneficiaries appealed.

ISSUE: When a settlor reserves a power to revoke his trust in a particular manner or under particular circumstances, can he revoke it only in that manner or under those circumstances?

HOLDING AND DECISION: (McGregor, J.) Yes. When a settlor reserves a power to revoke his trust in a particular manner or under particular circumstances, he can revoke it only in that manner or under those circumstances. Applying the common law presumption that a testator has revoked his will if it is last seen in the testator's possession and cannot be found after his death, the trial court correctly held that Pilafas had revoked his will and died intestate. However, Pilafas reserved the power to amend or revoke the trust agreement by an instrument in writing delivered to the trustee. Because no evidence was presented showing that the decedent complied with the required method of revocation, the inter vivos trust was not revoked and remains valid. Affirmed in part, reversed in part, and remanded.

EDITOR'S ANALYSIS: Unlike the execution of a will, the creation of a trust involves the present transfer of property interests in the trust corpus to the beneficiaries. The Restatement (Second) of Trusts § 330 makes it clear that a trust is revocable only if the settlor expressly reserves a power to revoke, and the terms of the trust strictly define and limit the reserved power of revocation. When not bound by previous decisions or legislative enactments, the court of appeals announced that it followed the Restatement.

[For more information on revocation of trusts, see Casenote Law Outline on Wills, Trusts & Estates, Chapter 5, § III, Trusts.]

QUICKNOTES

REVOCABLE TRUST - The holding of property by one party for the benefit of another pursuant to an instrument in which the creator reserves the right to revoke the trust.

INTER VIVOS TRUST - Property that is held by one person for the benefit of another and which is created by an instrument that takes effect during the life of the grantor.

ESTATE RESIDUE - That property which remains following the distribution of the assets of the testator's estate.

NOTES:

STATE STREET BANK & TRUST CO. v. REISER
Bank (P) v. Beneficiary (D)
Mass. Ct. App., 7 Mass. App. 633, 389 N.E.2d 768 (1979).

NATURE OF CASE: Action to reach the assets of an inter vivos trust to pay a debt.

FACT SUMMARY: The Bank (P) brought an action against Reiser (D) designed to reach the assets of an inter vivos trust, which Dunnebier had established before his death, in order to pay a debt Dunnebier owed the Bank (P) for a personal loan it had given him.

CONCISE RULE OF LAW: Where a person places property in trust and reserves the right to amend and revoke or to direct disposition of principal and income, the settlor's creditors may, following the death of the settlor, reach in satisfaction of the settlor's debts to them, to the extent not satisfied by the settlor's estate, those assets owned by the trust over which the settlor had such control at the time of his death as would have enabled him to use the trust assets for his own benefit.

FACTS: In 1971, Wilfred Dunnebier created an inter vivos trust, reserving the power to amend or revoke it and the right during his lifetime to direct the disposition of principal and income. He then placed the capital stock of five closely held corporations into the trust and executed a will leaving his residuary estate to the trust. Thirteen months thereafter, Dunnebier obtained an unsecured $75,000 personal loan from the Bank (P) after an officer went over a financial statement furnished by Dunnebier and visited single-family home divisions built by the aforementioned corporations. There was no intent to defraud in his failure to call attention to the fact that he had placed the stock of his corporations in a trust. When he died, his estate did not have sufficient funds to pay the loan off, so the Bank (P) sought to reach the assets of the trust.

ISSUE: Are there circumstances in which a creditor of the settlor of a trust can reach the assets of an inter vivos trust to pay the personal debts of the deceased settlor?

HOLDING AND DECISION: (Kass, J.) Yes. Equitable principles dictate that where a person places property in trust and reserves the right to amend and revoke or to direct disposition of principal and income, the settlors creditors may, following his death, reach in satisfaction of his debts to them, to the extent not satisfied by his estate, those assets owned by the trust over which he had such control at the time of his death as would have enabled him to use the trust assets for his own benefit. Assets which pour over into such a trust as a consequence of the settlor's death or after the settlor's death are not similarly subject to the reach of creditors. Reversed.

EDITOR'S ANALYSIS: The rule in all but a few states is that a trust is deemed irrevocable absent language in the instrument itself giving rise to an express or implied power of revocation. A small number of states, like California and Oklahoma, have statutes specifying that all trusts are deemed revocable unless expressly made irrevocable.

[For more information on creditors of the settlor, see Casenote Law Outline on Wills, Trusts & Estates, Chapter 11, § IV, Trusts.]

QUICKNOTES

INTER VIVOS TRUST - Property that is held by one person for the benefit of another and which is created by an instrument that takes effect during the life of the grantor.

SETTLOR - The grantor or donor of property that is to be held in trust for the benefit of another.

CREDITOR - A person or party to whom a debt or obligation is owed.

NOTES:

CLYMER v. MAYO
Administrator (P) v. Beneficiary (D)
393 Mass. 754, 473 N.E.2d 1084 (1985).

NATURE OF CASE: Appeal from judgment construing will and inter vivos trust.

FACT SUMMARY: Mayo (D) and his wife were divorced, and Mayo's (D) wife died after she executed a will and a revocable trust naming Mayo (D) as a beneficiary.

CONCISE RULE OF LAW: In the absence of a contrary intent, a divorce will revoke provisions of a spouse's pourover trust that favor the former spouse.

FACTS: Mayo's (D) wife executed a will naming Mayo (D) as its principal beneficiary. The residue of her estate was to pour over into a revocable inter vivos trust she created simultaneously with the will. If Mayo (D) survived her, the trust estate was divided into two parts: Trust A, a marital deduction trust, and the balance to Trust B. Mayo (D) was the income beneficiary of Trust A and was entitled to invade the trust principal at his or the trustee's discretion. Trust B provided that the balance of the trust's assets were to be held for Mayo's (D) benefit for life and then pass at his death to his wife's nieces and nephews. At the trust's creation, the trust was unfunded except for property which would pour over under her will's residuary clause. The trust was never funded. Mayo (D) and his wife were divorced. Clymer (P), the administrator of the decedent's estate, petitioned the court to determine the impact of the divorce on the estate's administration. The trial court held that the trust was valid even though it was unfunded; Mayo (D) did not take under Trust A because the transfer was intended for the marital deduction for estate tax purposes, and that objective became impossible after the divorce; and Mayo (D) was entitled to take his life income interest under Trust B because his wife failed to revoke the trust provisions benefiting Mayo (D). On appeal, it was argued that Mayo (D) should not take his life interest under Trust B since a Massachusetts statute provided that a divorce revoked any dispositions made by will to the former spouse.

ISSUE: In the absence of a contrary intent, does a divorce revoke provisions of a spouse's pourover trust that favor the former spouse?

HOLDING AND DECISION: (Hennessey, J.) Yes. In the absence of a contrary intent, a divorce will revoke provisions of a spouse's pourover trust that favor the former spouse. The appellant argues that the statute in question only revokes dispositions by will and not dispositions by trust. However, the decedent's will and trust were integrally related components of a single testamentary scheme. The trust, like the will, "spoke" only at the decedent's death. Therefore, Mayo's (D) interest in the trust was revoked by operation of the statute at the same time as his interest under the will was revoked. So ordered.

EDITOR'S ANALYSIS: Recent statutes provide that a divorce revokes any provision in a revocable trust in favor of an ex-spouse who predeceases the settlor. See, e.g., Okla. Stat. Ann. Ch. 60, 175 (Supp. 1989). In Dollar Savings & Trust Co. v. Turner, 39 Ohio St. 3d 182, 529 N.E.2d 1261 (1988), the court held that an antilapse statute, which by its language applied only to devises by will, applied equally to revocable trusts.

[For more information on revocation by divorce, see Casenote Law Outline on Wills, Trusts & Estates, Chapter 5, § VI, Change of Circumstances.]

QUICKNOTES

INTER VIVOS TRUST - Property that is held by one person for the benefit of another and which is created by an instrument that takes effect during the life of the grantor.

RESIDUARY CLAUSE (OF WILL) - A clause contained in a will disposing of the assets remaining following distribution of the estate.

MARITAL DEDUCTION - A tax deduction under federal law for transfers of property made between spouses.

NOTES:

CRUZAN v. DIRECTOR, MISSOURI DEPARTMENT OF HEALTH
Guardians (P) v. Government (D)
497 U.S. 261 (1990).

NATURE OF CASE: Appeal from reversal of authorization for termination of medical treatment of an incompetent adult.

FACT SUMMARY: After Nancy Cruzan (P) sustained injuries in an automobile accident, which left her in a persistent vegetative state, her parents (P) sought court authorization to terminate her medical treatment.

CONCISE RULE OF LAW: A state may constitutionally require clear and convincing evidence of an incompetent's desire to have food and water withheld if he or she is in a persistent vegetative state.

FACTS: Nancy Cruzan (P) was rendered incompetent as a result of severe injuries sustained in an automobile accident and was hospitalized in a persistent vegetative state. Her parents (P), as co-guardians, sought a court order directing the withdrawal of Nancy's (P) artificial feeding and hydration equipment after it became apparent that she had virtually no chance of recovering her cognitive faculties. The trial court gave the parents (P) authorization for termination. The Supreme Court of Missouri reversed, finding that Nancy's (P) statements to her roommate regarding her desire to live or die under certain conditions did not constitute clear proof of her intent as required by state law. The Cruzans (P) appealed.

ISSUE: May a state constitutionally require clear and convincing evidence of an incompetent's desire to have food and water withheld if he or she is in a persistent vegetative state?

HOLDING AND DECISION: (Rehnquist, C.J.) Yes. A state may constitutionally require clear and convincing evidence of an incompetent's desire to have food and water withheld if he or she is in a persistent vegetative state. Missouri has adopted a clear and convincing standard to assure that the action of a surrogate conforms as closely as possible to the wishes expressed by the patient while competent. Such a requirement is not forbidden by the Constitution. Here, the testimony at trial did not amount to clear and convincing proof of Nancy's (P) desire to have hydration and nutrition withdrawn. Moreover, there is no automatic assurance that the view of close family members will necessarily be the same as Nancy's (P) would have been had she been confronted with these circumstances while competent. Affirmed.

CONCURRENCE: (Scalia, J.) It would be preferable to announce, clearly and promptly, that the federal courts have no business in this field. American law has always accorded the state the power to prevent, by force if necessary, suicide, including suicide by refusing to take appropriate measures necessary to preserve one's life.

EDITOR'S ANALYSIS: This case, although highly publicized, framed the issue on such narrow grounds that its holding does not threaten removal of feeding tubes in jurisdictions outside of Missouri. Although the decision permits Missouri to erect procedural safeguards, it does not bar other states from requiring fewer safeguards, which is, in fact, the trend. After this decision was handed down, the Cruzans (P) presented new evidence of Nancy's (P) intent, whereupon the State (D) withdrew from the case, and Nancy's (P) feeding tube was removed. She died less than two weeks later.

NOTES:

CHAPTER 6
INTERPRETATION OF WILLS

QUICK REFERENCE RULES OF LAW

1. **Admission of Extrinsic Evidence.** A will duly executed and allowed by the court must, under the statute of wills, be accepted as the final expression of the intent of the person executing it. (Mahoney v. Grainger)

   [For more information on admission of extrinsic evidence, see Casenote Law Outline on Wills, Trusts & Estates, Chapter 6, § III, Ambiguity.]

2. **Admission of Extrinsic Evidence.** A witness to a will must witness a real interest to make a will at the time the witness signs a will in order to satisfy the statutory requirement of witnessing the execution of a will. (Fleming v. Morrison)

   [For more information on witnesses to a will, see Casenote Law Outline on Wills, Trusts & Estates, Chapter 4, §I, Wills.]

3. **Admission of Extrinsic Evidence.** Parol evidence is inadmissible to show a scrivener's mistake in drafting a will or codicil.. (Connecticut Junior Republic v. Sharon Hospital)

   [For more information on the parol evidence rule, see Casenote Law Outline on Wills, Trusts & Estates, Chapter 6, § VII, Bank Accounts.]

4. **Admission of Extrinsic Evidence.** When an uncertainty arises upon the face of a will, it cannot always be determined whether the will is ambiguous or not until the circumstances surrounding the writing of the will are first considered. (Estate of Russell)

   [For more information on ambiguity and surrounding circumstances, see Casenote Law Outline on Wills, Trusts & Estates, Chapter 6, § III, Ambiguity.]

5. **Death of Beneficiary Before Death of Testator.** An antilapse statute applies unless a contrary contention is indicated by the will of the testator. (In re Estate of Ulrickson)

   [For more information on antilapse statutes, see Casenote Law Outline on Wills, Trusts & Estates, Chapter 2, § II, Lapse.]

6. **Death of Beneficiary Before Death of Testator.** Where necessary to effectuate the intentions of the testator, a court may substitute the words "and" and "or" for one another when either of those words appears in a will. (Jackson v. Schultz)

7. **Death of Beneficiary Before Death of Testator.** Where the number of beneficiaries to a gift is certain, and the share each is to receive is also certain and in no way dependent for its amount upon the number who shall survive, it is not a gift to a class but to the individuals. (Dawson v. Yucus)

   [For more information on class gifts, see Casenote Law Outline on Wills, Trusts & Estates, Chapter 2, § II, Lapse.]

8. **Death of Beneficiary Before Death of Testator.** A bequest to a named individual and an identifiable group of other persons constitutes a class gift, and if any member of the class, including the named individual, fails to survive until the time that the bequest vests, the other members are entitled to share equally in the bequest. (In re Moss)

[For more information on class gifts, see Casenote Law Outline on Wills, Trusts & Estates, Chapter 2, § II, Lapse.]

9. **Changes in Property After Execution of Will: Specific and General Devises Compared.** When a testator disposes, during his lifetime, of the subject of a specific gift of real estate contained in a revocable inter vivos trust, that gift is held to be adeemed by extinction. (Wasserman v. Cohen)

[For more information on doctrine of ademption, see Casenote Law Outline on Wills, Trusts & Estates, Chapter 9, § I, Ademption.]

MAHONEY v. GRAINGER
Parties not identified
Mass. Sup. Ct., 283 Mass. 189, 186 N.E. 86 (1933).

NATURE OF CASE: Appeal from a decree denying a petition for distribution of a legacy under a will.

FACT SUMMARY: After a trial judge found that a testatrix's sole heir at law was her maternal aunt, ruling that statements of the testatrix were admissible only insofar as they gave evidence of the material circumstances surrounding the testatrix at the time of the execution of the will, her first cousins appealed the ruling, contending they were her heirs at law.

CONCISE RULE OF LAW: A will duly executed and allowed by the court must, under the statute of wills, be accepted as the final expression of the intent of the person executing it.

FACTS: Sullivan told her attorney she wanted to make a will. She left the bulk of her estate to two first cousins and told the attorney that the rest of the estate should be shared equally by "about twenty-five first cousins." The attorney subsequently drafted the will containing a residuary clause stating in part: "All the rest and residue of my estate, both real and personal property, I give, devise and bequeath to my heirs at law living at the time of my decease." After Sullivan's death, the trial judge found that Sullivan's sole heir at law at the time of her death was her maternal aunt, Frances Greene. The first cousins argued that Sullivan's statement regarding the twenty-five first cousins should be admitted to prove her testamentary intention. However, the trial judge ruled that the statements were not admissible to prove intention and dismissed the cousins' petition. They appealed.

ISSUE: Must a will duly executed and allowed by the court, under the statute of wills, be accepted as the final expression of the intent of the person executing it?

HOLDING AND DECISION: (Rugg, C.J.) Yes. A will duly executed and allowed by the court must, under the statute of wills, be accepted as the final expression of the intent of the person executing it. It is only where testamentary language is not clear in its application to facts that evidence may be introduced in order to clarify the language. In this case, there is no doubt as to Sullivan's heirs at law. The aunt alone falls within that description. The cousins are excluded. The circumstance that the plural word "heirs" was used does not prevent one individual from taking the entire gift. Decree affirmed.

EDITOR'S ANALYSIS: Most courts subscribe to the rule that when an instrument has been proved and allowed as a will, oral testimony as to the meaning and purpose of a testator cannot be used to disturb the plain meaning of a will. The fact that a will does not conform to the instructions given to the draftsman who prepared it, by reason of mistake or otherwise, does not authorize a court to reform or alter the will or remold it by amendments. Where no doubt exists as to the property bequeathed or the identity of the beneficiary, there is no room for extrinsic evidence.

[For more information on admission of extrinsic evidence, see Casenote Law Outline on Wills, Trusts & Estates, Chapter 6, § III, Ambiguity.]

QUICKNOTES

TESTATRIX - A woman who dies having drafted and executed a will or testament.

RESIDUARY CLAUSE (OF WILL) - A clause contained in a will disposing of the assets remaining following distribution of the estate.

EXTRINSIC EVIDENCE - Evidence that is not contained within the text of a document or contract but which is derived from the parties' statements or the circumstances under which the agreement was made.

NOTES:

FLEMING v. MORRISON
Parties not identified
187 Mass. 120, 72 N.E. 499 (1904).

NATURE OF CASE: Appeal from admission of will to probate.

FACT SUMMARY: Testator, who had a will drawn up and executed, but witnessed by one rather than the required three witnesses, did so to create a fake will purporting to give all of his property to Mary Fleming (P), thereby inducing her to sleep with him without giving her anything.

CONCISE RULE OF LAW: A witness to a will must witness a real interest to make a will at the time the witness signs a will in order to satisfy the statutory requirement of witnessing the execution of a will.

FACTS: The testator had his attorney draft a will and witness his signing of it bequeathing all of his wealth to Mary Fleming (P). Immediately after the will had been signed and witnessed by his attorney, the testator told his attorney that he had no intention of getting two more witnesses to validate the will because he intended that the will be a fake which he intended to use to induce Fleming (P) to sleep with him. (The attorney testified later that he witnessed a lack of testamentary intent and deduced that the testator had this same lack of intent when he witnessed the will.) Later, the testator changed his mind and sought to validate the will by having two more witnesses sign it to meet the statutory requirement of three witnesses. Objectors to this will appealed its admission to probate.

ISSUE: Can a witness to a will be a sufficient witness if the witness knows that the testator did not intend to make the will when the witness signed it?

HOLDING AND DECISION: (Loring, J.) No. To meet the statutory requirement of three witnesses to make a valid will, each witness must believe that the testator fully believes that the testator intends that the document witnessed is to be his will at the time each witness signs the will. Since the first witness knew that the document was intended to be a fake, the first witness cannot be counted. Without three witnesses, the will cannot be probated.

EDITOR'S ANALYSIS: It should be noted that witnesses to a will are a crucial element of a will's validity. An important exception to the statute of frauds is the allowance of parole evidence in the form of a witness' recollection to determine the validity of a will.

[For more information on witnesses to a will, see Casenote Law Outline on Wills, Trusts & Estates, Chapter 4, §I, Wills.]

QUICKNOTES

UNDUE INFLUENCE - Improper influence that deprives the individual freedom of choice or substitutes another's choice for the person's own choice.

TESTAMENTARY INTENT - A determination that the document was intended to be a will and as such, reflects the writer's true wishes.

ANIMUS TESTANDI - Testamentary intent; the intent to make a will.

NOTES:

CONNECTICUT JUNIOR REPUBLIC v. SHARON HOSPITAL

Charity (P) v. Remainder beneficiary (D)

Conn. Sup. Ct., 188 Conn. 1, 448 A.2d 190 (1982).

NATURE OF CASE: Appeal from admission of will to probate.

FACT SUMMARY: Connecticut Junior Republic (P) contended that extrinsic evidence was admissible to prove a scrivener's error in Emerson's will.

CONCISE RULE OF LAW: Parol evidence is inadmissible to show a scrivener's mistake in drafting a will or codicil.

FACTS: Emerson executed a will in 1960 in which he designated Sharon Hospital (D) and six other charities as remainder beneficiaries. In 1969, he instructed his attorney to delete six of the charities and to substitute Connecticut Junior Republic (P) and 10 other charities. In 1975, he instructed the attorney to structure the gifts for tax purposes but not to change the beneficiaries. The attorney did so yet mistakenly substituted Sharon Hospital (D) and the other 1960 beneficiaries for the 1969 beneficiaries. Emerson signed the codicil without noticing the error. After Emerson's death, the will was admitted to probate with the court holding that extrinsic evidence of a scrivener's error was inadmissible to alter the stated beneficiaries. Connecticut Junior Republic (P) appealed.

ISSUE: Is parol evidence admissible to show a scrivener's error in drafting a will or codicil?

HOLDING AND DECISION: (Healey, J.) No. Parol evidence is inadmissible to show a scrivener's error in drafting a will or codicil. Such evidence cannot be used to alter the provisions of a facially unambiguous will. The construction of a will is based solely on its wording. As a result, regardless of its ability to show Emerson's true intention, the extrinsic evidence of the attorney's error was inadmissible. Affirmed.

DISSENT: (Peters, J.) Wills are always held inadmissible to probate where their provisions are induced by fraud, duress, or undue influence because it is felt the testamentary process is distorted by a third party's interference with the testator's true intent. This case presents an analogous situation, and extrinsic evidence should be allowed.

EDITOR'S ANALYSIS: In re Estate of Ikuta, 639 P.2d 400 (1981), the court readily altered a testamentary instrument based on a scrivener's error. In that case, the court substituted "youngest" for the word "oldest" (sic), finding that the latter word made no sense and was clearly a scrivener's error. In recent years, several jurisdictions, including Texas and West Virginia, have freely remedied scrivener's mistakes.

[For more information on the parol evidence rule, see Casenote Law Outline on Wills, Trusts & Estates, Chapter 6, § VII, Bank Accounts.]

QUICKNOTES

REMAINDER - An interest in land that remains after the termination of the immediately preceding estate.

ANNUITY TRUST - A trust that pays a fixed amount, notwithstanding the amount of its principal.

PAROL EVIDENCE RULE - Doctrine precluding parties to an agreement from introducing evidence of prior or contemporaneous agreements in order to repudiate or alter the terms of a written contract.

CODICIL - A supplement to a will.

NOTES:

ESTATE OF RUSSELL
Parties not identified
Cal. Sup. Ct., 69 Cal. 2d 200, 444 P.2d 353 (1968).

NATURE OF CASE: Appeal from a determination of heirship.

FACT SUMMARY: The testator left her $10 gold piece and diamonds to Hembree, her only heir-at-law, and the residue of her estate to Charles Quinn and Roxy Russell, the latter being her dog, who predeceased her.

CONCISE RULE OF LAW: When an uncertainty arises upon the face of a will, it cannot always be determined whether the will is ambiguous or not until the circumstances surrounding the writing of the will are first considered.

FACTS: The testatrix left her $10 gold piece to her sister, Hembree, who was her only heir-at-law, and the residue of her estate to Charles Quinn and Roxy Russell. Charles was a longtime friend and confidante, while Roxy was testatrix' Airedale dog. Roxy predeceased the testatrix but was alive at the time of execution of the will. Extrinsic evidence was introduced to establish Roxy's identity. The trial court found that it was the testatrix' intention that Charles was to receive the entire residue and that the gift to Roxy was merely precatory in nature. It further found that there was no lapse of the gift to Charles but that the gift was to maintain Roxy. Hembree appealed, arguing that the gift of one-half of the residue to a dog was clear and unambiguous; that it was void and passed to her under the laws of intestate succession; and that the admission of extrinsic evidence did not cure the invalidity of the gift.

ISSUE: When an uncertainty arises upon the face of a will, can it always be determined whether the will is ambiguous or not until the circumstances surrounding its writing are first considered?

HOLDING AND DECISION: (Sullivan, J.) No. When an uncertainty arises upon the face of a will, it cannot always be determined whether the will is ambiguous or not until the circumstances surrounding the writing of the will are first considered. Extrinsic evidence is admissible to explain any ambiguity arising on the face of a will or to resolve a latent ambiguity which does not so appear. A latent ambiguity is one that does not appear on the face of the will but is disclosed by some collateral fact. Once shown, extrinsic evidence may be introduced to resolve it. A patent ambiguity, on the other hand, appears on the face of the will, and circumstances of execution may be considered to determine the testator's intentions. Also, when a will is clear on its face, no extrinsic evidence can be admitted, and it cannot be shown that something not expressed in the will was intended. The trend, however, tends to be to admit evidence to show the meaning of words even though no ambiguity appears on the face of the will. The exclusion of intrinsic evidence regarding surrounding circumstances merely

because no ambiguity appears can easily lead to giving the will a meaning never intended. California Probate Code § 105, which says that if after the admission of extrinsic evidence the will is not susceptible to two or more meanings no ambiguity exists, simply delineates the manner of ascertaining testator's intention. Here, the trial court's conclusion was unreasonable. No words gave the residuary all to Charles or appeared to be merely precatory in nature. A distribution in equal shares to two persons cannot be said to be for one to use whatever portion is necessary in behalf of the other. No extrinsic evidence should have been admitted which would lead to a meaning to which the will was not reasonably susceptible. As for the gift to Roxy, it was clearly void so that Roxy's gift lapsed and passed to the heirs-at-law by intestacy. Hembree, as the only heir-at-law, should take the gift. Reversed and remanded.

DISSENT: (McComb, J.) Dissented for reasons presented by presiding Justice Brown in his opinion, Court of Appeal, Fourth Appellate District, Division One, 4 Civ. 9840, unpublished.

EDITOR'S ANALYSIS: Few definite guidelines can be given as to interpretation of wills. Rules and "trends" are conflicting. The rules of the case above apply not only to wills but to contracts and deeds also. They are important in evidence cases as well. What evidence to admit is usually the tough question. The student can only consider the appropriate statutory provisions and the various theories presented in the cases and resolve the problem in his own mind.

[For more information on ambiguity and surrounding circumstances, see Casenote Law Outline on Wills, Trusts & Estates, Chapter 6, § III, Ambiguity.]

QUICKNOTES
TESTATRIX - A woman who dies having drafted and executed a will or testament.
RESIDUE - That property which remains following the distribution of the assets of the testator's estate.

EXTRINSIC EVIDENCE - Evidence that is not contained within the text of a document or contract but which is derived from the parties' statements or the circumstances under which the agreement was made.

NOTES:

IN RE ESTATE OF ULRIKSON

Nieces and nephews of deceased (P) v. Probate court (D)

Minn. Sup. Ct., 290 N.W.2d 757 (1980).

NATURE OF CASE: Appeal from the application of an antilapse statute.

FACT SUMMARY: Appellants contended that the Minnesota antilapse statute should not apply due to the implied intent of Ulrikson to bequeath equal gifts to the surviving nieces and nephews and providing an implicit condition of survivorship on her siblings.

CONCISE RULE OF LAW: An antilapse statute applies unless a contrary contention is indicated by the will of the testator.

FACTS: Bellida Ulrikson died testate in 1976 with a will drafted in 1971. She made specific bequest of $1,000 each to various nieces and nephews of her siblings both living and deceased. She also provided a residuary clause which provided that she bequeath to her then-living brother and sister, Melvin Hovland and Rodine Helger, the remainder of her estate. The clause also indicated that in the event that either one of them shall predecease her, then the other surviving brother or sister shall take the entire residuary portion of the estate. Prior to Ulrikson's death, both Melvin Hovland and Rodine Helger died. Melvin Hovland left two surviving children, Erickson and Barth, respondents herein. Ulrikson had two other siblings who had predeceased her and who left among them three children. The three children of the predeceased siblings challenged the probate court's determination that the Minnesota antilapse statute applied to allow Erickson and Barth to take the entire residuary estate. They contended that by providing for providership, Ulrikson provided a condition of survivorship for the then-living siblings to take the residuary estate. Because Ulrikson had provided equal shares for all of the remaining nephews and nieces, it was argued by the appellants that she did not intend the antilapse statute to apply. The probate court found the antilapse statute to apply and granted the entire residuary estate to Erickson and Barth. The remaining nieces and nephews appealed.

ISSUE: Does an antilapse statute apply unless a contrary intention is indicated by the will?

HOLDING AND DECISION: (Yetka, J.) Yes. An antilapse statute applies unless a contrary intention is indicated by the will. The law clearly prefers testacy over intestacy. As a result, courts were obligated to interpret wills to uphold the validity of the will rather than to invalidate it. Thus, looking at the will from this aspect, it appears relatively clear that Ulrikson intended for her then-living siblings to take more than the other remaining nephews and nieces. She did not clearly evidence an intent to defeat the antilapse statute, and therefore, the issue of Hovland must take the residue of the estate. Affirmed.

EDITOR'S ANALYSIS: This case illustrates a common thread in the interpretation of wills throughout most jurisdictions of the country. It has long been held that courts will attempt to uphold a will if such is consistent with the statutory scheme, and a reasonable interpretation which validates the will drawn from its language. Further, if one portion of the will is found to be invalid, courts will attempt to excise that portion so that the remainder of the will can be upheld. This is a common antilapse statute whereby the original legatees predeceased the testator and leave issue. If the gift were to lapse, it would be put into the residuary clause and be distributed as if no will were in existence. If the antilapse statute applies, the gift to the original legatees pass to their issue.

---

*[For more information on antilapse statutes, see **Casenote Law Outline on Wills, Trusts & Estates, Chapter 2, § II, Lapse.**]*

QUICKNOTES

ANTI-LAPSE STATUTE - State statute providing for the substitution of a recipient of a devise made pursuant to a testamentary instrument, if the beneficiary of the gift predeceases the testator and no alternative disposition is made.

RESIDUE - That property which remains following the distribution of the assets of the testator's estate.

SPECIFIC BEQUEST - A transfer of property that is accomplished by means of a testamentary instrument.

RESIDUARY CLAUSE (OF WILL) - A clause contained in a will disposing of the assets remaining following distribution of the estate.

NOTES:

JACKSON v. SCHULTZ
Seller (P) v. Purchaser (D)
Del. Ch. Ct., 38 Del. Ch. 332, 151 A.2d 284 (1959).

NATURE OF CASE: Suit seeking specific performance of a land sale contract.

FACT SUMMARY: Schultz (D) contracted to purchase property from Jackson (P) but later claimed that Bullock's will had not vested title to the property in Jackson (P).

CONCISE RULE OF LAW: Where necessary to effectuate the intentions of the testator, a court may substitute the words "and" and "or" for one another when either of those words appears in a will.

FACTS: Leonard Bullock's will bequeathed all his property to his wife. The dispositive portion of the bequest utilized the words "to her and her heirs and assigns forever." His wife, Bessie, predeceased Bullock, but her children (P) survived both Bessie and Leonard, who was stepfather of the children (P). After Bullock's death, the children (P) contracted to sell Bullock's house to Schultz (D), but Schultz (D) later refused to perform the contract. Claiming that the children (P) did not have title to the house, Schultz (D) argued that a gift to a named person "and her heirs and assigns forever" did not, according to ordinary rules of construction, give the heirs any interest by way of substitution in the event of the named devisee's failure to survive the testator. Bessie's children (P), contending that Bessie's interest had, upon Bullock's death, vested in the children (P), then sued Jackson (P) for specific performance of the contract for the sale of the house. Ultimately, the children (P) moved for a summary judgment against Schultz (D).

ISSUE: Does a gift to a named devisee "and his heirs and assigns forever" vest in the heirs if the named devisee predeceases the testator?

HOLDING AND DECISION: (Marvel, V.C.) Yes. In this case, Bessie's children (P) acquired, by way of substitution, Bessie's interest in the property which Bullock owned at the time of his death. Ordinarily, when the word "and" precedes the phrase "heirs and assigns," the heirs take nothing if the named devisee predeceases the testator. In this situation, the words "heirs and assigns" are deemed to be words of limitation, designed to restrict the quantity of the estate devised by the testator. However, where the word "or" precedes "heirs and assigns," the heirs do enjoy the right to take by substitution if the named devisee dies before the testator. And the courts of this jurisdiction have held that, where necessary to effectuate the intentions of the testator, the words "and" and "or" may be substituted for one another where either appears in a will. In this case, Bullock seems to have preferred his wife's children (P) rather than his own blood relatives. Therefore, "or" should be substituted for "and" in

Bullock's will, and his stepchildren's (P) motion for summary judgment should be granted.

EDITOR'S ANALYSIS: At least one court has rejected the approach adopted by Jackson v. Schultz. In Hofing v. Willis, 31 Ill. 2d 365, 201 N.E. 2d 852 (1964), the court held that the inclusion of the words "and assigns" precluded the insertion of the word "and" in place of the word "or." While a substitutionary gift in favor of the designated beneficiary's heir might have been consonant with the testator's intentions, the Hofing court reasoned, the existence of an additional substitutionary gift to the assignees of the named beneficiary would have been inconsistent with the gift to the heirs.

QUICKNOTES

SPECIFIC PERFORMANCE - An equitable remedy whereby the court requires the parties to perform their obligations pursuant to a contract.

SUBSTITUTIONARY GIFT - A gift that is made to a specific class of persons and pursuant to which, if any member of that class is deceased, the gift is to pass to that member's children in substitution for the original gift.

NOTES:

DAWSON v. YUCUS
Beneficiary (P) v. Executrix (D)
Ill. App. Ct., 97 Ill. App. 2d 101, 239 N.E.2d 305 (1968).

NATURE OF CASE: Appeal from a judgment for defendants in an action to construe a will.

FACT SUMMARY: Wilson (P), the remaining beneficiary of a will, argued that the gift was made to a class and therefore, as survivor of the class, he was entitled to the entire interest bequeathed to the class.

CONCISE RULE OF LAW: Where the number of beneficiaries to a gift is certain, and the share each is to receive is also certain and in no way dependent for its amount upon the number who shall survive, it is not a gift to a class but to the individuals.

FACTS: Nelle Stewart left a duly executed will containing ten clauses. The second clause gave the one-fifth interest in farm lands that Stewart inherited from her husband to two of his nephews, Stewart Wilson and Gene Burtle. Each was to receive one-half of Stewart's one-fifth interest. After the will was admitted to probate, Wilson (P) filed suit against the executrix, Yucus (D), to construe the will, alleging that the devise was a class gift, that Burtle had died after the date of execution of the will but before the testatrix, and that Wilson (P), as the survivor of the class, was entitled to the entire 1/5 interest in the farm. Burtle's two children, Dawson (P) and Burtle (P), were subsequently substituted as plaintiffs. The trial court held that clause two did not create a class gift, and therefore the gift to Burtle lapsed and passed into the residue of the estate upon his death. Dawson (P) and Burtle (P) appealed.

ISSUE: Where the number of beneficiaries to a gift is certain, and the share each is to receive is also certain and in no way dependent for its amount upon the number who shall survive, is it a gift to a class?

HOLDING AND DECISION: (Jones, J.) No. Where the number of beneficiaries to a gift is certain, and the share each is to receive is also certain and in no way dependent for its amount upon the number who shall survive, it is not a gift to a class but to the individuals. In this case, Stewart named the individuals, giving them each a specified portion of her interest in the farm, thus making certain the number of beneficiaries and the share each was to receive. The shares in no way depend upon the number who shall survive Stewart's death. She did, however, create a survivorship gift of the residue of her estate, thus indicating she knew how to manifest such an intent. Hence, the language of clause two, phrased differently, was intended to create a gift to individuals distributively. Affirmed.

EDITOR'S ANALYSIS: A testator is deemed to be "group minded," that is, intends to create a class gift, if she uses a generic class label such as "to my nephews" in devising her property. Stewart stated in her bequest in clause two that she believed the farm lands should go back to her late husband's "side of the house." Wilson argued unsuccessfully that this phrase, together with the extrinsic evidence admitted by the court as to Stewart's intentions, clearly required class gift construction.

[For more information on class gifts, see Casenote Law Outline on Wills, Trusts & Estates, Chapter 2, § II, Lapse.]

QUICKNOTES

REMAINDER - An interest in land that remains after the termination of the immediately preceding estate.

RESIDUE - That property which remains following the distribution of the assets of the testator's estate.

CLASS GIFT - A gift to a group of unspecified persons whose number, identity, and share of the gift will be determined sometime in the future.

EXTRINSIC EVIDENCE - Evidence that is not contained within the text of a document or contract but which is derived from the parties' statements or the circumstances under which the agreement was made.

NOTES:

IN RE MOSS
Parties not identified
Ct. App., 2 Ch. 314 (1899).

NATURE OF CASE: Suit seeking declaratory relief.

FACT SUMMARY: Moss bequeathed certain property in trust for his wife for life, then in trust for his niece and the children (D) of his sister. His wife later bequeathed the residue of her estate to Kingsbury (P).

CONCISE RULE OF LAW: A bequest to a named individual and an identifiable group of other persons constitutes a class gift, and if any member of the class, including the named individual, fails to survive until the time that the bequest vests, the other members are entitled to share equally in the bequest.

FACTS: By his will, Moss gave his interest in the Daily Telegraph newspaper to his wife Elizabeth and his niece, Elizabeth Jane Fowler, in trust. The income from this asset was to be paid to his wife for life. Thereafter, Moss' share of the Telegraph was to be held in trust for Fowler and all children of Moss' sister, Emily Walter, who should attain the age of twenty-one. Fowler predeceased Moss, but his wife survived him. Eventually, Moss' wife bequeathed her residuary estate, including her interest in her husband's share of the Telegraph, to George Kingsbury (P). After the death of Mrs. Moss, Kingsbury (P) filed an action seeking a declaration that the gift by Moss to Fowler and the children (D) of Walter was not a class gift and had lapsed in its entirety when Fowler failed to survive Moss. From an order giving one-sixth of the gift to Kingsbury (P), the five children (D) of Emily Walter, all of whom had turned twenty-one prior to Mrs. Moss' death, appealed.

ISSUE: If the testator bequeaths property to a named individual and an identifiable group of other persons but the named individual fails to survive the testator, are the members of the group entitled to receive the bequest?

HOLDING AND DECISION: (Lindley, M.R.) Yes. A bequest to a named individual and an identifiable group of other persons constitutes a class gift, and if any member of the class, including the named individual, fails to survive until the time that the bequest vests, the other members are entitled to share equally in the bequest. Whether Emily Walter's children (D) are considered a class or not, it is apparent that Moss desired his share of the Telegraph to go to Fowler, to the children (D), and to no one else. Since Fowler died before Moss, the five children (D) are each entitled to one-fifth of Moss' interest in the Telegraph.

CONCURRENCE: (Jeune, Sir F.H.) The Lindley decision is correct and requires no amplification.

CONCURRENCE: (Romer, L.J.) The bequest in Moss' will was a class gift. If a bequest is to a specific person and a class of other persons described by the testator, it cannot be doubted that the testator intends the named person to receive the gift even if the members of the class die and, on the other hand, intends the members of the class to enjoy the gift despite the demise of the named individual. Thus, although Fowler predeceased Moss, the five children (D) of Emily Walter are entitled to receive all of Moss' interest in the Telegraph.

EDITOR'S ANALYSIS: Countless courts and commentators have wrestled with the issue of whether or not a given bequest constitutes a class gift. Most tests for determining whether or not a class gift has been created necessarily focus upon the intent of the testator. In this context, any intent-based formula might be objected to as fanciful since few testators stop to consider whether the language they employ will satisfy the legal requisites of a class gift. But, it is the intentions of the testator which should control the descent of his property, and attempts to ascertain those intentions, however imperfectly conceived, must be undertaken. The Restatement of Property § 279 provides as workable a test as any for determining whether a class gift has been created. According to the Restatement standard, a class gift will be found to exist if the grantor can be demonstrated to have intended that there be a possibility that the number of recipients of the gift would fluctuate over time.

[For more information on class gifts, see Casenote Law Outline on Wills, Trusts & Estates, Chapter 2, § II, Lapse.]

QUICKNOTES

CLASS GIFT - A gift to a group of unspecified persons whose number, identity, and share of the gift will be determined sometime in the future.
RESIDUE - That property which remains following the distribution of the assets of the testator's estate.

RESIDUARY ESTATE - That portion of the estate which remains after all the estate has been distributed through the satisfaction of all claims and is conditional upon something remaining after the claims on the testator's estate are satisfied.

NOTES:

WASSERMAN v. COHEN

Trust beneficiary (P) v. Trustee (D)

Mass. Sup. Ct., 414 Mass. 172, 606 N.E.2d 901 (1993).

NATURE OF CASE: Appeal from dismissal of an action for declaratory judgment against the surviving trustee of a revocable inter vivos trust.

FACT SUMMARY: Wasserman (P) sought the proceeds from the sale of a building which would have been conveyed to her through a revocable inter vivos trust at the settlor's death had the settlor not sold the building prior to her death.

CONCISE RULE OF LAW: When a testator disposes, during his lifetime, of the subject of a specific gift of real estate contained in a revocable inter vivos trust, that gift is held to be adeemed by extinction.

FACTS: Drapkin created a memorial trust, naming herself both settlor and trustee. She funded the trust with "certain property" delivered on the date of execution, retaining the right to add property by inter vivos transfer and by will. Drapkin also reserved the right to amend or revoke the trust and to withdraw property from the trust. When she executed the trust, Drapkin held record title to an apartment building. However, Drapkin sold the property before she died and never conveyed her interest in the property to the trust. Wasserman (P) brought an action for declaratory judgment, requesting that Cohen (D) be ordered to pay to Wasserman (P) the proceeds from the sale of the building. The probate judge dismissed the action. Wasserman (P) appealed.

ISSUE: When a testator disposes, during his lifetime, of the subject of a specific gift of real estate contained in a revocable inter vivos trust, is that gift held to be adeemed by extinction?

HOLDING AND DECISION: (Lynch, J.) Yes. When a testator disposes, during his lifetime, of the subject of a specific gift of real estate contained in a revocable inter vivos trust, that gift is held to be adeemed by extinction. To be effective, a specific legacy or devise must be in existence and owned by the testator at the time of her death. A trust is construed according to the same rules traditionally applied to wills. Here, Drapkin created the trust along with her will as part of a comprehensive estate plan. There is no reason to apply a different rule because she conveyed the property under the terms of the trust rather than her will. Thus, the doctrine of ademption applies to the trust, and the devise of the apartment building was adeemed by Drapkin. Affirmed.

EDITOR'S ANALYSIS: Wasserman (P) had argued that deciding ademption questions based on a determination that a devise is general or specific is overly formalistic and fails to serve the testator's likely intent. However, the court found that, at least in regard to the conveyance of real estate, determining whether a devise is general or specific is the proper first step in deciding questions of ademption. The court noted that the so-called harsh results of the doctrine can easily be avoided by careful draftsmanship, and its existence must be recognized by any competent practitioner.

[For more information on doctrine of ademption, see Casenote Law Outline on Wills, Trusts & Estates, Chapter 9, § I, Ademption.]

QUICKNOTES

INTER VIVOS TRUST - Property that is held by one person for the benefit of another and which is created by an instrument that takes effect during the life of the grantor.

ADEMPTION - Revocation of a specific devise or bequest made pursuant to a testamentary instrument if the particular property is not part of the decedent's estate at the time of death.

SETTLOR - The grantor or donor of property that is to be held in trust for the benefit of another.

RESIDUARY ESTATE - That portion of the estate which remains after all the estate has been distributed through the satisfaction of all claims and is conditional upon something remaining after the claims on the testator's estate are satisfied.

NOTES:

NOTES

CHAPTER 7
RESTRICTIONS ON THE POWER OF DISPOSITION:
PROTECTION OF THE SPOUSE AND CHILDREN

QUICK REFERENCE RULES OF LAW

1. **Rights of the Surviving Spouse.** When a person dies, property that he gave during his lifetime to an heir shall be treated as an advancement against the heir's share of the estate only if declared in a contemporaneous writing by the decedent or acknowledged in writing by the heir to be an advancement. (King v. King)

   [For more information on elective share, see Casenote Law Outline on Wills, Trusts and Estates, Chapter 3, § III, Elective Share.]

2. **Rights of the Surviving Spouse.** The survivor of a homosexual relationship alleged to be a "spousal relationship" is not entitled to exercise a right of election against the decedent's will. (In re Estate of Cooper)

   [For more information on elective share, see Casenote Law Outline on Wills, Trusts and Estates, Chapter 3, § III, Elective Share.]

3. **Rights of the Surviving Spouse.** A trust created with the purpose of defeating a spouse's elective share will be voided if the settlor retained substantial control over the trust assets. (Seifert v. Southern National Bank of South Carolina)

   [For more information on elective share, see Casenote Law Outline on Wills, Trusts and Estates, Chapter 3, § III, Elective Share.]

4. **Rights of the Surviving Spouse.** The surviving spouse has no claim against the assets of a valid inter vivos trust created by the deceased spouse even when the deceased spouse allowed retained substantial rights and powers under the trust instrument. (Sullivan v. Burkin)

   [For more information on testamentary living trusts, see Casenote Law Outline on Wills, Trusts & Estates, Chapter 4, § III, Trusts.]

5. **Rights of the Surviving Spouse.** Where a statutory election to take a widow's share is of greater pecuniary value, the court should render such an election on behalf of an incompetent widow rather than the bequest under the will. (In re Estate of Clarkson)

   [For more information on election by guardian, see Casenote Law Outline on Wills, Trusts & Estates, Chapter 3, § III, Elective Share.]

6. **Rights of the Surviving Spouse.** The right of election of a surviving spouse may be waived by a written waiver, and, unless the waiver provides to the contrary, a waiver of all rights in the property or estate of a present or prospective spouse is a waiver of all rights to an elective share. (Briggs v. Wyoming National Bank)

   [For more information on elective share, see Casenote Law Outline on Wills, Trusts and Estates, Chapter 3, § III, Elective Share.]

7. **Rights of the Surviving Spouse.** If a testator fails to provide by will for a surviving spouse who married the testator after the execution of the will, the omitted spouse shall receive a statutorily prescribed share of the estate. (Estate of Shannon)

[For more information on the omitted spouse, see Casenote Law Outline on Wills, Trusts & Estates, Chapter 3, § VI, Omitted Spouse.]

8. **Rights of Issue Omitted from the Will.** When a testator fails to provide in his will for any of his children born after making the will, the child shall receive a share of the estate equal in value to that he would have received if the testator had died intestate, unless it appears the omission was intentional. (Azcunce v. Estate of Azcunce)

   [For more information on omitted children, see Casenote Law Outline on Wills, Trusts and Estates, Chapter 3, § I, Protection of Children.]

9. **Rights of Issue Omitted from the Will.** To bring a legal malpractice action, the plaintiff must either be in privity with the attorney or must be an intended third-party beneficiary. (Espinosa v. Sparber, Shevin, Shapo, Rosen & Heilbronner)

KING v. KING
Children of deceased (P) v. Widow (D)
Ohio Ct. App., 82 Ohio App. 3d 747, 613 N.E.2d 251 (1992).

NATURE OF CASE: Appeal from a judgment declaring an inter vivos gift of real property not an advancement against a donee's share of an estate.

FACT SUMMARY: Before his death, Elizabeth King's (D) husband made an inter vivos transfer of real property to her, which his children (P) from a previous marriage contended was an advancement against the statutory share she elected to take against the will.

CONCISE RULE OF LAW: When a person dies, property that he gave during his lifetime to an heir shall be treated as an advancement against the heir's share of the estate only if declared in a contemporaneous writing by the decedent or acknowledged in writing by the heir to be an advancement.

FACTS: Before his death, Glenn King transferred a piece of real property by deed to his wife, Elizabeth King (D), telling her that he did not want that property to go through his probate estate. Glenn's will devised all his real property and certain personal property to Elizabeth (D), with the remainder of his personal property going to his children (P) from a previous marriage. As executrix, Elizabeth (D) filed an inventory of assets of the estate, which did not include the previously transferred property. She then elected to take against the will, increasing her share of the estate assets. Glenn's children (P) filed this action for declaratory judgment, asking the court to find that the inter vivos gift of real property was an advancement. The trial court found the gift was not an advancement. The children (P) appealed.

ISSUE: When a person dies, shall property that he gave during his lifetime to an heir be treated as an advancement against the heir's share of the estate only if declared in a contemporaneous writing by the decedent or acknowledged in writing by the heir to be an advancement?

HOLDING AND DECISION: (Grady, J.) Yes. When a person dies, property that he gave during his lifetime to an heir shall be treated as an advancement against the heir's share of the estate only if declared in a contemporaneous writing by the decedent or acknowledged in writing by the heir to be an advancement. Here, there was no such writing. While there is some evidence that Glenn King transferred the real property to Elizabeth (D) in anticipation of her receipt of the property after his death, the warranty deed he executed did not state that he intended the conveyance to be an advancement against Elizabeth King's (D) share of his estate. The deed thus does not satisfy state law requirements of the statute and, therefore, does not in itself create an advancement. Affirmed.

EDITOR'S ANALYSIS: Where a spouse elects not to take under the will but to take a statutory share, the spouse takes as if the testator had died intestate. Under Ohio law, a statutory share equals one-third of the estate. An advancement is an irrevocable gift made by a person during his or her lifetime to an heir, by way of anticipation of the whole or part of the estate which the heir would receive in the event of the person's death intestate and, as such, must be counted against an intestate share.

[For more information on elective share, see Casenote Law Outline on Wills, Trusts and Estates, Chapter 3, § III, Elective Share.]

QUICKNOTES

ELECTIVE SHARE - Election by the surviving spouse to take either what the deceased spouse gave under the will or a share of the deceased spouse's estate as set forth by statute.

INTER VIVOS TRANSFER - A transfer of property that is effectuated between living persons.

ADVANCEMENT - Money or property given by a parent to a child with the intent that it be deducted from the share the child is to receive upon the parent's death.

NOTES:

IN RE ESTATE OF COOPER
Same-sex lover of deceased (P) v. Court (D)
N.Y. A.P.. Div., 187 A.D.2d 128, 592 N.Y.S.2d 797 (1993).

NATURE OF CASE: Appeal from a decree denying the right of a spouse's election to the surviving member of a same-sex relationship.

FACT SUMMARY: After Cooper's death, Chin (P), his current same-sex lover, petitioned the court to elect to take a statutory share of Cooper's estate as a "surviving spouse" rather than take his share under the will.

CONCISE RULE OF LAW: The survivor of a homosexual relationship alleged to be a "spousal relationship" is not entitled to exercise a right of election against the decedent's will.

FACTS: Cooper died testate, leaving a portion of his estate to his current homosexual lover, Chin (P), and the other portion to his former homosexual lover. Chin (P), submitting evidence of a "spousal relationship," petitioned the court for the statutory right of election against Cooper's will. Chin (P) alleged that the only reason he and Cooper were not married was that the state unconstitutionally made it impossible for two people of the same sex to obtain a marriage license. He argued further that interpreting the term "surviving spouse" to exclude homosexual life partners violated the equal protection clause of the state constitution. The court held that persons of the same sex have no constitutional rights to enter into a marriage with each other, and the survivor of such a relationship had no right to elect against a decedent's will. Chin (P) appealed.

ISSUE: Is the survivor of a homosexual relationship entitled to exercise a right of election against the decedent's will?

HOLDING AND DECISION: (Mangano, J.) No. The survivor of a homosexual relationship is not entitled to exercise a right of election against the decedent's will. Where a testator disposes of his entire estate by will and is survived by a spouse, the surviving spouse may elect to take a one-third share of the net estate if the decedent is survived by one or more issue. In all other cases, the spouse is entitled to one-half of such net estate. However, the term "surviving spouse" does not include homosexual life partners. Here, any equal protection analysis must be measured by the rational basis standard. That standard has been applied in other similar instances in refuting challenges to classifications based on sexual orientation. Purported homosexual marriages do not give rise to any statutory rights, and no constitutional rights have been abrogated or violated by so holding. Accordingly, the decree is affirmed.

EDITOR'S ANALYSIS: In a 1993 Hawaii case, three same-sex couples brought suit, claiming that the Hawaii law that denied marriage licenses to same-sex couples was a denial of equal protection. Unlike the Cooper court, the Hawaii Supreme Court applied a strict scrutiny standard and held that the state must have a "compelling" interest in forbidding such marriages. Baehr v. Lewin, 852 P.2d 44 (Haw. 1993). The case was remanded to give the state an opportunity to substantiate its compelling interest.

[For more information on elective share, see Casenote Law Outline on Wills, Trusts and Estates, Chapter 3, § III, Elective Share.]

QUICKNOTES

ELECTIVE SHARE - Election by the surviving spouse to take either what the deceased spouse gave under the will or a share of the deceased spouse's estate as set forth by statute.

EQUAL PROTECTION - A constitutional guarantee that no person shall be denied the same protection of the laws enjoyed by other persons in life circumstances.

RATIONAL BASIS REVIEW - A test employed by the court to determine the validity of a statute in equal protection actions, whereby the court determines whether the challenged statute is rationally related to the achievement of a legitimate state interest.

NOTES:

SEIFERT v. SOUTHERN NATIONAL BANK OF SOUTH CAROLINA
Widow (P) v. Bank (D)
S.C. Sup. Ct., 305 S.C. 353, 409 S.E.2d 337 (1991).

NATURE OF CASE: Appeal from finding that inter vivos trust should not be included in probate estate in declaratory judgment action.

FACT SUMMARY: Seifert (P) challenged a revocable inter vivos trust which her husband had created, and over which he had reserved substantial control.

CONCISE RULE OF LAW: A trust created with the purpose of defeating a spouse's elective share will be voided if the settlor retained substantial control over the trust assets.

FACTS: Seifert's (P) husband created a revocable trust that increased in value to approximately $800,000. His will left no other assets in the estate apart from a half-interest in the house and a life interest in the income of a smaller trust for Seifert (P). The beneficiaries of the inter vivos trust were two daughters from a previous marriage. The trust was designed so that the trustee's powers were limited and subject to approval by Seifert's (P) husband during his lifetime. After her husband died, Seifert (P) challenged the validity of the trust and sought to have its corpus added to the husband's estate, over which she intended to assert her elective share. The trial court held the trust valid, and Seifert (P) appealed.

ISSUE: Will a trust created with the purpose of defeating a spouse's elective share be voided if the settlor retains substantial control over the trust assets?

HOLDING AND DECISION: (Toal, J.) Yes. A trust created with the purpose of defeating a spouse's elective share will be voided if the settlor retained substantial control over the trust assets. A trust in which a settlor does not in fact part with the powers he had over the property prior to the creation of the trust has, in substance, not created a trust at all; the trust is illusory. Consequently, such a trust created to take property out of an estate will be voided, and the trust corpus will revert to the estate, out of which the surviving spouse can take the elective share. Here, the trust created by Seifert's (P) husband was completely revocable, and the trustee could not exercise any supervisory powers without the settlor's consent. This was an illusory trust, so its corpus must revert to the estate. Reversed and remanded.

EDITOR'S ANALYSIS: Following Seifert, surviving spouses could conceivably gain one-half of decedent's intestate property when a revocable trust fails — much more than they would take if limited to a one-third elective share. The South Carolina legislature foreclosed that option in 1991 by passing a law to ensure that inter vivos trusts found by courts to be illusory were not thereby rendered totally invalid; the assets of such trusts merely became part of the probate estate subject to the elective share. The law also provided that non-illusory, revocable inter vivos trusts were valid will substitutes.

[For more information on elective share, see Casenote Law Outline on Wills, Trusts and Estates, Chapter 3, § III, Elective Share.]

QUICKNOTES

INTER VIVOS TRUST - Property that is held by one person for the benefit of another and which is created by an instrument that takes effect during the life of the grantor.

ELECTIVE SHARE - Election by the surviving spouse to take either what the deceased spouse gave under the will or a share of the deceased spouse's estate as set forth by statute.

SURVIVING SPOUSE - The spouse who remains living after the death of the other spouse.

NOTES:

SULLIVAN v. BURKIN
Widow (P) v. Successor trustree (D)
Mass. Sup. Jud. Ct., 390 Mass. 864, 460 N.E.2d 571 (1984).

NATURE OF CASE: Appeal from a dismissal of a complaint for determination of estate assets.

FACT SUMMARY: Sullivan (P) contended that the value of real estate placed in trust by her late husband should be considered part of his estate for purposes of providing her a portion of the estate.

CONCISE RULE OF LAW: The surviving spouse has no claim against the assets of a valid inter vivos trust created by the deceased spouse even when the deceased spouse allowed retained substantial rights and powers under the trust instrument.

FACTS: Sullivan's (P) husband, the decedent, executed during his life a deed of trust by which he transferred real estate to a trust with himself as sole trustee. The net income of the trust was payable to him during his life, and the trustee was instructed to pay to him all or such part of the principal that he might request. Upon his death, the trust indicated that the trustee was to pay the principal amount and any undistributed income to third parties. Sullivan executed a will wherein he stated that he intentionally neglected to make any provision for his wife, Sullivan (P). Following her husband's death, Sullivan (P) made a claim against the estate, contending that the property in the trust should be considered part of the estate. Burkin (D) was the successor in interest to the third parties to whom the decedent left the residual of the trust. The probate court held that a valid inter vivos trust was created and that the property of the trust was not to be considered part of the estate. Sullivan (P) appealed.

ISSUE: May a surviving spouse claim against the assets of a valid inter vivos trust created by the deceased spouse even when the deceased spouse allowed retained substantial rights and powers under the trust instrument?

HOLDING AND DECISION: (Wilkins, J.) No. The surviving spouse may not claim against the assets of a valid inter vivos trust created by the deceased spouse even when the deceased spouse allowed retained substantial rights and powers under the trust instrument. Merely because the inter vivos trust was testamentary does not indicate that it was invalid. Merely because the settlor retained a broad power to modify or revoke the trust, the law of the state is quite clear in upholding inter vivos trusts which become testamentary in nature. Further, the widow has no special interest which should be recognized in breaking the trust. As a result, because this trust was created under the then-established law, the assets of the trust cannot be applied to the estate. Affirmed.

EDITOR'S ANALYSIS: The court indicated quite clearly that although it felt obligated to apply the general rule in this case, it announced that in the future any inter vivos trust created or amended after the date of this opinion shall no longer follow the previously announced rule. In the future, if the settlor retains the same type of substantial rights that the decedent did in the principal case, then the assets of the trust will be considered part of the estate for purposes of distribution to the heirs of the estate.

[For more information on testamentary living trusts, see Casenote Law Outline on Wills, Trusts & Estates, Chapter 4, § III, Trusts.]

QUICKNOTES

INTER VIVOS TRUST - Property that is held by one person for the benefit of another and which is created by an instrument that takes effect during the life of the grantor.

SUCCESSOR TRUSTEE - A trustee who succeeds a previous trustee.

REMAINDER INTEREST - An interest in land that remains after the termination of the immediately preceding estate.

NOTES:

IN RE ESTATE OF CLARKSON
Guardian (P) v. Court (D)
193 Neb. 201 (1975).

NATURE OF CASE: Appeal from a court decision that an incompetent beneficiary should take under the will.

FACT SUMMARY: Mrs. Clarkson (P), an incompetent, could elect to take a fee interest in 1/4 of her husband's estate or the income interest in 1/4 of the estate under the will.

CONCISE RULE OF LAW: Where a statutory election to take a widow's share is of greater pecuniary value, the court should render such an election on behalf of an incompetent widow rather than the bequest under the will.

FACTS: Mrs. Clarkson (P) was incompetent due to her advanced age and senility. Mrs. Clarkson's (P) husband died, leaving her 1/4 of his estate in trust. A life estate in the interest, plus the power to invade the corpus for her needs, was provided by the will. Under state statutes, a widow was given a 1/4 share of her husband's estate it she elected to take against the will. A guardian ad litem appointed for Mrs. Clarkson (P) recommended that she elect to take the statutory share since it was of a greater pecuniary value to her. The court disagreed and ordered that she take under the will to better effectuate testator's plan and to protect the interest of remaindermen. The court found that the amount provided under the trust was sufficient to care for her adequately.

ISSUE: Should a court order an incompetent widow to elect against the will when such an election is of a greater pecuniary value?

HOLDING AND DECISION: (Spencer, J.) Yes. A majority of jurisdictions provide that a court should consider numerous factors in determining whether an incompetent widow should elect to take under or against the will, i.e., testator's plan, remaindermen rights, whether the widow would have acceded to her husband's wishes if she were competent, etc. We find that such an analysis is unpersuasive and not in accordance with our statutes. The sale consideration should be which election is in the best interest of the incompetent. A fee interest in 1/4 of the estate is of a greater pecuniary benefit than an income interest in 1/4 of the estate. In such cases, the greater interest should be awarded, and the court should elect for the widow on this basis. Reversed.

DISSENT: (McGowan, J.) Mr. Clarkson left his wife (P) her statutory share in trust knowing she was hopelessly incompetent. All of the corpus could be used for her benefit if necessary. In such cases, the widow should be required to elect under the will. An equitable approach on a case-by-case basis is a far sounder approach.

EDITOR'S ANALYSIS: "Best interests of the incompetent" is normally read as being determined based on all relevant facts and circumstances on a case-by-case basis. Kinnett v. Hood, 25 Ill. 2d 600 (1962). However, courts subscribing to the majority view are unable to delineate the factors to be judged. Often the needs of the surviving spouse, the nature of decedent's estate plan, and the question of how the widow would probably have selected had she been competent are considered the most relevant. See Kinnett.

[For more information on election by guardian, see Casenote Law Outline on Wills, Trusts & Estates, Chapter 3, § III, Elective Share.]

QUICKNOTES
ELECTIVE SHARE - Election by the surviving spouse to take either what the deceased spouse gave under the will or a share of the deceased spouse's estate as set forth by statute.

GUARDIAN AD LITEM - Person designated by the court to represent an infant or ward in a particular legal proceeding.

NOTES:

BRIGGS v. WYOMING NATIONAL BANK
Widower (P) v. Trustee Bank (D)
Wyo. Sup. Ct., 836 P.2d 263 (1992).

NATURE OF CASE: Appeal from a summary judgment dismissing a declaratory judgment action.

FACT SUMMARY: After his wife died, Briggs (P) contested the validity of the living trust agreement he had signed, which included a waiver of his right to contest the trust into which his wife had placed most of her assets.

CONCISE RULE OF LAW: The right of election of a surviving spouse may be waived by a written waiver, and, unless the waiver provides to the contrary, a waiver of all rights in the property or estate of a present or prospective spouse is a waiver of all rights to an elective share.

FACTS: Briggs (P) and his wife kept their accounts, holdings, and income separate from one another. Mrs. Briggs transferred the major portion of her assets into a living trust agreement drawn up by her attorney. The agreement included a waiver of Briggs' (P) right to contest the establishment of the trust. Before signing the agreement, Briggs (P) was advised to review its contents with another attorney. He declined to do so. After his wife's death, Briggs (P) sought a judgment declaring the trust invalid and petitioned to take his elective share of her estate instead. The beneficiaries (D) counterclaimed that, for violating the "no contest" clause, Briggs (P) should take nothing from the trust. The court entered summary judgment for the trustees, Wyoming National Bank (D) and the beneficiaries (D), declaring the trust agreement, including the no contest clause, to be valid but dismissed the counterclaim. All parties appealed.

ISSUE: May the right of election of a surviving spouse be waived by a written waiver, and is a waiver of all rights in the property or estate of a present or prospective spouse a waiver of all rights to elective share?

HOLDING AND DECISION: (Macy, J.) Yes. The right of election of a surviving spouse may be waived by a written waiver, and, unless the waiver provides to the contrary, a waiver of all rights in the property or estate of a present or prospective spouse is a waiver of all rights to elective share. This is a provision of Wyoming's elective share statute. A waiver must be manifested in some unequivocal manner. Here, Briggs (P) unequivocally and affirmatively stated that he consented to whatever his wife desired to do. He cannot now complain that he did not understand what he was doing because he did not read the agreement or have the advice of an attorney. Moreover, the waiver contained in the trust agreement did not violate the state's elective share statute. Furthermore, Mrs. Briggs' unambiguous intent that anyone who challenged the trust would lose his or her share must govern. Thus, the counterclaim should not have been dismissed. Affirmed in part, reversed in part, and remanded.

DISSENT: (Urbigkit, C.J.) By his own admission, Briggs (P) did not fully understand the legal documents he signed. It is not clear that even if he had carefully read what he signed he would have understood that his signature effectively waived his elective share. Furthermore, Briggs (P) had a good-faith and valid argument that the trust violated the elective share statute. He should not be penalized for seeking an answer to this legal question. The district court thus correctly dismissed the counterclaim.

EDITOR'S ANALYSIS: The Uniform Probate Code essentially tracks the rule applied in this case permitting waiver of the right of election, provided the waiver is voluntary and there has been fair disclosure. In Dainton v. Watson, 658 P.2d 79 (Wyo. 1983), the court declared that it joined the majority of other states by upholding the validity of a no contest clause even though the contest was made in good faith and with probable cause. Briggs (P) did not question the holding in Dainton but maintained that the court should join the majority of other states which refuse to uphold a no contest clause if the challenged provision is in contravention of the law.

[For more information on elective share, see Casenote Law Outline on Wills, Trusts and Estates, Chapter 3, § III, Elective Share.]

QUICKNOTES

ELECTIVE SHARE - Election by the surviving spouse to take either what the deceased spouse gave under the will or a share of the deceased spouse's estate as set forth by statute.

NOTES:

ESTATE OF SHANNON
Surviving spouse (P) v. Court (D)
Cal. Ct. App., 224 Cal. App. 3d 1148, 274 Cal. Rptr. 338 (1990).

NATURE OF CASE: Appeal from an order denying a petition for a determination of heirship as an omitted spouse.

FACT SUMMARY: When Russell Shannon died, after marrying Lila (P) and without changing the will he had executed twelve years before the marriage, Lila (P) argued that she should be entitled to estate distribution as an omitted surviving spouse.

CONCISE RULE OF LAW: If a testator fails to provide by will for a surviving spouse who married the testator after the execution of the will, the omitted spouse shall receive a statutorily prescribed share of the estate.

FACTS: Twelve years after executing his last will and testament, Russell Shannon, a widower, married Lila (P). Russell died less than two years later, without making any changes in his will, which named his daughter Beatrice as executrix and sole beneficiary. Lila (P) filed a petition for determination of entitlement to estate distribution as an omitted surviving spouse, which the probate court denied. Lila (P) appealed. When Lila (P) died while the appeal was pending, her son was named executor of her estate and substituted in her place as appellant.

ISSUE: If a testator fails to provide by will for a surviving spouse who married the testator after the execution of the will, shall the omitted spouse receive a statutorily prescribed share of the estate?

HOLDING AND DECISION: (Huffman, J.) Yes. If a testator fails to provide by will for a surviving spouse who married the testator after the execution of the will, the omitted spouse shall receive a statutorily prescribed share of the estate. The rule reflects a strong statutory presumption of revocation of the will as to the omitted spouse based upon public policy. Because Russell failed to provide for Lila (P) in his will, she is an omitted spouse. The will on its face does not manifest any intent by Russell to disinherit Lila (P). Furthermore, a general disinheritance clause in a will is insufficient to avoid the statutory presumption. Finally, no provision was made for Lila (P) outside the will, nor did she make a valid agreement waiving her right to share in Russell's estate. Thus, Beatrice has not rebutted the presumption of revocation. Reversed and remanded.

EDITOR'S ANALYSIS: The rule applied here is found in § 6560 of the California Probate Code, which essentially tracks the 1990 Uniform Probate Code. Under the statute, an omitted spouse receives a share of the estate as if the deceased had died intestate. The exceptions to that rule are listed in § 6561 and occur where the will clearly shows that the omission was intentional, the testator provided for the spouse by transfer outside the will in lieu of a testamentary provision, or the spouse made a valid waiver of the right to share in the testator's estate.

[For more information on the omitted spouse, see Casenote Law Outline on Wills, Trusts & Estates, Chapter 3, § VI, Omitted Spouse.]

QUICKNOTES

SURVIVING SPOUSE - The spouse who remains living after the death of the other spouse.

DISINHERITANCE CLAUSE - A clause in a testamentary instrument expressly denying a person, who would ordinarily be an heir of the testator, from the right to take a portion of the estate.

NOTES:

AZCUNCE v. ESTATE OF AZCUNCE

After-born child of deceased (P) v. Estate (D)

Fla. Dist. Ct. App., 586 So. 2d 1216 (1991).

NATURE OF CASE: Appeal from an order denying a petition to obtain a statutory share.

FACT SUMMARY: When Azcunce died shortly after executing a second codicil to his will, republishing the original will, Patricia (P), who had been born prior to the execution of the second codicil, petitioned the court for a share of her father's estate as a pretermitted child.

CONCISE RULE OF LAW: When a testator fails to provide in his will for any of his children born after making the will, the child shall receive a share of the estate equal in value to that he would have received if the testator had died intestate, unless it appears the omission was intentional.

FACTS: Azcunce executed a will, establishing a trust for his surviving spouse and his then-born children. The will contained no provision for after-born children. Azcunce subsequently executed two codicils which republished all the terms of the original will, without altering the testamentary disposition or making provision for after-born children. Between the execution of the two codicils, Azcunce's fourth child, Patricia (P), was born. Azcunce died shortly after executing the second codicil. After the will and the two codicils were admitted to probate, Patricia (P) filed this petition, seeking a statutory share of her father's estate as a pretermitted child. The trial court denied the petition. This appeal followed.

ISSUE: When a testator fails to provide in his will for any of his children born after making the will, shall the child receive a share of the estate equal in value to that he would have received if the testator had died intestate, unless it appears the omission was intentional?

HOLDING AND DECISION: (Hubbart, J.) Yes. When a testator fails to provide in his will for any of his children born after making the will, the child shall receive a share of the estate equal in value to that he would have received if the testator had died intestate, unless it appears the omission was intentional. Without dispute, Patricia (P) was a pretermitted child both at the time her father's will was executed and at the first time the first codicil was executed. However, when the second codicil republished the original will and first codicil, Patricia's (P) prior status as a pretermitted child was destroyed, inasmuch as she was alive at the time. Presumably, if her father had wished to provide for Patricia (P), he would have done so in the second codicil. Because he did not, Patricia (P) was, in effect, disinherited. Affirmed.

EDITOR'S ANALYSIS: The rule of § 732.302, Florida Statutes (1985) was applied here by the court of appeals. Such pretermitted heir statutes are intended to protect children from being unintentionally disinherited. Patricia (P) had argued that the will and the two codicils were somehow ambiguous and that the court should have accepted parol evidence that her father intended to provide for her. The court found utterly no ambiguity that would authorize the taking of parol evidence.

[For more information on omitted children, see Casenote Law Outline on Wills, Trusts and Estates, Chapter 3, § I, Protection of Children.]

QUICKNOTES

CODICIL - A supplement to a will.

PRETERMITTED - Omitted; usually refers to an heir who is unintentionally omitted from a testator's will.

STATUTORY SHARE - The statutory scheme pursuant to which property is distributed in the absence of a valid will.

NOTES:

ESPINOSA v. SPARBER, SHEVIN, SHAPO, ROSEN & HEILBRONNER

After-born child (P) v. Law firm (D)

Fla. Sup. Ct., 612 So. 2d 1378 (1993).

NATURE OF CASE: Appeal from a dismissal with prejudice, due to lack of privity, of an action for legal malpractice.

FACT SUMMARY: After Rene Azcunce died without providing in his will for his after-born child (P), his wife brought this legal malpractice action on the child's (P) behalf against Rene's attorney, Roskin (D), and his law firm (D).

CONCISE RULE OF LAW: To bring a legal malpractice action, the plaintiff must either be in privity with the attorney or must be an intended third-party beneficiary.

FACTS: Rene Azcunce contacted his attorney, Roskin (D), in order to include his latest child, Patricia (P), in his will. Roskin (D) drafted a new will that provided for Patricia (P) and restructured the trust. However, due to a disagreement between Rene and Roskin (D), Rene never signed the second will. Instead, he executed a second codicil drafted by Roskin (D), which did not provide for the after-born child, Patricia (P). After Rene's death, his wife brought this malpractice action on behalf of Patricia (P) and the estate against Roskin (D) and the law firm (D). The trial court dismissed the complaint with prejudice for lack of privity, entering summary judgment for Roskin (D) and his firm (D). The court of appeal reversed the dismissal with regard to the estate but affirmed it with regard to Patricia (P) and certified the question of standing to the supreme court.

ISSUE: To bring a legal malpractice action, must the plaintiff either be in privity with the attorney or be an intended third-party beneficiary?

HOLDING AND DECISION: (McDonald, J.) Yes. To bring a legal malpractice action, the plaintiff must either be in privity with the attorney or must be an intended third-party beneficiary. Because Patricia (P) cannot be described as one in privity with Roskin (D) or as an intended third-party beneficiary, a lawsuit alleging professional malpractice cannot be brought on her behalf. Rene's estate, however, standing in the shoes of the testator and clearly satisfying the privity requirement, may maintain a legal malpractice action against Roskin (D). Thus, the certified question is answered in the negative, and the decision of the district court is approved.

EDITOR'S ANALYSIS: Standing in legal malpractice actions is limited to those who can show that the testator's intent, as expressed in the will, is frustrated by the negligence of the testator's attorney. Unfortunately, although Rene did not express in his will and codicils any intention to exclude Patricia (P), he did not express any affirmative intent to provide for her either.

Because the client is no longer alive and is unable to testify, the task of identifying any intended third-party beneficiaries, under that limited exception to the strict privity requirement, causes an evidentiary problem.

QUICKNOTES

CODICIL - A supplement to a will.

PRETERMITTED - Omitted; usually refers to an heir who is unintentionally omitted from a testator's will.

PRIVITY - Commonality of rights or interests between parties.

THIRD-PARTY BENEFICIARY - A party who benefits from a promise made pursuant to a contract although he is not a party to the agreement.

EXTRINSIC EVIDENCE - Evidence that is not contained within the text of a document or contract but which is derived from the parties' statements or the circumstances under which the agreement was made.

NOTES:

CHAPTER 8
TRUSTS: CREATION, TYPES, AND CHARACTERISTICS

QUICK REFERENCE RULES OF LAW

1.   Creation of a Trust. Where the existence of a confidential relationship and an oral agreement to reconvey has been established, it is up to the other party, through clear and convincing proof, to negate the presumption of a constructive trust. (Jimenez v. Lee)

[For more information on provisions of the trust instrument, see Casenote Law Outline on Wills, Trusts & Estates, Chapter 12, § VI, Sales by Fiduciaries.]

2.   Creation of a Trust. A mere promise to give periodic gifts in the future will not support a finding that a trust has been established. (Unthank v. Rippstein)

[For more information on intent to create a trust, see Casenote Law Outline on Wills, Trusts & Estates, Chapter 4, § III, Trusts.]

3.   Creation of a Trust. Where a promise to declare a trust of property not yet in existence is unsupported by consideration, and the intention to hold the property in trust is not manifested until sometime after its acquisition by declarant, the property is not received in trust and is therefore taxable to the declarant. (Brainard v. Commissioner)

[For more information on the creation of a trust, see Casenote Law Outline on Wills, Trusts & Estates, Chapter 4, § III, Trusts.]

4.   Creation of a Trust. A gift of property to be acquired in the future is valid and effective if the donor manifests an irrevocable intention to make a present transfer of his interest. (Speelman v. Pascal)

[For more information on the creation of a gift, see Casenote Law Outline on Wills, Trusts & Estates, Chapter 4, § II, Gifts.]

5.   Creation of a Trust. Where the beneficiaries of a noncharitable trust cannot adequately be determined, the trust fails. (Clark v. Campbell)

[For more information on designation of trust beneficiaries, see Casenote Law Outline on Wills, Trusts & Estates, Chapter 4, § III, Trusts.]

6.   Creation of a Trust. An "honorary trust" is valid where it is for a valid purpose and the trustee accepts the testator's wishes, even though there is no beneficiary who can enforce the trust. (In re Searight's Estate)

[For more information on honorary trusts, see Casenote Law Outline on Wills, Trusts & Estates, Chapter 10, § VIII, Charitable Trusts.]

7.   Creation of a Trust. Where the existence of a confidential relationship and an oral agreement to reconvey has been established, it is up to the other party, through clear and convincing proof, to negate the presumption of a constructive trust. (Hieble v. Hieble)

[For more information on constructive trusts, see Casenote Law Outline on Wills, Trusts & Estates, Chapter 6, § VIII, Other Inter Vivos Transfers.]

8.   Creation of a Trust. Where a will upon its face shows that the devisee takes the legal title only and not the beneficial interest, and the trust is not sufficiently defined by the will to take effect, the equitable interest goes by way of resulting trust to the heirs or next of kin as property of the deceased not disposed of by his will. (Olliffe v. Wells)

[For more information on resulting trust, see Casenote Law Outline on Wills, Trusts & Estates, Chapter 6, § VIII, Other Inter Vivos Transfers.]

9.   Discretionary Trusts. Where a trust gives the trustee a discretionary power to pay amounts of the principal for the comfortable support and maintenance of a beneficiary, the trustee has a duty to inquire into the financial resources of that beneficiary so as to recognize his needs. (Marsman v. Nasca)

[For more information on discretionary trusts, see Casenote Law Outline on Wills, Trusts and Estates, Chapter 10, § V, Discretionary Trusts.]

10.   Spendthrift Trusts: Creditors' Rights. Public policy requires that the spendthrift provisions of a trust be overridden by a beneficiary's obligation to support his wife and children, and valid claim for such support can be enforced against that portion of the trust realizable by the beneficiary. (Shelley v. Shelley)

[For more information on alimony and child support, see Casenote Law Outline on Wills, Trusts & Estates, Chapter 11, § V, Spendthrift Provisions.]

11.   Modification and Termination of Trusts. A trust may be terminated if all of the beneficiaries agree, none of the beneficiaries is under a legal disability, and the trust's purposes would not be frustrated by doing so. (In re Trust of Stuchell)

[For more information on deviations from the trust terms, see Casenote Law Outline on Wills, Trusts & Estates, Chapter 10, § VI, Deviations from the Trust Terms.]

12.   Modification and Termination of Trusts. In construing a will, the testator's intention must be determined by what the will actually says and not by what the testator would have said if he had further explained his intentions. (Hamerstrom v. Commerce Bank of Kanss City)

[For more information on deviations from the trust terms, see Casenote Law Outline on Wills, Trusts & Estates, Chapter 10, § VI, Deviations from the Trust Terms.]

13.   Modification and Termination of Trusts. An active trust may not be terminated, even with the consent of all the beneficiaries, if a material purpose of the settlor remains to be accomplished. (In re Estate of Brown)

[For more information on termination of trusts, see Casenote Law Outline on Wills, Trusts & Estates, Chapter 10, § VII, Premature Termination of Trusts.]

14.   Charitable Trusts. For a charitable trust to be valid, it must provide relief for poor or needy or otherwise benefit or advance the social interest of the community. (Shenandoah Valley National Bank v. Talyor)

[For more information on the creation of a charitable trust, see Casenote Law Outline on Wills, Trusts & Estates, Chapter 10, § VIII, Charitable Trusts.]

15.   Charitable Trusts. Where a will gives real property for a general charitable purpose, the gift may be reformed cy pres when compliance with a particular purpose grafted on to the general purpose is impracticable. (In re Neher)

[For more information on doctrine of cy pres, see Casenote Law Outline on Wills, Trusts & Estates, Chapter 10, § VIII, Charitable Trusts.]

16.   Charitable Trusts. The cypres doctrine applies only where the purpose of a trust has become illegal, impossible, or permanently impracticable of performance. (In re Estate of Buck)

JIMENEZ v. LEE
Parties not identified
274 Ore. 457 (1976).

NATURE OF CASE: Action for an accounting.

FACT SUMMARY: Jimenez (P) sought an accounting from her father, Lee (D), for his use of trust funds to satisfy his legal support obligations to her.

CONCISE RULE OF LAW: Where funds are held in trust for a specific purpose, the trustee will be liable for all expenditures not related to that purpose.

FACTS: Jimenez's (P) grandmother purchased a $1,000 savings bond shortly after Jimenez's (P) birth in the joint names of Jimenez (P) and/or her father, Lee (D). The bond was for Jimenez's (P) educational needs. Another $500 bond was purchased by a third party for Jimenez's (P) education. Lee (D) subsequently cashed the bonds in and invested the proceeds in common stock, which Lee (D) held as custodian for Jimenez (P) under the Uniform Gift to Minors Act. Lee (D) had held these funds as trustee and could only use them for a proper trust purpose, Jimenez's (P) education. Jimenez (P) sought an accounting. Lee (D) alleged that no trust existed and that all funds had been used for Jimenez's (P) benefit.

ISSUE: May a trustee use trust funds for the benefit of the beneficiary but for purposes not authorized under the trust?

HOLDING AND DECISION: (O'Connell, C.J.) No. A trustee may only use trust funds in a manner authorized under the trust. He may not expand his powers to include unauthorized uses. The evidence indicates that the bonds were to be used for Jimenez's (P) education and were held in trust by Lee (D) for this purpose. The evidence clearly establishes that Lee (D) could not expand his powers by using the bonds to purchase stock, with Lee (D) acting as custodian under the Uniform Gift to Minors Act. The stock is directly traceable to the bonds, and the trust is impressed on the stock. As trustee, Lee (D) was obligated to keep exact records of all expenditures made for Jimenez's (P) education. Failure to keep accurate records can result in a surcharge to the trustee for unaccounted sums. The trustee is also liable for expenditures not related to the purpose of the trust. Use of the trust funds for gifts, medical expenses, clothing, etc., are not related to Jimenez's (P) educational needs. Lee (D) is liable for all such expenditures. Remanded for a determination of exactly how much of the trust corpus was used for Jimenez's (P) educational expenses.

EDITOR'S ANALYSIS: Jimenez is important for a number of reasons. First, it points up the importance of keeping adequate records of expenditures. Even if the trustee has acted entirely properly, he will be liable for any unaccounted-for funds. White v.

Rankin, 46 N.Y.S. 228 (1897). Next, Jimenez indicates that the trustee must be able to establish that all expenditures are within the areas permitted under the trust instrument. Bogart on Trusts and Trustees § 972(1) (1962).

_____

[For more information on provisions of the trust instrument, see Casenote Law Outline on Wills, Trusts & Estates, Chapter 12, § VI, Sales by Fiduciaries.]

NOTES:

UNTHANK v. RIPPSTEIN
Promisee (P) v. Executor (D)
386 S.W.2d 134 (1964).

NATURE OF CASE: Action to declare a trust.

FACT SUMMARY: Craft sent a letter to Rippstein (P) promising to give her $200 per month.

CONCISE RULE OF LAW: A mere promise to give periodic gifts in the future will not support a finding that a trust has been established.

FACTS: Craft sent Rippstein (P) a letter a few days before his death promising to give her $200 per month. The letter stated that Craft's estate would be liable for such payments if he died. Rippstein (P) alleged that the letter created an enforceable trust. Unthank (D), the executor of Craft's will, alleged that this was an unenforceable gift or a voluntary trust which was unenforceable for lack of consideration.

ISSUE: Is a mere promise to make payments in the future enforceable as a trust?

HOLDING AND DECISION: (Steakley, J.) No. A gift or voluntary trust is merely a promise, without consideration to make payments in the future. As such, it is unenforceable under the rules governing gifts. It is not a trust since there is no res and no intention expressed to hold all of the alleged trustor's property liable for payment. Upon the death of the promisor, the promise cannot be enforced against the estate since the gift of payments after death is a will substitute lacking the requisite testamentary requirements. The gift is unenforceable.

EDITOR'S ANALYSIS: Before a trust may be found to be enforceable, the equitable title must sufficiently rest in the beneficiary so as to allow him to maintain an action for the conversion of the trust property. Flick v. Baldwin, 141 Tex. 340. Where there is no specific trust res to which the trust is to attach, the beneficiary has no beneficial interest in any particular property. Additionally, of course, the absence of a trust res would, in and of itself, cause the trust to fail in most instances.

[For more information on intent to create a trust, see Casenote Law Outline on Wills, Trusts & Estates, Chapter 4, § III, Trusts.]

QUICKNOTES

HOLOGRAPHIC CODICIL - A handwritten provision added to a testamentary instrument.

VOLUNTARY TRUST - A trust established by a settlor voluntarily, as opposed to by operation of law, with the intent to make a gift of the trust property for the benefit of another.

TRUST CORPUS - The aggregate body of assets placed into a trust.

NOTES:

BRAINARD v. COMMISSIONER OF INTERNAL REVENUE
Taxpayer (D) v. IRS (P)
91 F.2d 880 (7th Cir. 1937).

NATURE OF CASE: Appeal from decision ordering payment of a tax deficiency.

FACT SUMMARY: Brainard (D) declared a trust in favor of members of his family, then entered into securities transactions, the profits from which he credited to the trust account.

CONCISE RULE OF LAW: Where a promise to declare a trust of property not yet in existence is unsupported by consideration, and the intention to hold the property in trust is not manifested until sometime after its acquisition by declarant, the property is not received in trust and is therefore taxable to the declarant.

FACTS: In December of 1927, Brainard (D), in contemplation of trading in the stock market, consulted an attorney and was advised that he could establish a trust in favor of the members of his family. After discussing this prospect with his wife and mother, he declared a trust of any profits to be received from his securities dealings during the year 1928. It was agreed that Brainard (D) would assume all losses resulting from the ventures but that any profits remaining after Brainard (D) had deducted a reasonable compensation for his services would be divided equally among his wife, mother, and two children, then aged one and three. At the conclusion of a year of successful trading, Brainard (D) claimed almost $10,000 as compensation for his services and reported that amount as income for the year 1928. The remaining profits were reported in approximately equal amounts in the tax returns of the members of his family although, except for minimal payments to taxpayer's (D) mother, the beneficiaries did not receive any cash from the transactions. The Board of Tax Appeals held that all of the income from the transactions was taxable to Brainard (D), and when the Commissioner (P) sought to collect the alleged deficiency, Brainard (D) brought this appeal.

ISSUE: When a trust is declared of property not yet in existence, and the promise to create the trust is not supported by consideration, is the property taxable to the declarant upon acquisition?

HOLDING AND DECISION: (Sparks, J.) Yes. An interest not yet in existence cannot constitute the property of a trust, and, although a person can bind himself to create a trust of property which he anticipates acquiring, such an agreement is binding only if supported by consideration. Since Brainard (D), at the time of his declaration, constituted a mere promise to create a trust in the future, and since the declaration was gratuitous, it was not supported by consideration. Therefore, no trust was created at the time of taxpayer's (D) declaration. Although a trust would have arisen at the time that the property came into existence if, at that time, Brainard (D) had manifested an intention that it be held in trust, it is generally held that silence does not constitute conduct from which the intent to impress a trust may be inferred. In the present case, the Board of Tax Appeals correctly determined that the first action manifesting an intent to form a trust at the time of or subsequent to taxpayer's (D) acquisition of the property was the act of crediting the profits to the books of the beneficiaries. Prior to that time, Brainard's (D) declaration of a trust was merely gratuitous and could not be enforced against him. Since the trust did not come into existence until the time of taxpayer's (D) bookkeeping entries, the profits, at the time of their acquisition, constituted property of the taxpayer (D) and not of the trust. Therefore, because between acquisition of the property and formation of the trust there intervened this period during which Brainard (D) was owner of the profits, they were properly taxed to him as part of his income.

EDITOR'S ANALYSIS: Brainard v. Commissioner of Internal Revenue is one of the leading cases standing for the rule that an attempt to establish a trust in property not yet in existence is ineffective unless supported by consideration. The significant element of the case is that the trust was declared voluntarily and for that reason was unenforceable. The trust would have been effective had Brainard (D), simultaneous with his acquiring the property which he proposed to place in trust, manifested an intention that a trust attach. Of course, once Brainard (D) was in possession of the trust property, he could have declared a valid trust at any time, and his prior declaration would have been superfluous. Therefore, the case may be read as standing for the proposition that a declaration of trust of property not yet in existence is, as a practical matter, of no import at all unless supported by consideration.

[For more information on the creation of a trust, see Casenote Law Outline on Wills, Trusts & Estates, Chapter 4, § III, Trusts.]

QUICKNOTES

CONSIDERATION - Value given by one party in exchange for performance, or a promise to perform, by another party.

EXECUTORY CONTRACT - A contract in which performance of an obligation has yet to be rendered.

SPEELMAN v. PASCAL
Assigned (P) v. Widow of producer (D)
N.Y. Ct. App., 10 N.Y.2d 313, 222 N.Y.S.2d 324, 178 N.E.2d 723 (1961).

NATURE OF CASE: Action to enforce a gift of future profits.

FACT SUMMARY: Prior to his death, Pascal's (D) husband sent Speelman (P) a letter in which he promised to give Speelman (P) a share of the profits from his future production of a musical.

CONCISE RULE OF LAW: A gift of property to be acquired in the future is valid and effective if the donor manifests an irrevocable intention to make a present transfer of his interest.

FACTS: Pascal, a theatrical producer, owned an exclusive license to create stage and film versions of a musical based on George Bernard Shaw's "Pygmalion." About two years before this license was due to expire, Pascal sent a letter to Speelman (P) (also known as Kingman) in which he promised her shares of his profits from the anticipated productions. Although Pascal died several months later, arrangements were later made, through his estate, for the production of the well-known and highly successful musical "My Fair Lady." Speelman (P) then sought to enforce Pascal's promise to give her a share of the production's profits, but Pascal's widow (D) claimed that the gift was not enforceable since it had referred to profits which were not yet in existence. The trial court rendered judgment in favor of Speelman (P), but Mrs. Pascal (D) appealed.

ISSUE: May a valid gift be created of property which is not yet in existence?

HOLDING AND DECISION: (Desmond, J.) Yes. A gift of property to be acquired in the future is valid and effective if the donor manifests an irrevocable intention to make a present transfer of his interest. This rule enjoys general acceptance in this jurisdiction. In this case, delivery of Pascal's letter constituted an adequate expression of his intention to make a present gift of future profits from his anticipated production. Accordingly, the gift to Speelman (P) is enforceable, and the judgment of the lower court must be affirmed.

EDITOR'S ANALYSIS: Perhaps the most significant distinction between gifts and trusts is that the former is ineffective without delivery. Almost any type of property, tangible or intangible, may be the subject of a gift or a trust. When interests in property not yet in existence are involved, however, the donor or trustor must make a present and irrevocable transfer of his interest in the property to be acquired. If the donor or trustor retains any interest in the future property or maintains any control over its distribution, the gift or trust will likely be deemed ineffective. Virtually every Anglo-American jurisdiction recognizes and applies this rule.

[For more information on the creation of a gift, see Casenote Law Outline on Wills, Trusts & Estates, Chapter 4, § II, Gifts.]

QUICKNOTES

LICENSEES - Persons known to an owner or occupier of land, who come onto the premises voluntarily and for a specific purpose although not necessarily with the consent of the owner.

ASSIGNMENT - A transaction in which a party conveys his or her entire interest in property to another.

CONSIDERATION - Value given by one party in exchange for performance, or a promise to perform, by another party.

NOTES:

CLARK v. CAMPBELL
Parties not identified
82 N.H. 281 (1976).

NATURE OF CASE: Will contest.

FACT SUMMARY: The trustees of the estate were directed to give decedent's personal effects to the friends they knew she wished to receive them.

CONCISE RULE OF LAW: Where the beneficiaries of a noncharitable trust cannot adequately be determined, the trust fails.

FACTS: Decedent left her personal property to her trustees in trust to "make disposal by way of memento . . . to such of my friends as they, my trustees, shall select." Decedent further stated that her trustees were familiar with her friends and her wishes. Heirs alleged that the trust was void for lack of definite beneficiaries or ascertainable standards to identify them.

ISSUE: Must there be a definite beneficiary of a trust or ascertainable standards for determining the identity of beneficiaries?

HOLDING AND DECISION: (Snow, J.) Yes. To be valid, a trust must have an identifiable beneficiary, or there must be adequate standards provided under the trust instrument for their identification in the future. "Friends" is too indefinite a class of beneficiaries. Appointment of property by the trustee could not be opposed, in most cases, since the permissible class is too vague for the court to determine whether the distribution was proper. The trust therefore fails, and the trustee holds for the taker under the will. The bequest was a trust and not an outright gift to the trustee.

EDITOR'S ANALYSIS: The attorney general of the state administers charitable trusts and can protect against trustee abuses. Therefore, charitable trusts will not fail for lack of a definite beneficiary. Harrington v. Pier, 105 Wis. 485. Personal wishes conveyed to the trustee by the testator are not sufficient to render an otherwise indefinite description of beneficiaries definite. Olliffe v. Wells, 130 Mass. 221.

[For more information on designation of trust beneficiaries, see Casenote Law Outline on Wills, Trusts & Estates, Chapter 4, § III, Trusts.]

QUICKNOTES

UNJUST ENRICHMENT - The unlawful acquisition of money or property of another for which both law and equity require restitution to be made.

CESTUI QUE TRUST - Beneficiary; the party for whose benefit a trust is established.

NOTES:

IN RE SEARIGHT'S ESTATE
Department of taxation (P) v. Executor (D)
87 Ohio App. 417 (1950).

NATURE OF CASE: Appeal from probate decision.

FACT SUMMARY: The testator, by will, left $1,000 to his executor (D) to pay another to care for his dog for the rest of the dog's life; the probate court found it was a valid trust and that the recipient of the dog could be taxed only on the dog's worth ($5), over the Department of Taxation's (P) objection that it was not a trust and the $1,000 was taxable.

CONCISE RULE OF LAW: An "honorary trust" is valid where it is for a valid purpose and the trustee accepts the testator's wishes, even though there is no beneficiary who can enforce the trust.

FACTS: The testator, by will, left $1,000 to his executor (D) to pay Florence Hand $0.75 per day to care for his dog for the rest of the dog's life. The probate court found that it was a valid "honorary trust" and that Florence could be charged inheritance tax on the value of the dog ($5) only. The Department of Taxation (P) objected that there was no valid trust created since there was no ascertainable beneficiary who could enforce the trust, and it violated the rule against perpetuities and that the full $1,000 was taxable to Florence.

ISSUE: Is an "honorary trust" valid where it is for a valid purpose and the trustee accepts the testator's wishes, even though there is no beneficiary who can enforce the trust?

HOLDING AND DECISION: (Hunsicker, J.) Yes. Normally, attempts to create a trust where there is no ascertainable beneficiary will fail, but an exception permits an "honorary trust" to survive. The requirements are that the trust have some legal purpose and that the trustee accepts the wishes of the testator. Here, the testator attempted to further no illegal purpose but rather a worthy one, and Florence accepted the dog and the responsibilities of care. The transfer into trust does not violate the rule against perpetuities since there is only $1,000 plus accumulated interest involved, which, at $0.75 per day, would be exhausted within 5 years. (The R.A.P. requires the transfer to vest within a life or lives in being, plus twenty-one years.) And since Florence did not receive any gift under the trust except the dog, worth $5, she can only be taxed on that amount. Any amount remaining after the dog dies will be taxed to the remaindermen under the trust.

EDITOR'S ANALYSIS: Most jurisdictions do not recognize "honorary trusts." But no jurisdiction recognizes such a trust where the testator "requests" or "hopes" that the trustee will perform the stated tasks in the purported trust instrument. This would be an aleatory suggestion which the trustee could ignore while keeping the transfer into trust for his own benefit. It would then be void due to no affirmative trust intent.

[For more information on honorary trusts, see Casenote Law Outline on Wills, Trusts & Estates, Chapter 10, § VIII, Charitable Trusts.]

QUICKNOTES

RULE AGAINST PERPETUITIES - The doctrine that a future interest that is incapable of vesting within twenty-one years of lives in being at the time it is created is immediately void.

CHARITABLE TRUST - A trust that is established for the benefit of a class of persons or for the public in general.

NOTES:

HIEBLE v. HIEBLE
Mother (P) v. Son (D)
164 Conn. 56 (1972).

NATURE OF CASE: Action to impose a constructive trust.

FACT SUMMARY: In fear that cancer could reoccur, Mrs. Hieble (P) conveyed real property to her son (D) and daughter on the oral condition that they would reconvey it if she had no reoccurrence of the cancer for five years.

CONCISE RULE OF LAW: Where the existence of a confidential relationship and an oral agreement to reconvey has been established, it is up to the other party, through clear and convincing proof, to negate the presumption of a constructive trust.

FACTS: Mrs. Hieble (P) conveyed real property to her son (D) and daughter after finding out that she had cancer. There was an oral agreement that the property would be reconveyed to her if no further cancer was found five years after it had been operated on and removed. Mrs. Hieble (P) was to continue to use the property, and she paid all taxes and upkeep on it. The daughter reconveyed her share of the property, but the son (D) subsequently refused to reconvey. Mrs. Hieble (P) brought an action to compel the reconveyance. Mrs. Hieble (P) alleged that the property was held by the son (D) in a constructive trust. The son (D) alleged that there was no fiduciary or special confidential relationship and that there was insufficient evidence on which to base a trust.

ISSUE: Will a constructive trust be imposed where a fiduciary or confidential relationship exists and the evidence indicates that reconveyance was actually promised?

HOLDING AND DECISION: (Shapiro, J.) Yes. Before a constructive trust will be imposed, there must be a showing that a fiduciary or confidential relationship existed between the parties. A mere familial relationship may not automatically qualify as a confidential relationship. In this case, however, a classic example of a confidential relations arose: a mother had just gone through a recent operation which could have been terminal, the parties are mother and child, and the son (D) reassured his mother of his faithfulness. Both the testimony and the conduct of the parties clearly established the existence of the oral agreement. Where the owner of an interest in land makes a transfer of it to another in trust for the transferor and no written memorandum exists, a constructive trust will be imposed to require reconveyance where a confidential relationship exits. Judgment for Mrs. Hieble (P).

EDITOR'S ANALYSIS: In Ray v. Winter, 67 Ill. 2d 296 (1976), Ray alleged that he had confidentially told Winter about a business opportunity but that he did not have funds to take advantage of it. Winter promised Ray 40 areas of land when he could afford to pay for it. The court found that there was no past relationship between the parties which would support a finding that a confidential or fiduciary relationship existed. A mere oral agreement will generally not create such a relationship.

[For more information on constructive trusts, see Casenote Law Outline on Wills, Trusts & Estates, Chapter 6, § VIII, Other Inter Vivos Transfers.]

QUICKNOTES

CONSTRUCTIVE TRUST - A trust that arises by operation of law whereby the court imposes a trust upon property lawfully held by one party for the benefit of another, as a result of some wrongdoing by the party in possession so as to avoid unjust enrichment.

PAROL EVIDENCE RULE - Doctrine precluding parties to an agreement from introducing evidence of prior or contemporaneous agreements in order to repudiate or alter the terms of a written contract.

NOTES:

OLLIFFE v. WELLS
Family of deceased (P) v. Executor (D)
Mass. Sup. Jud. Ct., 130 Mass. 221 (1881).

NATURE OF CASE: Action to have legacy of estate residue declared lapsed and to have property distributed among heirs at law and next of kin.

FACT SUMMARY: Testator devised residue of estate to the executor with an instruction to distribute it, according to his discretion, so as to carry out the testator's preexpressed wishes.

CONCISE RULE OF LAW: Where a will upon its face shows that the devisee takes the legal title only and not the beneficial interest, and the trust is not sufficiently defined by the will to take effect, the equitable interest goes by way of resulting trust to the heirs or next of kin as property of the deceased not disposed of by his will.

FACTS: Testatrix left a will, and after giving various legacies, she devised to Wells (D), the named executor, the residue of the estate, which the executor was empowered to distribute in such manner as in his discretion was best calculated to carry out the wishes of the testatrix as expressed to him. In an action by the heirs at law (P) and next of kin (P) of the testatrix to have the executor (D) distribute the residue to them, the executor (D) claimed that, prior to her death, the testatrix orally instructed him to give the residue to charities.

ISSUE: Where a will, on its face, gives legal title but not any beneficial interest to a devisee, and there is no express trust indicated, will a resulting trust arise in favor of heirs or next of kin?

HOLDING AND DECISION: (Gray, C.J.) Yes. The purported trust in favor of the charities did not appear on the face of will; therefore, it cannot be established by extrinsic evidence. Thus, the executor (D) only has discretion in the manner of distribution; he cannot choose the beneficiaries. Since the trust cannot be carried out, the bequest falls within the residue of the estate and goes to the heirs (P) and next of kin (P). If the charities had been expressly named, they could have enforced the trust against the executor (D), who received only a legal title, and no beneficial interest, in the devise.

EDITOR'S ANALYSIS: Where a testamentary trust fails for any reason, the assets that were to be a part of that trust must still be distributed. In some instances, the testator's will may provide for the distribution of such assets. But if no contingent provision was prepared, the assets must pass intestate. This has resulted, in some cases, in the assets going to heirs or next of kin specifically excluded by the testator. A statement by a testator, in his will, that certain individuals are not to share in his estate does not constitute a testamentary scheme.

[For more information on resulting trust, see Casenote Law Outline on Wills, Trusts & Estates, Chapter 6, § VIII, Other Inter Vivos Transfers.]

QUICKNOTES

RESIDUARY ESTATE - That portion of the estate which remains after all the estate has been distributed through the satisfaction of all claims and is conditional upon something remaining after the claims on the testator's estate are satisfied.

DEVISEE - A person upon whom a gift of real or personal property is conferred by means of a testamentary instrument.

EXTRINSIC EVIDENCE - Evidence that is not contained within the text of a document or contract but which is derived from the parties' statements or the circumstances under which the agreement was made.

NOTES:

MARSMAN v. NASCA
Wife of beneficiary (P) v. Trustee (D)
Mass. App. Ct., 30 Mass. App. Ct. 789, 573 N.E.2d 1025 (1991).

NATURE OF CASE: Appeal from judgment imposing constructive trust for breach of trust.

FACT SUMMARY: Because Farr (D), as trustee of Cappy Marsman's trust, did not inquire into Cappy's financial circumstances, Cappy was forced to give up the house he lived in as a means of solving his financial difficulties.

CONCISE RULE OF LAW: Where a trust gives the trustee a discretionary power to pay amounts of the principal for the comfortable support and maintenance of a beneficiary, the trustee has a duty to inquire into the financial resources of that beneficiary so as to recognize his needs.

FACTS: Sara Marsman set up a trust that provided for her husband, Cappy, after her death. Farr (D), as trustee, had discretionary power to pay out amounts of the principal as he deemed advisable but failed to adequately explain that power to Cappy. Because Cappy was denied access to the principal, financial difficulties caused him to transfer his house to Sara's daughter, Sally, and her husband, Marlette (D), reserving a life estate for himself. After Cappy's death, Marlette (D), now sole owner due to Sally's death, told Margaret (P), Cappy's second wife, to vacate the premises. Margaret (P) brought an action in the probate court, which held that Farr (D) had breached his duty to inquire into Cappy's finances. Marlette (D) was ordered to convey the house to Margaret (P), and Farr (D) was ordered to reimburse Marlette (D) for upkeep expenses. Marlette (D) and Farr (D) appealed.

ISSUE: Where a trust gives the trustee a discretionary power to pay amounts of the principal for the comfortable support and maintenance of a beneficiary, does the trustee have a duty to inquire into the financial resources of that beneficiary so as to recognize his needs?

HOLDING AND DECISION: (Dreben, J.) Yes. Where a trust gives the trustee a discretionary power to pay amounts of the principal for the comfortable support and maintenance of a beneficiary, the trustee has a duty to inquire into the financial resources of that beneficiary so as to recognize his needs. A life beneficiary is to be maintained in accordance with his normal standard of living. Had Farr (D) met his duties either of inquiry or of distribution under the trust, Cappy would not have lost his home. However, Sally and Marlette (D) cannot be charged as constructive trustees of the property. But the payments of principal which would have made it possible for Cappy to keep the house can be deemed to be a constructive trust in favor of his estate. Vacated and remanded for a determination of the amount to be paid Cappy's estate from the trust.

EDITOR'S ANALYSIS: Here, Farr (D) was directed by the trust agreement to pay Cappy enough for his "comfortable support," yet Farr (D) failed to do so. Prudence and reasonableness are the standard of conduct for trustees of a discretionary trust. However, a desire to save for a beneficiary's future medical needs does not warrant a persistent policy of miserliness toward those beneficiaries.

[For more information on discretionary trusts, see Casenote Law Outline on Wills, Trusts and Estates, Chapter 10, § V, Discretionary Trusts.]

QUICKNOTES

DISCRETIONARY TRUST - A trust pursuant to which the trustee is authorized to make decisions regarding the investment of the trust funds and the distribution of such funds to beneficiaries.

TENANCY BY THE ENTIRETY - The ownership of property by a husband and wife whereby they hold undivided interests in the property with right of survivorship.

CONSTRUCTIVE TRUST - A trust that arises by operation of law whereby the court imposes a trust upon property lawfully held by one party for the benefit of another, as a result of some wrongdoing by the party in possession so as to avoid unjust enrichment.

EXCULPATORY CLAUSE - A clause in a contract relieving one party from liability for certain unlawful conduct.

NOTES:

SHELLEY v. SHELLEY
Ex-wife of beneficiary (P) v. Beneficiary bank (D)
Ore. Sup. Ct., 223 Ore. 328, 354 P.2d 282 (1960).

NATURE OF CASE: Suit for declaration of rights to trust proceeds.

FACT SUMMARY: Grant Shelly's (D) father created a trust for his benefit containing "spendthrift" provisions. His two former wives and their children sought to reach the trust income and principal to satisfy court-ordered alimony and child support obligations.

CONCISE RULE OF LAW: Public policy requires that the spendthrift provisions of a trust be overridden by a beneficiary's obligation to support his wife and children, and valid claim for such support can be enforced against that portion of the trust realizable by the beneficiary.

FACTS: By the terms of his will, Grant Shelly's (D) father created a testamentary trust for the benefit of Grant (D). The U.S. National Bank of Portland (D) was made trustee and was given complete control over the trust assets. U.S. National (D) was directed to pay the income from the trust to Grant (D) and to make payments of principal to him when, "in its discretion," he was competent to manage the funds on his own. The trust further provided that the trustee could make emergency payments for the benefit of Grant (D) or his children for unusual or extraordinary expenses. The trust contained a spendthrift clause that precluded the alienation of an interest in the trust by the trust beneficiary. This clause further immunized the trust from the claims of any of the beneficiary's creditors. Grant was first married and then divorced from Patricia (P). The decree of divorce awarded child support payments to their two children but no alimony. Grant (D) then married and divorced Betty (P), and that decree awarded alimony as well as child support to their children. Grant (D) ceased making the court-ordered payments to any of his children or to Betty (P). Betty (P) brought suit against Grant (D) and U.S. National (D) to have the trust income and, if necessary, the principal paid by U.S. National (D) to satisfy the alimony and child support obligations. Patricia (P) joined the suit on behalf of her children. Grant (D), by this time, had disappeared, and the suit was opposed by U.S. National (D) alone.

ISSUE: Does public policy require that the spendthrift provisions of a trust be overridden to satisfy the obligation of a beneficiary to support his wife and children?

HOLDING AND DECISION: (O'Connell, J.) Yes. The validity of spendthrift trusts is long established in this state to protect the assets and income of a trust from the reaches of creditors. But the right of a settlor to bequeath his property without interference is not absolute. Courts have traditionally refused to enforce trusts that violate the rule against perpetuities or are designed to further an unlawful objective. While a spendthrift trust is immunized against the claims of ordinary creditors, the wife and children of the beneficiary of such a trust cannot be grouped with those creditors. It would violate public policy to allow the beneficiary of such a trust to continue to enjoy the fruits of the trust while his family becomes a public charge. This is particularly true of the obligation of child support. Alimony is somewhat different in that the ability of the ex-wife to support herself, the length of the marriage, and other factors must be taken into account before such payments are ordered. However, once an alimony order is entered, it becomes as much an obligation of the husband as a child support order. In this case, Grant's (D) right to the income is absolute and as such is available for payment of the child support and alimony obligations to any reasonable extent. The right to invade the principal is not as sure. Grant (D) had no right to the principal unless U.S. National (D), as trustee, determined he was entitled thereto. Therefore, it is not reachable by his dependents since their claim derives through him. However, the children have a direct claim under the provision providing for emergency payments to Grant (D) or his children. We find that the failure of Grant (D) to provide any support at all constitutes such an emergency. This direct access is not available for the alimony payments since there is no comparable provision for Grant's (D) wife.

EDITOR'S ANALYSIS: Spendthrift trusts are created by settlors who do not have faith in the ability of the beneficiary to manage his assets. Some states have refused to enforce such trusts on the grounds that they operate as a fraud on creditors. The states that do recognize the validity of these trusts do so on the basis that a creditor is under the obligation to make inquiry as to the terms of the trust if they will look to its assets as security. If credit was extended without reference to the trust, then the creditor cannot now complain that he was misled. Some few jurisdictions have compromised and will allow a limited attachment of the trust income for creditors.

[For more information on alimony and child support, see Casenote Law Outline on Wills, Trusts & Estates, Chapter 11, § V, Spendthrift Provisions.]

QUICKNOTES

TRUST CORPUS - The aggregate body of assets placed into a trust.

RULE AGAINST PERPETUITIES - The doctrine that a future interest that is incapable of vesting within 21 years of lives in being at the time it is created is immediately void.

IN RE TRUST OF STUCHELL
Life income beneficiary (P) Court (D)
Or. Ct. App., 104 Or. App. 332, 801 P.2d 852 (1990).
Review denied, 311 Or. 166, 806 P.2d 1153.

NATURE OF CASE: Appeal from a dismissal of a petition to modify a trust.

FACT SUMMARY: A life-income beneficiary of a trust sought court approval of an agreement to modify the trust, allowing it to continue if her mentally retarded son survived her since a direct distribution to him would impact his ability to qualify for public assistance.

CONCISE RULE OF LAW: A trust may be terminated if all of the beneficiaries agree, none of the beneficiaries is under a legal disability, and the trust's purposes would not be frustrated by doing so.

FACTS: Stuchell established a testamentary trust with his granddaughter as one of two surviving life-income beneficiaries. On the death of the last income beneficiary, the remainder was to be distributed equally to the granddaughter's four children or to their lineal descendants. One of those children, Harrell, was mentally retarded and unable to live independently without assistance. If the remainder were distributed directly to Harrell, he would no longer qualify for public assistance. Thus, his mother requested that the court approve an agreement made by the other income beneficiary and remaindermen. The court dismissed the petition for modification. The granddaughter appealed.

ISSUE: May a trust be terminated if all of the beneficiaries agree, none of the beneficiaries is under a legal disability, and the trust's purposes would not be frustrated by doing so?

HOLDING AND DECISION: (Buttler, J.) Yes. A trust may be terminated if all of the beneficiaries agree, none of the beneficiaries is under a legal disability, and the trust's purposes would not be frustrated by doing so. However, in this case, the granddaughter, relying on Restatement (Second) of Trusts § 167(1) (1959), urged the court to extend the rule to permit modification. However, comment b to that section states that the court will not permit or direct the trustee to deviate from the terms of the trust merely because such deviation would be more advantageous to the beneficiaries than compliance. Here, the only purpose of the proposed amendment is to make the trust more advantageous to the beneficiaries. The most obvious advantage would be to the three remaindermen who have consented to the amendment. Since there is no authority for a court to approve the proposed modification, the trial court did not err in dismissing the petition. Affirmed.

EDITOR'S ANALYSIS: By its terms, the Restatement's rule applies only to the termination of a trust under very limited circumstances. Section 167(1) of the Restatement allows a court to permit the trustee to deviate from the terms of a trust if circumstances not known or anticipated by the settlor would defeat the purposes of the trust. The court noted that even if the Restatement rule were to be adopted as the law in Oregon, the limitation imposed by the comment would preclude permitting the proposed amendment.

[For more information on deviations from the trust terms, see Casenote Law Outline on Wills, Trusts & Estates, Chapter 10, § VI, Deviations from the Trust Terms.]

QUICKNOTES
REMAINDER BENEFICIARY - A person who is to receive property that is held in trust after the termination of a preceding income interest.

LIFE-INCOME BENEFICIARY - A person who is the recipient of income generated by certain property for the duration of the person's life, the remainder of which is to pass on to another individual upon the income beneficiary's death.

NOTES:

HAMERSTROM v. COMMERCE BANK OF KANSAS CITY
Parties not identified
Mo. Ct. App., 808 S.W.2d 434 (1991).

NATURE OF CASE: Appeal from a judgment denying a petition for deviation.

FACT SUMMARY: Due to inflation, her husband's retirement, and increased health care costs, Hamerstrom (P) filed a petition to increase the monthly sum she received as a life beneficiary of a testamentary trust, but the trial court denied the petition on the ground that it failed to benefit the trust's unascertained contingent remaindermen.

CONCISE RULE OF LAW: In construing a will, the testator's intention must be determined by what the will actually says and not by what the testator would have said if he had further explained his intentions.

FACTS: Hamerstrom (P), life beneficiary of a trust, acquired the consent of the trust's remaindermen to a proposed deviation increasing her monthly payment from $150 to $2,000 due to inflation, her husband's retirement, and increased health care costs. The trust was to end at Hamerstrom's (P) death, with any remainder going to her husband, should he survive her, and, if not, to their two sons, or the balance to whichever son survived the other. Hamerstrom (P) filed a petition for deviation. The trial court appointed a guardian ad litem who opposed the action, contending that the deviation did not benefit the trust's unascertained contingent remaindermen. The trial court denied the request for deviation and for attorney fees. Hamerstrom (P) appealed.

ISSUE: In construing a will, must the testator's intention be determined by what the will actually says and not by what the testator would have said if he had further explained his intentions?

HOLDING AND DECISION: (Ulrich, J.) Yes. In construing a will, the testator's intention must be determined by what the will actually says and not by what the testator would have said if he had further explained his intentions. Hamerstrom's (P) husband and their two sons are the specifically named remaindermen of the trust, which makes no specific provision for or mention of the "heirs" or "issue" of the two sons. The testator's intent to limit the distribution of his estate to those persons he specifically identified within the will is evident. Since the possible issue of the two sons are not beneficiaries, the agreement of the adult beneficiaries, present and contingent, was sufficient under the statute to modify the trust as requested. Reversed and remanded.

EDITOR'S ANALYSIS: Under the law in England and some of the Commonwealth countries, revocation of a trust on any terms is possible so long as all the beneficiaries agree to its termination. The settlor's intent may be set aside after his death since the trust is then considered the property of the beneficiaries, not the settlor. Contrast that with the approach taken in this country, the so-called Claflin Doctrine, where courts seek to fulfill the settlor's intent even after the settlor's death.

[For more information on deviations from the trust terms, see Casenote Law Outline on Wills, Trusts & Estates, Chapter 10, § VI, Deviations from the Trust Terms.]

QUICKNOTES

REMAINDERMAN - A person who has an interest in property to commence upon the termination of a present possessory interest.

GUARDIAN AD LITEM - Person designated by the court to represent an infant or ward in a particular legal proceeding.

NOTES:

IN RE ESTATE OF BROWN

Nephew / trust beneficiary (P) v. Probate court (D)
148 Vt. 94, 528 A.2d 752 (1987).

NATURE OF CASE: Appeal from judgment terminating trust.

FACT SUMMARY: The lifetime beneficiaries of Brown's trust petitioned the court to terminate the trust.

CONCISE RULE OF LAW: An active trust may not be terminated, even with the consent of all the beneficiaries, if a material purpose of the settlor remains to be accomplished.

FACTS: Andrew Brown died after transferring his entire estate into a trust. The trust income and principal were to be used to provide an education for the children of Brown's nephew, Woolson. After that purpose was accomplished, the trust income and principal were to be used for the care and maintenance of Woolson and his wife so that they could live in the style they were accustomed. At their death, the remainder was to pass the Woolsons' children. The trustee complied with the terms of the trust by using the proceeds for the education of the Woolsons' children and applying the proceeds to benefit Woolson and his wife after the education purpose was completed. Woolson and his wife petitioned the probate court for termination of the trust, arguing that the sole remaining purpose of the trust was to maintain their lifestyle and that the distribution of the assets was necessary to accomplish this purpose. The remaindermen, Woolson's children, filed consents to the proposed termination. The probate court denied Woolson's petition to terminate, and Woolson appealed. The superior court reversed, concluding that the only material trust purpose, the education of the children, had been accomplished. The trustee appealed.

ISSUE: May an active trust be terminated, even with the consent of all the beneficiaries, if a material purpose of the settlor remains to be accomplished?

HOLDING AND DECISION: (Gibson, J.) No. An active trust may not be terminated, even with the consent of all the beneficiaries, if a material purpose of the settlor remains to be accomplished. Here, the termination cannot be compelled because a material purpose remains to be accomplished. The trust instrument had two purposes. First, it provided for the education of Woolson's children. It is clear that the educational purpose of the trust was achieved. The second purpose was the assurance of lifelong income for the beneficiaries through the discretion of the trustee. The trustee has to use all the income and such part of the principal as is necessary for this purpose. This purpose would be defeated if termination of the trust were allowed. Reversed.

EDITOR'S ANALYSIS: Some courts will allow the termination of a testamentary trust by a compromise agreement between the beneficiaries and heirs entered into soon after the testator's death. In one case, the court allowed such a compromise regardless of whether a material purpose of the trust was defeated by the trust's termination (Budin v. Levy, 343 Mass. 644, 180 N.E. 2d 74 (1982).

[For more information on termination of trusts, see Casenote Law Outline on Wills, Trusts & Estates, Chapter 10, § VII, Premature Termination of Trusts.]

QUICKNOTES

REMAINDERMAN - A person who has an interest in property to commence upon the termination of a present possessory interest.

RESIDUARY BENEFICIARIES - Person specified pursuant to will to receive the portion of the estate remaining following distribution of the assets and the payment of costs.

SUPPORT TRUST - A trust pursuant to which the trustee is authorized to only distribute such funds as are required for the support of the beneficiary.

SPENDTHRIFT TRUST - A trust formed for the beneficiary's support, but with restrictions imposed so as to safeguard against the beneficiary's abuse.

LIFE-INCOME BENEFICIARY - A person who is the recipient of income generated by certain property for the duration of the person's life, the remainder of which is to pass on to another individual upon the income beneficiary's death.

NOTES:

SHENANDOAH VALLEY NATIONAL BANK v. TAYLOR
Heir-at-law (P) v. Trustee / bank (D)
Va. Sup. Ct. App., 192 Va. 135, 63 S.E.2d 786 (1951).

NATURE OF CASE: Suit challenging validity of a testamentary trust.

FACT SUMMARY: A testator created a perpetual trust, the income of which was to be paid in equal shares to each student in a particular grade school just before Christmas and Easter. Although the payments were purportedly for educational purposes, an heir challenged the validity of the trust.

CONCISE RULE OF LAW: For a charitable trust to be valid, it must provide relief for poor or needy or otherwise benefit or advance the social interest of the community.

FACTS: The terms of the testator's will left the bulk of his $86,000 estate to the Shenandoah Valley National Bank (D), as trustee to administer a perpetual trust. The trust funds were to be invested and the income was to be paid to all the first-, second-, and third-grade students in a particular local grade school. The payments were to be made in equal shares to each student directly and were to be distributed just before the Christmas and Easter vacations. The trust directed that the money so distributed was to be used by each student for the furtherance of his or her education. Although the testator had no children or other close relative, Taylor (P), a distant relative and heir at law, brought suit challenging the validity of the trust as not being charitable and therefore violative of the rule against perpetuities.

ISSUE: For a charitable trust to be valid, must it provide relief for the poor or needy or otherwise benefit or advance the social interest of the community?

HOLDING AND DECISION: (Miller, J.) Yes. There is a fundamental difference between a trust that is charitable and one that is benevolent. A benevolent trust, while it may be praiseworthy, is a private enterprise and is subject to the rule against perpetuities. A charitable trust is public and is not subject to the rule. For a perpetual charitable trust to be valid, it must provide relief to the poor or needy or otherwise benefit or advance the social interest of the community. The most common examples of such interests include the relief of poverty, the advancement of education, the advancement of religion, the promotion of health, and governmental or municipal purposes. The keystone is the accomplishment of a purpose which is beneficial to the community. While the testator's scheme would surely delight the recipients, there is no way that the stated purpose of educational advancement can be assured. The timing of the payments and the ages of the children practically assure the opposite. This trust cannot be classified as charitable, and as it violates the rule against perpetuities, it must fail.

EDITOR'S ANALYSIS: A perpetual charitable trust may validly be directed toward a small ascertainable group so long as the recipients are qualified as to actual need. Such provisions as providing for the support of needy widows and children of the deceased ministers of a particular church have been upheld for example. Where no need test is applied, the group benefited must be needy by definition, such as young seamstresses (upheld at a time before minimum wage laws). Generally, the larger the class, the less strict the application of the needs test.

[For more information on the creation of a charitable trust, see Casenote Law Outline on Wills, Trusts & Estates, Chapter 10, § VIII, Charitable Trusts.]

QUICKNOTES
TESTAMENTARY TRUST - A trust created by will and only effective after the grantor's death, since the assets that comprise the corpus of the trust are assumed to vest at that time.

CHARITABLE TRUST - A trust that is established for the benefit of a class of persons or for the public in general.

PERPETUAL TRUST - A trust which is to continue for as long as its purpose is necessary.

RULE AGAINST PERPETUITIES - The doctrine that a future interest that is incapable of vesting within twenty-one years of lives in being at the time it is created is immediately void.

NOTES:

IN RE NEHER
Parties not identified
N.Y. Ct. App., 279 N.Y. 370, 18 N.E.2d 625 (1939).

NATURE OF CASE: Appeal from the denial of a petition for a decree to construe and reform a charitable gift.

FACT SUMMARY: When Red Hook Village (P) found it did not have the resources to establish and maintain a hospital on property willed to the Village (P) by Ella Neher, the Village (P) petitioned the court for permission to establish instead an administration building designated as the Herbert Neher Memorial Hall.

CONCISE RULE OF LAW: Where a will gives real property for a general charitable purpose, the gift may be reformed cy pres when compliance with a particular purpose grafted on to the general purpose is impracticable.

FACTS: Ella Neher's will gave her home in Red Hook Village (P) to the Village (P) to be used as a memorial to the memory of her husband. She further directed that the property be used as a hospital to be known as the "Herbert Neher Memorial Hospital." The Village (P) accepted the gift but later discovered that it was without the resources necessary to establish and maintain a hospital on the property. Furthermore, a modern hospital in a neighboring village adequately served the needs of both communities. Instead, the Village (P) petitioned the court for leave to erect and maintain a building for the administration purposes of the Village (P) to be designated as the Herbert Neher Memorial Hall. The court denied the petition. The appellate division affirmed. The Village (P) appealed.

ISSUE: Where a will gives real property for a general charitable purpose, may the gift be reformed cy pres when compliance with a particular purpose grafted on to the general purpose is impracticable?

HOLDING AND DECISION: (Loughran, J.) Yes. Where a will gives real property for a general charitable purpose, the gift may be reformed cy pres when compliance with a particular purpose grafted on to the general purpose is impracticable. When taken as a whole, the true construction of the paragraph outlining the gift in Neher's will is that the paramount intention was to give the property for a general charitable purpose rather than a particular charitable purpose. Neher's gift to the Village (P) did not specify what sort of medical or surgical care should be provided. The direction grafted on to the general gift, that the property be used for a hospital, may be ignored where, as here, the Village (P) finds compliance with that direction impracticable due to a lack of resources. Reversed.

EDITOR'S ANALYSIS: Application of the doctrine of cy pres allows a charitable trust to continue rather than fail. The doctrine's application occurs where the court can discern a primary general charitable intent and where the altered charitable purpose falls within the general charitable intent of the settlor. Such reformation allows the donor's general intent to be carried out even where changes unforeseen by the settlor eliminate the need for the gift's original intended use.

[For more information on doctrine of cy pres, see Casenote Law Outline on Wills, Trusts & Estates, Chapter 10, § VIII, Charitable Trusts.]

QUICKNOTES
CHARITABLE TRUST - A trust that is established for the benefit of a class of persons or for the public in general.

DOCTRINE OF CYPRESS - Equitable doctrine applied in order to give effect to an instrument, which would be unlawful if enforced strictly, as close to the drafter's intent as possible without violating the law.

NOTES:

IN RE ESTATE OF BUCK

San Francisco foundation (P) v. Court (D)

California Superior Court, Marin County, 1986.

NATURE OF CASE: Petition for application of cy pres doctrine to change trust purpose.

FACT SUMMARY: After Mrs. Buck's will left the residue of her multimillion-dollar estate to the San Francisco Foundation to be used exclusively for the benefit of Marin County, California and its residents, the Foundation petitioned the court to use part of the estate for the benefit of other Bay Area counties.

CONCISE RULE OF LAW: The cy pres doctrine applies only where the purpose of a trust has become illegal, impossible, or permanently impracticable of performance.

FACTS: In 1973 Beryl Buck, a childless widow and a Marin County, California resident, died. Buck's will left the residue of her estate to the San Francisco Foundation to be used for exclusively nonprofit charitable, religious, or educational purposes in providing care for the needy in Marin County, California, and for other nonprofit charitable, religious, or educational purposes in that county. At the time of her death, her estate was valued at approximately $9,000,000. However, by 1984 it had appreciated to over $300,000,000. In 1984, the Foundation brought suit, asking judicial authorization to spend a portion of the Buck Trust income on the other four Bay Area counties. The cy pres petition was based on the theory that the posthumous increase in value of the estate was an unanticipated change in circumstances. The Foundation claimed that if Buck had predicted such an event she would have reduced her gift to Marin County. Marin County officials objected to the Foundation's petition. At trial, a Foundation expert testified that the surprise increase in value of the Buck estate and a finding that the Buck funds were being spent inefficiently justified application of the cy pres doctrine. All the parties except for forty-six individuals and charitable organizations and the four counties (called Objectioner-Beneficiaries) agreed to a settlement. The court then turned to the application of the cy pres doctrine.

ISSUE: Does the cy pres doctrine apply only where the purpose of a trust has become illegal, impossible, or permanently impracticable of performance?

HOLDING AND DECISION: (Thompson, J.) Yes. The cy pres doctrine applies only where the purpose of a trust has become illegal, impossible, or permanently impracticable of performance. The purpose of the cy pres doctrine is to prevent the failure of valid charitable trust gifts. The impossibility or impracticability prerequisite requires a permanency of the impossibility or impracticability of carrying out the specific charitable purpose of the creator of the trust. Neither inefficiency nor ineffective

philanthropy constitutes impracticability. Cy pres may not be invoked upon the belief that the modified scheme would be more desirable or would constitute a better use of the income. Here, the residents of Marin County have substantial unmet needs which are within the scope of the purposes of the Buck Trust. Additionally, there are significant opportunities to spend Buck Trust funds on nonprofit charitable, religious, or educational purposes in Marin County. The entire income of the Buck Trust is insufficient and will remain insufficient to address all of Marin County's future needs. The petition for modification is denied.

EDITOR'S ANALYSIS: Commentators have urged the expanded use of judicial cy pres to change charitable trust provisions to maximize community benefits to meet changing community needs. See Johnson & Taylor, Revolutionizing Judicial Interpretation of Charitable Trusts: Applying Relational Contracts and Dynamic Interpretation to Cy Pres and America's Cup Litigation. 74 Iowa L. Rev. 545 (1989).

[For more information on the cy pres doctrine, see Casenote Law Outline on Wills, Trusts & Estates, Chapter 10, § VIII, Charitable Trusts.]

QUICKNOTES

RESIDUE - That property which remains following the distribution of the assets of the testator's estate.

DOCTRINE OF CYPRESS - Equitable doctrine applied in order to give effect to an instrument, which would be unlawful if enforced strictly, as close to the drafter's intent as possible without violating the law.

COMMUNITY TRUST - Funds held in trust for the benefit of the public.

CHARITABLE TRUST - A trust that is established for the benefit of a class of persons or for the public in general.

IMPRACTICABILITY - A doctrine relieving the parties to a contract from liability for nonperformance of their duties thereunder, if the subject matter of the contract ceases to exist.

IN RE WILSON

Parties not identified

N.Y. Ct. App., 59 N.Y.2d 461, 452 N.E.2d 1228, 465 N.Y.S.2d 900 (1983).

NATURE OF CASE: Consolidated appeals involving the administration of private charitable trust.

FACT SUMMARY: In separate cases, the courts had to deal with private charitable trusts whose purpose was financing the education of male students and the judicial use of the doctrine of cy pres to reform the trusts.

CONCISE RULE OF LAW: A provision in a charitable trust that is central to the testator's or settlor's charitable purpose and is not illegal should not be invalidated on public policy grounds unless that provision, if given effect, would substantially mitigate the general charitable effect of the gift.

FACTS: In two separate instances, charitable trusts were set up which specified that the funds they generated were to be used to provide financial support to male students who met certain requirements and wanted to continue their education. Court proceedings were instituted in relation thereto, one of the central issues being whether or not the Due Process Clause is violated when a court permits the administration of such private charitable trusts. In one case, a court had determined that the school whose students were to be certified as eligible for trust benefits had no obligation to provide a certified list of names, that the School Superintendent was no longer willing to do so, that this meant administration according to the literal terms of the trust was impossible, and that the cy pres power should be exercised to reform the trust by striking the certification clause. In the second case, a court was faced with a trustee who declined to administer the trust in the sex-biased fashion that was required by its terms. It determined that administration of the estate by a trustee appointed by the court would violate the Equal Protection Clause in view of the sex discrimination involved, that administration of the trust was impossible, and that cy pres power should be used to reform the trust by eliminating the gender restriction.

ISSUE: Should a provision in a charitable trust that is central to the testator's or settlor's charitable purpose and is not illegal be invalidated on public policy grounds unless that provision, if given effect, would substantially mitigate the general charitable effect of the gift?

HOLDING AND DECISION: (Cooke, C.J.) No. A provision in a charitable trust that is central to the testator's or settlor's charitable purpose and is not illegal should not be invalidated on public policy grounds unless that provision, if given effect, would substantially mitigate the general charitable effect of the gift. The gender-based discrimination practiced by the trusts at issue here is not attributable to the state and does not violate the Due Process Clause. A trust's discriminatory terms are not fairly attributable to the state when a court applies trust principles that permit private discrimination but do not encourage, affirmatively promote, or compel it. Resolution of the disputes encountered in these cases should proceed by applying the basic principle that when an impasse is reached in the administration of a trust due to an incidental requirement of its terms, a court may effect or permit the trustee to effect a deviation from the trust's literal terms. In one case, this can be done by letting the male students apply directly to the trustee, thus eliminating the incidental requirement of certification of the names by the School Superintendent. In the other, the court should simply replace the recalcitrant trustee with someone able and willing to administer the trust according to its terms, including the gender-based one. Thus, application of the power of cy pres to do away with the gender-based provision was premature and inappropriate. This is not an instance in which the restriction of the trusts serves to frustrate a paramount charitable purpose.

EDITOR'S ANALYSIS: Earlier, a Delaware court had rendered a decision in a case involving a scholarship fund at the University of Delaware that was limited to providing aid to women. The trustees of the state university administered this trust so there was no argument that state action existed, but the court concluded that sex discrimination in favor of women was permissible because its purpose was to compensate women for past acts of discrimination. Trustees of University of Delaware v. Gebelein, 420 A.2d 1191 (Del. Ch. 1980).

[For more information on restrictions in charitable gifts, see Casenote Law Outline on Wills, Trusts & Estates, Chapter 10, § VIII, Charitable Trusts.]

QUICKNOTES

CYPRESS POWER - Equitable doctrine applied in order to give effect to an instrument, which would be unlawful if enforced strictly, as close to the drafter's intent as possible without violating the law.

CHARITABLE TRUST - A trust that is established for the benefit of a class of persons or for the public in general.

EQUAL PROTECTION CLAUSE - A constitutional guarantee that no person should be denied the same protection of the laws enjoyed by other persons in like circumstances.

NOTES

CHAPTER 9
BUILDING FLEXIBILITY INTO TRUSTS: POWERS OF APPOINTMENT

QUICK REFERENCE RULES OF LAW

1. **Does the Appointive Property Belong to the Donor or the Donee?** A power of appointment which is unexercised may not be reached by a creditor of the trustee. (Irwin Union Bank & Trust Co. V. Long)

    [For more information on creditors of a trust, see Casenote Law Outline on Wills, Trusts & Estates, Chapter 11, § IV, Trusts.]

2. **Creation of a Power of Appointment.** Where there is a grant, devise, or bequest to one in general terms only, expressing neither fee nor life estate, and there is a subsequent limitation over what remains at the first taker's death, if there is also given to the first taker an unlimited and unrestricted power of absolute disposal, express or implied, the grant, devise, or bequest to the first taker is construed to pass a fee simple interest, and the attempted limitation over is void. (Sterner v. Nelson)

3. **Release of a Power of Appointment.** A contract promising to exercise a testamentary power of appointment in favor of a specific party is not specifically enforceable, and no damages may be awarded for its breach. (Seidel v. Werner)

4. **Exercise of a Power of Appoinment.** The fact that there has been a prior partial release of a general power does not obviate the application of that rule of construction which presumes that a general residuary clause in a will exercises a general power of appointment. (Beals v. State Street Bank & Trust Co.)

5. **Failure to Exercise a Power of Appointment.** When a beneficiary with powers of appointment appoints his portion of will proceeds to less than the full class of potential appointees, the nonappointed class members will take the beneficiary's share if the appointees are deceased. (Loring v. Marshall)

NOTES

IRWIN UNION BANK AND TRUST COMPANY v. LONG
Ex-wife of trustee (P) v. Bank (D)
Ind. Ct. App., 160 Ind. App. 509, 312 N.E.2d 908 (1974).

NATURE OF CASE: Appeal from order allowing execution on a portion of a trust corpus.

FACT SUMMARY: The trial court ordered that 4% of the trust corpus of a trust held as trustee by Phillip Long was subject to execution in favor of his ex-wife.

CONCISE RULE OF LAW: A power of appointment which is unexercised may not be reached by a creditor of the trustee.

FACTS: Phillip Long was made the trustee of a trust by his mother and was granted a right of appointment of 4% of the trust corpus. Long was subsequently sued by his wife, Victoria Long (P), for divorce, and a judgment in the amount of $15,000 was entered in favor of Victoria (P). Victoria (P) then filed an action to execute upon 4% of the trust corpus in which she contended that because Phillip had a right of appointment with regard to this percentage of the trust, it could be reached by his creditors. The trial court, over Union Bank's (D) objections that an unexercised right of appointment cannot be reached by creditors, issued the writ of execution. Union Bank (D) appealed.

ISSUE: May an unexercised right of appointment be reached by creditors of the trust deed?

HOLDING AND DECISION: (Lowdermilk, J.) No. An unexercised right of appointment may not be reached by creditors of the beneficiary. In the absence of a statute, the unexercised general right of appointment cannot be reached by creditors, as to hold to the contrary would allow creditors to force the exercise of said power upon the beneficiary. If the beneficiary chooses not to exercise the power, creditors cannot force him to do so. Where the power is a special power, the appointee derives no benefit therefrom, and, therefore, it cannot be reached by his creditors. As a result, the trial court erred in granting the writ of execution. Reversed.

EDITOR'S ANALYSIS: The principal case is cited and followed by the Restatement Second Property donative transfers. The basis upon which this case is determined is that a right of appointment is not property. Because the beneficiary does not derive any benefit from it, it cannot be attached by his creditors. The power of appointment is personal to the beneficiary and therefore cannot be alienated. As a result, it lacks a fundamental element of the concept of property and therefore cannot be attached.

[For more information on creditors of a trust, see Casenote Law Outline on Wills, Trusts & Estates, Chapter 11, § IV, Trusts.]

QUICKNOTES

TRUST CORPUS - The aggregate body of assets placed into a trust.

POWER OF APPOINTMENT - Power, created by another person in connection with a gratuitous transfer (often in trust), residing in a person (as trustee or otherwise) to affect the disposition or distribution of the property.

NOTES:

STERNER v. NELSON
Parties not identified
Neb. Sup. Ct., 210 Neb. 358, 314 N.W.2d 263 (1982).

NATURE OF CASE: Appeal from decision construing a will.

FACT SUMMARY: While Oscar Wurtele in his will gave his wife all of his property "absolutely with full power in her to make such disposition of said property as she may desire," he thereafter provided that whatever was left in her hands on her death would vest in his foster daughter, Sterner (P).

CONCISE RULE OF LAW: Where there is a grant, devise, or bequest to one in general terms only, expressing neither fee nor life estate, and there is a subsequent limitation over what remains at the first taker's death, if there is also given to the first taker an unlimited and unrestricted power of absolute disposal, express or implied, the grant, devise, or bequest to the first taker is construed to pass a fee simple interest, and the attempted limitation over is void.

FACTS: By the terms of his will, Oscar Wurtele bequeathed all of his property to his wife "absolutely with full power in her to make such disposition of said property as she may desire." He also therein provided that whatever of such property remained in his wife's possession at the time of her death would vest in his foster daughter, Sterner (P). An action was instituted that involved construction of these provisions, and the court granted a summary judgment to the effect that the wife had been granted a fee simple absolute.

ISSUE: Is an attempted limitation over, following a gift which is in fee with full power of disposition and alienation, void?

HOLDING AND DECISION: (Krivosha, C.J.) Yes. Where there is a grant, devise, or bequest to one in general terms only, expressing neither fee nor life estate, and there is a subsequent limitation over of what remains at the first taker's death, if there is also given to the first taker an unlimited and unrestricted power of absolute disposal, express or implied, the grant, devise, or bequest to the first taker is construed to pass a fee simple interest. The attempted limitation over, following a gift which is in fee with full power of disposition and alienation, is void. A testator simply cannot give an estate in fee simple by clear and concise language and subsequently diminish or destroy the devise by use of other language. That is the rule to apply here. Affirmed.

EDITOR'S ANALYSIS: The rule highlighted in this case is known as the rule of repugnancy. It has not been spared criticism and has been tagged as an arbitrary rule that serves no public policy, results in a complete frustration of the legitimate intention of the testator, and is productive of enormous amounts of unnecessary litigation. See C. J. Vanderbilt's dissent in Fox v. Snow, 6 N.J. 12 (1950).

QUICKNOTES

FEE SIMPLE ABSOLUTE - An estate in land characterized by ownership of the entire property for an unlimited duration and by absolute power over distribution.

JOINT TENANCY - An interest in property whereby a single interest is owned by two or more persons and created by a single instrument; joint tenants possess equal interests in the use of the entire property and the last survivor is entitled to absolute ownership.

NOTES:

SEIDEL v. WERNER
Executor (P) v. Widow (D)
81 Misc. 2d 220 (1975).

NATURE OF CASE: Action on a contract.

FACT SUMMARY: Werner promised to exercise his testamentary power of appointment in favor of his ex-wife, Harriet, pursuant to their divorce decree.

CONCISE RULE OF LAW: A contract promising to exercise a testamentary power of appointment in favor of a specific party is not specifically enforceable, and no damages may be awarded for its breach.

FACTS: Werner died, exercising his testamentary power by will in favor of his third wife, Edith. Werner's second wife, Harriet (D), alleged that Werner had promised to exercise his power in favor of her children as part of his settlement obligation under their divorce decree. The executor, Seidel (P), sought a declaratory judgment as to whether the contract under the divorce decree was valid and binding.

ISSUE: May a party enforce a contract under which the holder of a testamentary power promises to exercise it in a certain manner?

HOLDING AND DECISION: (Silverman, J.) No. Under state law, a contract requiring that a testamentary power be exercised in a specific manner is not specifically enforceable, and a damage action for its breach may not be maintained. This is based on policy reasons. The exercise of a testamentary power is to represent the holder's final judgment. The free and unfettered exercise of this judgment may not be contracted away by the holder since this would defeat the intention of the donor of the power. The divorce decree did not order that the power be exercised in a specific manner; it merely approved the property settlement agreement. Hence, it is not res judicata on the issue. There was no intention that Werner was to release the power since under the agreement he was obligated to exercise it in a certain manner by establishing a trust. Thus, there was no intent to allow the property to pass in fee directly to the children. The injured party may recover, in restitution, the value of any property or rights given in exchange for the unenforceable power. The claim is limited to assets in the promisor's estate. The power property passes to Edith (P).

EDITOR'S ANALYSIS: A contract under which the power is released will normally be enforced since once released, the holder can no longer exercise it. Matter of Haskell, 59 Misc. 2d 797 (1969). In analyzing power problems, it is always necessary to remember that power belongs to the donor until it is exercised or released by the donee. By statute or decisional law, every state allows the release of a power, generally because of estate tax considerations.

QUICKNOTES

POWER OF APPOINTMENT - Power, created by another person in connection with a gratuitous transfer (often in trust), residing in a person (as trustee or otherwise) to affect the disposition or distribution of the property.

TRUST REMAINDER - An interest in trust property that passes to a beneficiary after the expiration of a prior interest.

LIFE ESTATE - An interest in land measured by the life of the tenant or a third party.

NOTES:

BEALS v. STATE STREET BANK & TRUST CO.

Parties not identified

Mass. Sup. Jud. Ct., 367 Mass. 318, 326 N.E.2d 896 (1975).

NATURE OF CASE: Petition for instructions on distribution of a portion of a trust.

FACT SUMMARY: In an action seeking instructions on how a portion of a trust should be distributed, the Bank (P), as trustee, sought to determine if a power of appointment could be considered to have been exercised by a general residuary clause in a will.

CONCISE RULE OF LAW: The fact that there has been a prior partial release of a general power does not obviate the application of that rule of construction which presumes that a general residuary clause in a will exercises a general power of appointment.

FACTS: As trustee, the Bank (P) sought instructions on how a portion of a trust should be distributed. The central question was whether one Isabella had, by means of the general residuary clause in her will, exercised the power of appointment she had been given by the trust. While she had been given a general power of appointment, Isabella had subsequently partially released her general power of appointment. She released it "to the extent that such power empowers me to appoint to any one other than one or more of the . . . descendants me [sic] surviving of Arthur Hunnewell."

ISSUE: Does the fact that there has been a prior partial release of a general power obviate the application of that rule of construction which presumes that a general residuary clause in a will exercises a general power of appointment?

HOLDING AND DECISION: (Wilkins, J.) No. The fact that there has been a prior partial release of a general power of appointment does not obviate the application of that rule of construction which presumes that a general residuary clause in a will exercises a general power of appointment. That same rule has not been extended to special powers. In this case, the power initially given to Isabella was a power of general appointment which she reduced to what was effectively a special power by her own actions, which themselves amounted to treating the property as her own. Thus, the rule applicable to special powers is not on point, and it must be considered that Isabella did exercise her power of appointment by means of the general residuary clause in her will.

EDITOR'S ANALYSIS: A majority of jurisdictions take the approach adopted in the following provision of the Uniform Probate Code (§ 2-610): "A general residuary clause in a will, or a will making general disposition of all of the testator's property, does not exercise a power of appointment held by the testator unless specific reference is made to the power or there is some other indication of intention to include the property subject to the power." Since this case was heard, Massachusetts has adopted the Uniform Probate Code.

QUICKNOTES

POWER OF APPOINTMENT - Power, created by another person in connection with a gratuitous transfer (often in trust), residing in a person (as trustee or otherwise) to affect the disposition or distribution of the property.

RESIDUARY CLAUSE (OF WILL) - A clause contained in a will disposing of the assets remaining following distribution of the estate.

NOTES:

LORING v. MARSHALL

Parties not identified

Mass. Sup. Jud. Ct., 396 Mass. 166, 484 N.E.2d 1315 (1985).

NATURE OF CASE: Declaratory judgment action seeking determination of proper testamentary beneficiary.

FACT SUMMARY: Morse, beneficiary with power of appointment under Hovey's will, declined to appoint his portion of the proceeds to all potential appointees.

CONCISE RULE OF LAW: When a beneficiary with powers of appointment appoints his portion of will proceeds to less than the full class of potential appointees, the nonappointed class members will take the beneficiary's share if the appointees are deceased.

FACTS: Hovey's will made Morse a beneficiary thereof. The will, by its terms, gave Morse the power to appoint the proceeds of the testamentary trust created by the will to his wife and issue. Morse, in his will, left only a nominal legacy to his son and appointed his trust proceeds to his wife. Following the wife's death, both Morse's son and the trust's remaindermen made claim to the trust principal.

ISSUE: When a beneficiary with powers of appointment appoints his portion of will proceeds to less than the full class of potential appointees, will the nonappointed class members take the beneficiary's share if the appointees are deceased?

HOLDING AND DECISION: (Wilkins, J.) Yes. When a beneficiary with powers of appointment appoints his portion of will proceeds to less than the full class of potential appointees, the nonappointed class members will take the beneficiary's share if the appointees are deceased. If a will does not contain a provision creating a gift in default of appointment, it is presumed that a testator wished testamentary proceeds to remain within the class of beneficiaries and their potential appointees. If the beneficiaries and actual appointees no longer live, then the law presumes that the testator intended the proceeds to pass to the remaining potential appointees. Here, Morse's son is a living potential appointee, and, therefore, the proceeds are properly his. [The court then remitted the action to the trial court for a determination of executor and counsel fees.]

EDITOR'S ANALYSIS: The position taken by the court here appears to be the majority rule. It can be found in the Restatement, 2d of Property, Donative Transfers § 24.2. Essentially, the rule implies a donative intent on the part of the testator to the entire class of named potential appointees. This presumption can be rebutted, if the will so provides.

QUICKNOTES

POWER OF APPOINTMENT - Power, created by another person in connection with a gratuitous transfer (often in trust), residing in a person (as trustee or otherwise) to affect the disposition or distribution of the property.

REMAINDERMAN - A person who has an interest in property to commence upon the termination of a present possessory interest.

NOTES:

NOTES

CHAPTER 10
CONSTRUCTION OF TRUSTS: FUTURE INTERESTS
QUICK REFERENCE RULES OF LAW

1. **Construction of Trust Instruments.** A beneficiary of a discretionary trust may renounce his interest in the disposition. (In re Estate of Gilbert)

   [For more information on trust requirements, see Casenote Law Outline on Wills, Trusts, and Estates, Chapter 4, § III, Trusts.]

2. **Construction of Trust Instruments.** In construing a conveyance which vests title contingent upon an age restriction, the choice between a condition precedent and a condition subsequent shall be made with a view toward vesting the remainder rather than having it fail. (Edwards v. Hammond)

3. **Construction of Trust Instruments.** An inter vivos trust reserving to the settlor the income for life plus the power to revoke, with a remainder over at the death of the settlor, creates a vested interest in the remainderman subject to defeasance by the exercise of the power of revocation. (First National Bank of Bar Harbor v. Anthony)

4. **Construction of Trust Instruments.** Because the law favors the early vesting of devised estates, it will be presumed that words of survivorship relate to the death of the testator, if fairly capable of that construction. (Security Trust Co. V. Irvine)

5. **Construction of Trust Instruments.** A remainder to vest only upon the death without issue of the primary beneficiary is contingent in nature and cannot vest in the heirs of the remainderman unless he survives the primary beneficiary. (Lawson v. Lawson)

   [For more information on ambiguity in a will, see Casenote Law Outline on Wills, Trusts & Estates, Chapter 6, § III, Ambiguity.]

6. **Construction of Trust Instruments.** If a bequest is "to be paid" at the happening of a certain event, the money passes to the estate of the beneficiary even if he dies before the contingency occurs. (Clobberie's Case)

   [For more information on ambiguity in a will, see Casenote Law Outline on Wills, Trusts & Estates, Chapter 6, § III, Ambiguity.]

7. **Construction of Trust Instruments.** One who adopts a spouse or other adult cannot thereby make the adoptee an heir to an estate created by an existing testamentary instrument executed by an ancestor of the adopter. (Minary v. Citizens Fidelity Bank)

   [For more information on adult adoption, see Casenote Law Outline on Wills, Trusts & Estates, Chapter 2, § V, Adoption.]

8. **Construction of Trust Instruments.** The identity of heirs entitled to trust assets must be determined at the date of death of the named ancestor who predeceased the life tenant, not at the date of death of the life tenant. (Estate of Woodworth)

   [For more information on gifts, see Casenote Law Outline on Wills, Trusts and Estates, Chapter 4, § II, Gifts.]

9. **Construction of Trust Instruments.** Members of a class pursuant to a class gift are joint tenants with rights of survivorship unless a contrary intent is expressed in the will. (Dewire v. Haveles)

[For more information on class gifts, see Casenote Law Outline on Wills, Trusts & Estates, Chapter 2, § II, Lapse.]

10. Construction of Trust Instruments. A class gift should be closed when all existing beneficiaries attain a specific age. (Lux v. Lux)

[For more information on class gifts, see Casenote Law Outline on Wills, Trusts & Estates, Chapter 2, § II, Lapse.]

IN RE ESTATE OF GILBERT
Executor (P) v. Beneficiary
N.Y. Sup. Ct., 156 Misc. 2d 379, 592 N.Y.S.2d 224 (1992).

NATURE OF CASE: Motion to declare trust beneficiary's renunciation void.

FACT SUMMARY: When Lester (D), who was a beneficiary of discretionary trusts under his father's will, renounced his interest in the estate, the executor (P) moved to declare the renunciation premature and therefore invalid.

CONCISE RULE OF LAW: A beneficiary of a discretionary trust may renounce his interest in the disposition.

FACTS: Decedent was survived by a wife and four children. By will, he created two sets of discretionary trusts for the benefit of his children. One son, Lester (D), who had taken a vow of poverty, renounced his share of the estate. Lester (D) was a discretionary income beneficiary of two testamentary trusts. The executor (P) filed a motion to declare Lester's (D) renunciation void. The executor (P) argued that Lester (D) possessed no current property interest to renounce and that a renunciation could be made only after the trustees exercised their discretion to distribute income or principal.

ISSUE: May a beneficiary of a discretionary trust renounce his interest in the disposition?

HOLDING AND DECISION: (Roth, S.) Yes. A beneficiary of a discretionary trust may renounce his interest in the disposition. Renunciations are governed by statute. A statutory renunciation need not relate to specific property. Instead, the statute merely requires the disclaimant to renounce his or her interest in a trust. Therefore, a beneficiary of a discretionary trust may renounce his interest in the disposition. Assuming, arguendo, that in order to be effective the renounced interest must be in the nature of property, Lester's (D) renunciation would still be valid. Courts have recognized the right of a trust beneficiary to compel a distribution of funds where trustees abuse their discretion in refusing to make distributions. Therefore, a beneficiary who has the right to compel trustees to distribute trust property under certain circumstances arguably has a current interest which could be deemed property for the purpose of an effective renunciation. Motion denied.

EDITOR'S ANALYSIS: As important as the attempt to effectuate the intent of the testator is, an individual cannot be compelled to accept an inheritance against his will. Furthermore, once an individual has disclaimed or renounced his interest in an estate, most states by statute presume the individual to have predeceased the testator. This is preferable to attempting to litigate the testator's intent had he known the individual would renounce.

[For more information on trust requirements, see Casenote Law Outline on Wills, Trusts, and Estates, Chapter 4, § III, Trusts.]

QUICKNOTES

DISCRETIONARY TRUST - A trust pursuant to which the trustee is authorized to make decisions regarding the investment of the trust funds and the distribution of such funds to beneficiaries.

RENUNCIATION - The abandonment of a right or interest.

CONTINGENT REMAINDER - A remainder limited to a person not in being, not certain or ascertained, or so limited to a certain person that his right to the state depends upon some contingent event in the future.

GUARDIAN AD LITEM - Person designated by the court to represent an infant or ward in a particular legal proceeding.

NOTES:

EDWARDS v. HAMMOND

Parties not identified

Ct. Common Pleas, 3 Lev. 132, 83 Eng. Rep. 614 (1684).

NATURE OF CASE: Suit for ejectment from real property.

FACT SUMMARY: A grantor conveyed a life estate to himself, with the remainder to his eldest son if that son lived to age 21, and if the eldest did not survive to 21, then to the youngest son. The grantor died when the eldest son was 17, and the youngest son took possession, claiming title.

CONCISE RULE OF LAW: In construing a conveyance which vests title contingent upon an age restriction, the choice between a condition precedent and a condition subsequent shall be made with a view toward vesting the remainder rather than having it fail.

FACTS: In an area of England where the youngest son was the natural heir rather than the eldest son, a father conveyed a life estate to himself, with the remainder to go to his eldest son upon the father's death so long as that son lived to age 21. If the eldest son did not survive to 21, the remainder was to go to the heirs of the father, i.e., the youngest son. The father died when the eldest son was 17, and the youngest son took possession of the property and claimed title. The eldest son brought suit to eject the youngest from the property. The youngest son claimed the conveyance created a condition precedent to the eldest's taking title. The eldest son asserted that the condition was subsequent, which would vest title in him subject to divestment should he not reach age 21.

ISSUE: In construing a conveyance which vests title contingent upon an age restriction, should the choice between a condition precedent and a condition subsequent be made with a view toward vesting the remainder rather than having it fail?

HOLDING AND DECISION: Yes. The words of conveyance would appear to create a condition precedent to the eldest son's taking title. The youngest son contends his title vests, at least until the eldest reaches 21. Yet, the entire conveyance, taken as a whole, reveals an intent to vest title in the eldest at the father's death subject to a condition subsequent defeasing this title should the eldest not reach 21. In construing a conveyance which vests title contingent upon an age restriction, the choice between a condition precedent and a condition subsequent shall be made with a view toward vesting the remainder rather than having it fail. Accordingly, the eldest son has vested title and may eject the youngest.

EDITOR'S ANALYSIS: This rule, although almost 300 years old, is still followed by most courts today and is the rule of the Restatement (Second) of Property. While the rule would appear to be equally valid in cases of contingencies based on survival or other conditions, it was limited early to age restrictions by the English courts and by most American jurisdictions as well.

QUICKNOTES

EJECTMENT - An action to oust someone in possession of real property unlawfully and to restore possession to the party lawfully entitled to it.

ABEYANCE - Occurs when there is a lapse in succession of property and there is no owner in which the property currently vests.

CONDITION PRECEDENT - The happening of an uncertain occurrence, which is necessary before a particular right or interest may be obtained or an action performed.

CONDITION SUBSEQUENT - Potential future occurrence that extinguishes a party's obligation to perform pursuant to the contract.

NOTES:

FIRST NATIONAL BANK OF BAR HARBOR v. ANTHONY

Bank (P) v. Grandchildren of deceased (D)

Maine Sup. Jud. Ct., 557 A.2d 957 (1989).

NATURE OF CASE: Appeal from the denial of a claim to a remainder interest in an inter vivos trust.

FACT SUMMARY: When one of the three children provided for in a trust set up by their father, J. Franklin Anthony, died before the father, the son's three children (D) asserted, after their grandfather's death, that they were entitled to their father's one-third interest in the trust.

CONCISE RULE OF LAW: An inter vivos trust reserving to the settlor the income for life plus the power to revoke, with a remainder over at the death of the settlor, creates a vested interest in the remainderman subject to defeasance by the exercise of the power of revocation.

FACTS: J. Franklin Anthony established a revocable inter vivos trust with First National Bank (P). Upon the death of both J. Franklin and his wife, the corpus of the trust was to be divided equally among their three children, John, Peter (D), and Dencie (D). John died after his mother's death but prior to the death of his father, leaving three children (D). After J. Franklin's death, the Bank (P) filed a complaint, requesting construction of the Anthony Trust. John's heirs (D) asserted that their father's interest was vested, not contingent, at the time of its creation. Thus, they were entitled to his one-third interest in the trust. The court, however, held that the gift to John lapsed because his interest did not vest until J. Franklin's death. This appeal followed.

ISSUE: Does an inter vivos trust reserving to the settlor the income for life plus the power to revoke, with a remainder over at the death of the settlor, create a vested interest in the remainderman subject to defeasance by the exercise of the power of revocation?

HOLDING AND DECISION: (Roberts, J.) Yes. An inter vivos trust reserving to the settlor the income for life plus the power to revoke, with a remainder over at the death of the settlor, creates a vested interest in the remainderman subject to defeasance by the exercise of the power of revocation. In this case, J. Franklin made survival an explicit condition of any benefit to his wife but not to his children (D). Moreover, the plan of disposition effectively eliminated any further interest of J. Franklin in the trust principal unless he affirmatively chose to intervene. The language of the trust suggests a disposition to a predeceased child's estate rather than a reversion to the settlor's estate. Thus, John's (D) interest vested at the time of the creation of the trust. The judgment is vacated.

EDITOR'S ANALYSIS: The settlor's intention is critical in interpreting the terms of a trust and must be ascertained by analyzing the trust instrument. Only when the instrument is ambiguous can a court consider extrinsic evidence. Because the supreme court held that John's (D) interest vested at the time of the creation of the trust and did not, in fact, lapse, it did not consider whether Maine's antilapse statute would apply to an inter vivos trust.

QUICKNOTES

REMAINDER INTEREST - An interest in land that remains after the termination of the immediately preceding estate.

INTER VIVOS TRUST - Property that is held by one person for the benefit of another and which is created by an instrument that takes effect during the life of the grantor.

TESTAMENTARY TRUST - A trust created by will and only effective after the grantor's death, since the assets that comprise the corpus of the trust are assumed to vest at that time.

LIFE TENANT - An individual whose estate in real property is measured either by his own life or by that of another.

ANTI-LAPSE STATUTE - State statute providing for the substitution of a recipient of a devise made pursuant to a testamentary instrument, if the beneficiary of the gift predeceases the testator and no alternative disposition is made.

NOTES:

SECURITY TRUST CO. v. IRVINE
Trustee (P) v. Brother-in-law of deceased (D)
Del. Ch. Ct., 33 Del. Ch. 375, 93 A.2d 528 (1953).

NATURE OF CASE: Action to determine vesting of a residuary estate.

FACT SUMMARY: The testator gave a life estate to his surviving sisters and the remainder to his brothers and sisters, which appeared to include the two surviving sisters in the remainder class.

CONCISE RULE OF LAW: Because the law favors the early vesting of devised estates, it will be presumed that words of survivorship relate to the death of the testator, if fairly capable of that construction.

FACTS: The testator devised a portion of his estate to Security (P) as trustee for the benefit of his two unmarried sisters and his one married sister should she be widowed. The remainder was left to his "brothers and sisters, share and share alike, their heirs and assigns forever, the issue of any deceased brother or sister to take his or her parent's share." Of all the brothers and sisters, one of the two unmarried sisters was the last to die, that is to say, she outlived the remaindermen. Security (P) sought to determine whether or not the residuary estate left to the testator's brothers and sisters vested as of the date of his death or as of the date of death of the last life tenant and if vesting was as of the date of death of the testator, whether the life tenants took as members of the class of brothers and sisters receiving the residuary estate. (Irvine (D) was the surviving husband of the married, now deceased, sister.)

ISSUE: Because the law favors the early vesting of devised estates, will it be presumed that words of survivorship relate to the death of the testator, if fairly capable of the construction?

HOLDING AND DECISION: (Bramhall, V.C.) Yes. Because the law favors the early vesting of devised estates, it will be presumed that when words of survivorship do not unambiguously indicate an intention to the contrary, the heirs will be determined as of the date of the testator's death and not at some future date. The fact that a life tenant is a member of a class, in the absence of any clear indication in the will to the contrary, does not prevent the life tenant from participating in the remainder of the testator's estate as part of the class. Simply because a testator gives the tenant, in another part of his will, a life interest in his residuary estate is not sufficient to prevent the life tenant from participating in the remainder as part of the class. Here, the two sisters, although a part of the class of brothers and sisters, could share in the remainder. The will provided that in the event of the death of any life tenant, his share should go by substitution to his or her issue. Although it did not provide for disposition where a deceased life tenant was survived by no issue, the event of the death of such life

tenants did not cause the disposition to be divested from their estates.

EDITOR'S ANALYSIS: The rule favoring early vesting has been called useful in protecting the issue of remaindermen who die before their interests become possessory. Thus, the rule can act something like a modern antilapse statute by substituting the issue of a beneficiary who predeceases the testator. Rabin, The Law Favors the Vesting of Estates, Why?, 65 Colum. L. Rev. 467 (1965). The early vesting rule does have some disadvantages, the most glaring disadvantage being that transmissible remainders are subject to estate taxes. Schuyler, Drafting, Tax, and Other Consequences of the Rule of Early Vesting, 46 Ill. L. Rev. 407 (1951).

QUICKNOTES
RESIDUARY ESTATE - That portion of the estate which remains after all the estate has been distributed through the satisfaction of all claims and is conditional upon something remaining after the claims on the testator's estate are satisfied.

VESTING - The attaining of the right to pension or other employer-contribution benefits when the employee satisfies the minimum requirements necessary in order to be entitled to the receipt of such benefits in the future.

LIFE TENANT - An individual whose estate in real property is measured either by his own life or by that of another.

LIFE ESTATE - An interest in land measured by the life of the tenant or a third party.

NOTES:

LAWSON v. LAWSON

Siblings of deceased (P) v. Nieces and nephews (D)

N.C. Sup. Ct., 267 N.C. 643, 148 S.E.2d 546 (1966).

NATURE OF CASE: Petition seeking a partitioning of real property.

FACT SUMMARY: J. Rad Lawson devised property to his daughter, Opal, for life, remainder to her brothers (P) and sisters (P) if she died without children. When she died childless, her siblings (P) and the children (D) of her two deceased brothers all claimed an interest in the property.

CONCISE RULE OF LAW: A remainder to vest only upon the death without issue of the primary beneficiary is contingent in nature and cannot vest in the heirs of the remainderman unless he survives the primary beneficiary.

FACTS: J. Rad Lawson's will devised certain land to his daughter, Opal, for life and, at her death, to her children, if any. If Opal died without children, the property was to pass to her brothers (P) and sisters (P). Fifteen years after the death of her father, Opal died childless. She was survived by four brothers (P) and sisters (P) and by five nieces (D) and nephews (D) who were the children of two brothers who had predeceased Opal. Shortly after Opal's death, her brothers (P) and sisters (P), each claiming to own a one-quarter interest in the land devised to Opal by their father, petitioned for a partitioning of the property. The nieces (D) and nephews (D) opposed the petition, arguing that their fathers, the deceased brothers of Opal, had each acquired one-sixth interests in the property and had passed the same to their children, Opal's nieces (D) and nephews (D). Upon consideration of the facts, the trial judge concluded that the nieces (D) and nephews (D) had no interest in the property and that a partitioning should occur. From this judgment, the nieces (D) and nephews (D) appealed.

ISSUE: If a group of individuals are designated as recipients of a devise in the event that the primary beneficiary dies without issue, may the children of any of the individuals who fail to survive the primary beneficiary receive the share which their parents would have collected?

HOLDING AND DECISION: (Sharpe, J.) No. A remainder to vest only upon the death without issue of the primary beneficiary is contingent in nature and cannot vest in the heirs of the remainderman unless he survives the primary beneficiary. The individuals who were to succeed to Opal's interest could be determined only upon the happening of a stated event, i.e., her death. The remainder interest which all of Opal's siblings once hoped to enjoy was, therefore, a contingent one and never vested in the brothers who predeceased Opal or in their children, Opal's nieces (D) and nephews (D). Therefore, only Opal's surviving brothers (P) and sisters (P) may claim an interest in the property for which the partitioning is sought.

EDITOR'S ANALYSIS: A handful of authorities support the rule announced by the Lawson court. A far greater number, however, have adopted a contrary rule, according to which Opal Lawson's deceased brothers, and therefore their children, would have acquired an interest in the property devised to Opal despite the failure of her brothers to survive her. Lawson presents one of those too frequent cases which would not have arisen had the issue which it involved been effectively dealt with at the drafting stage.

[For more information on ambiguity in a will, see Casenote Law Outline on Wills, Trusts & Estates, Chapter 6, § III, Ambiguity.]

QUICKNOTES

REMAINDER - An interest in land that remains after the termination of the immediately preceding estate.

FEE SIMPLE - An estate in land characterized by ownership of the entire property for an unlimited duration and by absolute power over distribution.

LIFE TENANT - An individual whose estate in real property is measured either by his own life or by that of another.

NOTES:

CLOBBERIE'S CASE
Parties not identified
Ct. Ch., 2 Vent. 342, 86 Eng. Rep. 476 (1677).

NATURE OF CASE: Suit seeking an order construing a bequest.

FACT SUMMARY: Money was bequeathed to a woman at her age of 21 years or day of marriage, to be paid with interest. The woman died without marrying or attaining the age of twenty-one.

CONCISE RULE OF LAW: If a bequest is "to be paid" at the happening of a certain event, the money passes to the estate of the beneficiary even if he dies before the contingency occurs.

FACTS: Money was bequeathed to a certain woman at her age of 21 years or day of marriage, to be paid to her with interest. She died prior to marrying or attaining the age of twenty-one. It was argued that the bequest, instead of lapsing, should pass to the executor of her estate.

ISSUE: If a bequest is "to be paid" at the occurrence of a stated event, but the beneficiary dies before the contingency occurs, does the bequest pass to his estate?

HOLDING AND DECISION: (Finch, L.C.) Yes. If a bequest is "to be paid" at the happening of a certain event, the money passes to the estate of the beneficiary even if he dies before the contingency occurs. In this case, money was bequeathed to the woman at her age of 21 years or her wedding day and was to be paid with interest. Thus, upon her death, the money passed to the executor of her estate. If the money had merely been bequeathed at the occurrence of a stated event, the death of the beneficiary prior to its occurrence would have resulted in the loss of the money. But, where the money is "to be paid" at the occurrence of the designated event, it shall pass to the beneficiary's executors despite his failure to survive until the event takes place. Therefore, the bequest to the woman in this case passes to her executor.

EDITOR'S ANALYSIS: The rule in Clobberie's Case has long perplexed the student of future interests in property. The rule causes significantly different consequences to ensue from the most minute differences in language. The rule in Clobberie's Case is still applied by some courts, although it has been repeatedly modified and updated. Perhaps no case of comparable succinctness has enjoyed notoriety equivalent to that earned by Clobberie's Case.

[For more information on ambiguity in a will, see ***Casenote Law Outline on Wills, Trusts & Estates,*** *Chapter 6, § III, Ambiguity.]*

MINARY v. CITIZENS FIDELITY BANK & TRUST COMPANY
Daughter-in-law of deceased (P) v. Trustee (D)
Ky. Ct. App., 419 S.W.2d 340 (1967).

NATURE OF CASE: Action seeking to have a will provision construed.

FACT SUMMARY: Amelia Minary placed property in trust for eventual distribution "to my then-surviving heirs." One of Amelia's sons adopted his own wife (P), but the Bank (D) refused to distribute the trust property to the wife (P) as Amelia's heir.

CONCISE RULE OF LAW: One who adopts a spouse or other adult cannot thereby make the adoptee an heir to an estate created by an existing testamentary instrument executed by an ancestor of the adopter.

FACTS: Amelia Minary's will created a trust, the income of which was to be paid to her husband and her three sons. Upon the death of the last surviving beneficiary, the property which Amelia had placed in the trust was to be distributed "to my then-surviving heirs, according to the laws of descent and distribution then in force in Kentucky, and, if no such heirs, then to the First Christian Church, Louisville, Kentucky." Amelia died in 1932. Her husband passed away three years later. Two of her three sons had predeceased their father and had left no issue. Amelia's husband was survived by the couple's daughter and by Alfred, the last of the three sons who had been named beneficiaries of Amelia's trust. In 1934, Alfred married and, prior to his death, adopted his wife (P). When Alfred died in 1959, Myra (P), the wife, demanded that the Citizens Fidelity Bank & Trust Co. (D) distribute the corpus of Amelia's trust to her. A suit was eventually filed in which Myra (P) claimed to be, by virtue of having been adopted as Alfred's child, an heir of Amelia Minary. The trial court ruled that Myra (P) was an heir of Amelia, but the Trust Company (D) appealed.

ISSUE: May a party, by adopting her, make his spouse an heir of one of his ancestors?

HOLDING AND DECISION: (Osborne, J.) No. One who adopts a spouse or other adult cannot thereby make the adoptee an heir to an estate created by an existing testamentary instrument executed by an ancestor of the adopter. It is clear that any adopted person, including an adult adoptee, may inherit from his adoptive parent. Moreover, the adoptee may ordinarily inherit, through an adoptive parent, the estate of an adoptive ancestor. In this case, it is probable that Amelia Minary intended her heirs to include any adopted children of her sons. Nonetheless, despite precedent to the contrary, a descendant should not be able to frustrate the declared intentions of an ancestor by adopting an adult for the sole purpose of making them an heir of the ancestor. Such a tactic, although permitted by the adoption laws, would thwart the ancestor's testamentary scheme. Therefore, the finding that Myra (P) is an heir of Amelia Minary must be reversed.

EDITOR'S ANALYSIS: Adoption is entirely a creature of statute and was not recognized in earliest common law times. Traditionally, an adopted child was entitled to inherit from, but not through, its adoptive parents. The modern statutory trend, however, is to permit the adoptee to inherit from the ancestors of its adoptive parents. Of course, once a legal adoption has been consummated, the adopted child loses all right to inherit from or through its natural parents.

[For more information on adult adoption, see Casenote Law Outline on Wills, Trusts & Estates, Chapter 2, § V, Adoption.]

QUICKNOTES
RESIDUARY ESTATE - The portion of the estate remaining following distribution of the assets and the payment of costs.

NOTES:

ESTATE OF WOODWORTH

Parties not identified

Cal. Ct. App., 18 Cal. App. 4th 936 (1993).

NATURE OF CASE: Appeal from an order rejecting a claim to the remainder of a testamentary trust.

FACT SUMMARY: Because the trustee was uncertain as to whether the heirs at law of the ancestor named to take the remainder of the Woodworth trust should be determined at the date of the named ancestor's death or at the date of the life tenant's death, the trustee petitioned the court for that determination.

CONCISE RULE OF LAW: The identity of heirs entitled to trust assets must be determined at the date of death of the named ancestor who predeceased the life tenant, not at the date of death of the life tenant.

FACTS: Woodworth's will distributed a portion of his estate outright to his wife, Mamie Barlow Woodworth, with the balance to be administered as a testamentary trust with Mamie as the life tenant. Upon her death, any remainder of the trust estate was to go to Woodworth's sister, Elizabeth Plass, or to her heirs at law, if she no longer survived. Elizabeth died before Mamie but was survived by her husband, Ray Plass, a niece, and a nephew. Ray also died before Mamie, leaving the residue of his estate to the Regents of the University of California. At Mamie's death, the trustee petitioned the probate court as to the date for determining who would receive the distribution of the trust estate. Concluding that the heirs must be determined as of the date of death of the life tenant, Mamie, the court ordered the assets distributed to Elizabeth's niece and nephew. The Regents appealed.

ISSUE: Must the identity of heirs entitled to trust assets be determined at the date of death of the named ancestor who predeceased the life tenant, not at the date of death of the life tenant?

HOLDING AND DECISION: (DiBiaso, J.) Yes. The identity of heirs entitled to trust assets must be determined at the date of death of the named ancestor who predeceased the life tenant, not at the date of death of the life tenant. Nothing in the language of the other provisions of the decree of distribution revealed Woodworth's intent or desire. The general rule favoring early vesting was well-established long before Woodworth died. Nothing in the decree forecloses the possibility that Woodworth took into account the fact that Raymond Plass might succeed to a portion of the trust remainder. Moreover, the fact that the University, an entity, is not a relative of Elizabeth Plass or one of her heirs at law is not material. In addition, the language of the decree does not contain any expression of futurity in the description of the ancestor's heirs. Therefore, the Regents have a claim to the assets of the trust. Reversed.

EDITOR'S ANALYSIS: In the absence of any firm indication of testamentary intent, the rules of construction must be implemented in order to insure uniformity and predictability in the law. This is preferable to carrying out a court's ad hoc sense of what is, with perfect hindsight, acceptable in a particular set of circumstances. Here, at the time of Elizabeth Plass' death, her "heir at law" was her husband, Ray.

[For more information on gifts, see Casenote Law Outline on Wills, Trusts and Estates, Chapter 4, § II, Gifts.]

QUICKNOTES

TESTAMENTARY TRUST - A trust created by will and only effective after the grantor's death, since the assets that comprise the corpus of the trust are assumed to vest at that time.

REMAINDER - An interest in land that remains after the termination of the immediately preceding estate.

LIFE TENANT - An individual whose estate in real property is measured either by his own life or by that of another.

LIFE ESTATE - An interest in land measured by the life of the tenant or a third party.

DEFEASIBLE FEE SIMPLE ESTATE - A fee simple interest in land that is subject to being terminated upon the happening of a future event.

NOTES:

DEWIRE v. HAVELES
Parties not identified
Mass. Sup. Jud. Ct., 404 Mass. 274, 534 N.E.2d 782 (1989).

NATURE OF CASE: Action to declare rights in a residuary trust.

FACT SUMMARY: Haveles (D) contended the testator failed to manifest a contrary intent in his will that a right of survivorship should apply to a gift to the grandchildren; therefore, Dewire (P) was not entitled to share in her father's legacy.

CONCISE RULE OF LAW: Members of a class pursuant to a class gift are joint tenants with rights of survivorship unless a contrary intent is expressed in the will.

FACTS: Thomas Dewire died, leaving a widow, a son, Thomas Jr., and three grandchildren. He placed his estate in a residuary trust, the income payable to his widow for life and on her death to his son, Thomas Jr., his widow, and Thomas Jr.'s children. After the testator's death, Thomas Jr. had three more children by a second wife and then died. He was survived by six children, including Thomas III, who served as trustee until his death. Thomas III left one child, Jennifer. Upon Thomas III's death, an action was brought to determine the rights of the remaining grandchildren in the estate. Haveles (D) contended that Jennifer, the issue of Thomas III, could not take a share of the grandchildren's gift, as a class gift had been created for the grandchildren with a right of survivorship. Jennifer (P) contended that a contrary intent was manifested in the original will to supersede the joint tenancy, and, therefore, she was entitled to her father's share.

ISSUE: Does a class gift create a joint tenancy with right of survivorship in the absence of contrary intent expressed in the will?

HOLDING AND DECISION: (Wilkins, J.) Yes. A class gift creates a joint tenancy with right of survivorship unless a contrary intent is expressed in the will. Because the testator must have intended for the income of the trust to be paid out during the term of its existence, the only logical recipients of that income would be the issue, by right of representation, of deceased grandchildren, the same group of people who would take the trust assets upon termination of the trust. As a result, a contrary intent to the right of survivorship was expressed in the will, and, therefore, Jennifer (P) was entitled to her father's share of the estate.

EDITOR'S ANALYSIS: The court as a side issue indicated that this will violated the rule against perpetuities. This most confusing and ancient rule has been the source of many will invalidations. However, a will in this case survived under the general policy that upholds the balance of a will when one part is invalid. Had a joint tenancy been recognized in this case, Thomas III's share would have passed to his remaining cousins rather than passing on to his daughter.

[For more information on class gifts, see Casenote Law Outline on Wills, Trusts & Estates, Chapter 2, § II, Lapse.]

QUICKNOTES
RULE AGAINST PERPETUITIES - The doctrine that a future interest that is incapable of vesting within twenty-one years of lives in being at the time it is created is immediately void.

RIGHT OF SURVIVORSHIP - Between two or more persons, such as in a joint tenancy relationship, the right to the property of a deceased passes to the survivor.

JOINT TENANCY - An interest in property whereby a single interest is owned by two or more persons and created by a single instrument; joint tenants possess equal interests in the use of the entire property and the last survivor is entitled to absolute ownership.

CLASS GIFT - A gift to a group of unspecified persons whose number, identity, and share of the gift will be determined sometime in the future.

NOTES:

LUX v. LUX
Parties not identified
109 R.I. 592 (1972).

NATURE OF CASE: Will contest.

FACT SUMMARY: Lux left the residue of her estate to her grandchildren, some of whom might not be born until after her death.

CONCISE RULE OF LAW: A class gift should be closed when all existing beneficiaries attain a specific age.

FACTS: Lux's will left her estate to her husband, who predeceased her. A clause in her will provided for this contingency, leaving the residue of her estate to her grandchildren, per capita. Lux's real property was to be sold when the youngest grandchild reached age twenty-one. Until then, the property was to be held for their benefit. Lux had five grandchildren alive at her death. Lux's son informed the court that he intended to have more children. An attorney was appointed to act as guardian for the present grandchildren, and another attorney was appointed to represent the interest of persons having an interest who are not presently known or lives in being. The dispute centered on whether the gift of the real property was in fee or in trust, when the class gift was to close, and when the heirs were to be determined. Since there is a presumption that a person remains fertile, it is conceivable that the class might have to remain open until the son's death.

ISSUE: Should a class be closed when all of the existing beneficiaries have obtained the stated age?

HOLDING AND DECISION: (Kelleher, J.) Yes. First, we find that Lux did not intend to give the grandchildren a fee simple interest in the property. No specific words of art are necessary to create a testamentary trust. Nor is it necessary that all possible beneficiaries be named or a trustee appointed. Where, as here, when all of the facts are viewed in their entirety, it is clear that a trust was intended and that the court should be closed and the members determined, we find that when the youngest existing child reaches twenty-one, the class should be deemed closed. While there is a presumption of continued fertility, we adopt the rule of convenience, which requires that a class be closed when all existing members meet the testator/trustor's requirements. If necessary, the trustee may dispose of the real property and use the proceeds to purchase productive trust assets. Any income earned from trust assets shall be distributed in equal shares to all class members since this is the normal presumption when the trust instrument does not specify that the income is to be accumulated.

EDITOR'S ANALYSIS: The rule of convenience adopted in Lux only applies to situations involving the division of a specific sum to the class members. It does not apply where a fixed sum is to be awarded to each member of the class, i.e., a per capita gift. Where there is a per capita gift, the class closes at the date of death of the testator. Of course the rule of convenience is merely an aid to construction, and it will yield to an expression of the testate's intent. Earle's Estate, 369 Pa. 521 (1951).

[For more information on class gifts, see Casenote Law Outline on Wills, Trusts & Estates, Chapter 2, § II, Lapse.]

QUICKNOTES

CLASS GIFT - A gift to a group of unspecified persons whose number, identity, and share of the gift will be determined sometime in the future.

RESIDUARY CLAUSE (OF WILL) - A clause contained in a will disposing of the assets remaining following distribution of the estate.

TESTAMENTARY TRUST - A trust created by will and only effective after the grantor's death, since the assets that comprise the corpus of the trust are assumed to vest at that time.

NOTES:

CHAPTER 11
DURATION OF TRUSTS: THE RULE AGAINST PERPETUITIES

QUICK REFERENCE RULES OF LAW

1. **The Requirement of No Possibility of Remote Vesting.** An instrument creating a trust naming as beneficiaries children of an unnamed spouse violates the rule against perpetuities. (Dickerson v. Union National Bank of Little Rock)

2. **The Requirement of No Possibility of Remote Vesting.** Where a gift is made upon alternative contingencies, one of which must occur, if at all, within the period of perpetuities and the other of which may not, the gift is valid if the first contingency occurs. (First Portland National Bank v. Rodrique)

3. **Application of the Rule to Class Gifts.** In construing a will against the rule against perpetuities, the intention of the testator must first be discerned from the words of the will before it is determined whether or not the testamentary scheme satisfies the rule. (Ward v. Van der Loeff)

4. **Application of the Rule to Class Gifts.** In order for a class gift to be valid, the class must close within the period of the rule against perpetuities. If the ultimate takers of an interest are not described as a single class but rather as a group of subclasses, and if the share to which each separate subclass is entitled will finally be determined within the period of the rule, the gifts to the different subclasses are separable for the purposes of the rule. (American Security & Trust Co. v. Cramer)

5. **Application of the Rule to Powers of Appointment.** The rule against perpetuities is computed from the date of death of the settlor of an inter vivos trust where the power to revoke, alter, or amend the trust was retained. (Second National Bank of New Haven v. Harris Trust & Savings Bank)

6. **Perpetuities Reform.** When the preconditions to the vesting of a bequest have already occurred, its validity in terms of the rule against perpetuities should be evaluated according to what has actually come to pass rather than according to what could have transpired. (Merchants National Bank v. Curtis)

NOTES

DICKERSON v. UNION NATIONAL BANK OF LITTLE ROCK
Son (P) v. Executor / Bank (D)
Ark. Sup. Ct., 268 Ark. 292, 595 S.W.2d 677 (1980).

NATURE OF CASE: Appeal of dismissal of action seeking to invalidate a testamentary trust.

FACT SUMMARY: A will created a testamentary trust which was to continue until the death of the testator's sons and a possible widow of one son.

CONCISE RULE OF LAW: An instrument creating a trust naming as beneficiaries children of an unnamed spouse violates the rule against perpetuities.

FACTS: Dickerson's will created a trust. Named as beneficiaries were Dickerson's two sons and the widow, unnamed, of one of the sons. After the death of the last of these three individuals, the trust was to end, and the principal was to be distributed to the issue of the three. Cecil (P), one of the sons, brought an action to nullify the will as violative of the rule against perpetuities. The Chancery Court held the will valid and dismissed. Cecil (P) appealed.

ISSUE: Does an instrument creating a trust naming as beneficiaries children of an unnamed spouse violate the rule against perpetuities?

HOLDING AND DECISION: (Smith, J.) Yes. An instrument creating a trust naming as beneficiaries children of an unnamed spouse violates the rule against perpetuities. Under the rule, any remainder must vest within twenty-one years of a life in being at the time of the death of the testator. A common pitfall is the "unnamed widow," a problem existing here. This widow conceivably could be born after the testator's death, which would exclude her from being a measuring life. She might live longer than twenty-one years after her husband's death, which would cause any vesting of proceeds in her children after her death to violate the rule. While this is only a theoretical scenario, a mere theoretical possibility is all that is needed to invoke the rule. Reversed.

EDITOR'S ANALYSIS: The present action was brought several years after the probate proceeding on the will. The rule against perpetuities objection was not made at the probate proceeding. The trial court, besides holding the rule inapplicable on the merits, held this a waiver. The state supreme court disagreed, ruling that the rule was not waivable.

QUICKNOTES

HOLOGRAPHIC WILL - A will that is handwritten by the testator or testatrix.

RULE AGAINST PERPETUITIES - The doctrine that a future interest that is incapable of vesting within twenty-one years of lives in being at the time it is created is immediately void.

RES JUDICATA - The rule of law that a final judgment by a court precludes subsequent litigation between the parties regarding the same cause of action.

NOTES:

FIRST PORTLAND NATIONAL BANK v. RODRIQUE

Bank (P) v. Heirs (D)

Me. Sup. Ct., 172 A.2d 107 (1961).

NATURE OF CASE: Appeal from judgment regarding a complaint seeking an interpretation and construction of a will and codicil.

FACT SUMMARY: Because the trust provisions in a will contained alternative contingencies, one of which violated the rule of perpetuities, the Bank (P) sought an interpretation and construction of the will from the court.

CONCISE RULE OF LAW: Where a gift is made upon alternative contingencies, one of which must occur, if at all, within the period of perpetuities and the other of which may not, the gift is valid if the first contingency occurs.

FACTS: Charles Cressy died testate, survived by his widow, Alice Rodrique (D), four children from a previous marriage, and a foster daughter (D). His will contained alternative contingencies providing for distribution of the trust after twenty-five years. The first contingency stated that the trust was to end at Alice's (D) death if it had been in effect for twenty-five years. The second contingency provided for continuation of the trust for the requisite twenty-five-year period, even if Alice's (D) death occurred before the end of the twenty-five years. The Bank (P) sought an interpretation and construction of Cressy's will and codicil from the court. Alice (D), the personal representatives (D) of Cressy's children, who were deceased at the time, grandchildren (D), great-grandchildren (D), and unborn issue (D) were named as parties defendant and defendants.

ISSUE: Where a gift is made upon alternative contingencies, one of which must occur, if at all, within the period of perpetuities and the other of which may not, is the gift valid if the first contingency occurs?

HOLDING AND DECISION: (Dubord, J.) Yes. Where a gift is made upon alternative contingencies, one of which must occur, if at all, within the period of perpetuities and the other of which may not, the gift is valid if the first contingency occurs. In this case, the second contingency is in violation of the rule against perpetuities because the trust might continue for more than twenty-one years beyond all lives in being at Cressy's death. However, Alice (D), who is the life annuitant, has in fact survived the date of the void limitation, and the trust will terminate and all interests vest not later than her death. Thus, the provisions of the will containing the alternative contingencies do not violate the rule against perpetuities. Remanded.

EDITOR'S ANALYSIS: While other jurisdictions had determined the issue presented in the instant case, the supreme court noted that this was a question of first impression for the court. Until recently, courts would not apply "split contingencies rule," also known as the "alternative contingencies rule," unless the testator himself separated the contingencies in his will, as Cressy did in the above case. However, courts may now be more willing to do the separating themselves, thereby saving the valid contingent events and discarding the rest.

QUICKNOTES

RULE AGAINST PERPETUITIES - The doctrine that a future interest that is incapable of vesting within 21 years of lives in being at the time it is created is immediately void.

RESIDUARY CLAUSE (OF WILL) - A clause contained in a will disposing of the assets remaining following distribution of the estate.

CONTINGENCY - Based on the uncertain happening of another event.

ALTERNATIVE CONTINGENCY - One of two or more events which are uncertain of happening.

NOTES:

WARD v. VAN DER LOEFF

Parties not identified

House of Lords, 1924, A.C. 653 (1924).

NATURE OF CASE: Appeal from a determination of heirship under a will and codicil thereto.

FACT SUMMARY: Testator created a trust fund in favor of his nieces and nephews because he had no children, but the trust appeared to violate the rule against perpetuities because he failed to limit the class of his brothers and sisters whose children were the beneficiaries of the trust.

CONCISE RULE OF LAW: In construing a will against the rule against perpetuities, the intention of the testator must first be discerned from the words of the will before it is determined whether or not the testamentary scheme satisfies the rule.

FACTS: Testator left a 1915 will and a 1916 codicil thereto. By his will, testator left his estate in trust for his wife for life, remainder to his children. In the event there were no children, which was the case, his wife was given a power to appoint the trust fund among the children of testator's brothers and sisters. In default of such appointment, the trust would go in equal shares to those children. The codicil provided (1) that the wife's life interest would be terminable on her remarriage unless such remarriage was with a natural-born British subject, (2) that the power of appointment be revoked, and (3) that the trustees after the wife's death would hold the trust for the children of the brothers and sisters who were living at the time of the wife's death or born at any time afterward and before any one of such children attained a vested interest and being male attained the age of twenty-one or being female attained that age or married. The testator died in 1916, survived by his wife, his parents, two brothers, and two sisters (all four with living children). In 1921, the widow, Van Der Loeff (P), remarried to a Dutch citizen. Subsequent to her remarriage, one of his brothers had a son, Philip. The probate judge found that the codicil in favor of the brothers' and sisters' children violated the rule against perpetuities; that the codicil operated to revoke the residuary gift in the will only so far as the substituted provision in the codicil was valid; and that the gift in the will took effect but only as to those children born before the widow's remarriage, thus excluding Philip. The court of appeals affirmed the finding of voidness but found that the codicil revoked the gift in the children's favor and that there was intestacy as to the residuary estate as from the remarriage of the widow. This appeal followed.

ISSUE: In construing a will against the rule against perpetuities, must the intention of the testator be first discerned from the words of the will before it is determined whether or not the testamentary scheme satisfies the rule?

HOLDING AND DECISION: (Haldine, V.) Yes. First, the codicil violated the rule against perpetuities. Testator spoke of his brothers and sisters generally and did not exclude the children of other brothers and sisters of whole or half blood who might in contemplation of the law be born. He did not limit his will to brothers and sisters alive at his death. Second, the codicil, although inoperative to the extent the rule was violated, did not revoke the gift in the will to the children of the brothers and sisters. The revocation was confined to the power of appointment given to the widow. There was no independent expression of intention to revoke anything more than the power of appointment. As for the class of children eligible under the will, the period when distribution occurred was the time to determine distribution. Taking into account the valid portion of the codicil and the remarriage to a Dutch citizen, Philip was excluded. The probate court decree was reinstated.

CONCURRENCE: (Dunedin, L.) When it is sought to vary the meaning of a word denoting a class of relations from what the prima facie meaning of that word is, there are only two classes of cases from where one can depart from the primary meaning: first, where it is impossible that any person indicated by the prima facie meaning can take under the bequest and, second, where the will itself states that the prima facie meaning should not be used.

EDITOR'S ANALYSIS: Notice that the trust in the will did not violate the rule. There the trust would have clearly passed within twenty-one years of a life in being, the widow's life. In the codicil, the brothers and sisters were the measuring life, and their class was not closed. Under the rule, the gift must be valid for all members of the class; it cannot be partially valid and partially void. Some gifts to a class can be salvaged under the class closing rule. That rule closes a class prior to the time it closes physiologically. Under the "rule of convenience," the class will close when any member of the class becomes entitled to immediate possession and enjoyment.

QUICKNOTES

RULE AGAINST PERPETUITIES - The doctrine that a future interest that is incapable of vesting within twenty-one years of lives in being at the time it is created is immediately void.

CODICIL - A supplement to a will.

REMAINDER - An interest in land that remains after the termination of the immediately preceding estate.

NOTES:

AMERICAN SECURITY AND TRUST CO. v. CRAMER

Trustee (D) v. Heirs (P)

175 F. Supp. 367 (D.D.C. 1959).

NATURE OF CASE: Bill for instructions by trustee.

FACT SUMMARY: A trust, whose beneficiaries included the issue of testator's daughter, two of whom were alive at the time of testator's death and two who were born later, was attacked as violative of the rule against perpetuities.

CONCISE RULE OF LAW: In order for a class gift to be valid, the class must close within the period of the rule against perpetuities. If the ultimate takers of an interest are not described as a single class but rather as a group of subclasses, and if the share to which each separate subclass is entitled will finally be determined within the period of the rule, the gifts to the different subclasses are separable for the purposes of the rule.

FACTS: Testator provided that a trust be established for the benefit of his widow for life, and upon her death half of the corpus was to be held in trust for his daughter for life. Upon the daughter's death the income was to go to her children, and upon the death of each child to the persons who would be the heirs of such child. The daughter had four children. Two were born before and two after testator's death. The trustee brought an action desiring instructions as to the validity of the remainders to the heirs of the daughter's issue.

ISSUES: (1) Must a class close within the period of the rule against perpetuities in order for a class gift to be valid? (2) Will an invalid remainder taint an otherwise valid one and render it invalid?

HOLDING AND DECISION: (Youngdahl, J.) (1) Yes. In order for a class gift to be valid, the class must close within the period of the rule against perpetuities. Thus, the life estates to the testator's daughter's children had to vest, if at all, at the termination of the preceding life estates of the widow and the daughter. Since the daughter's children had to be born within her lifetime, and since she was a life in being, the class of daughter's children closed within the period of the rule. As to the remainders to the heirs of the children, the children of the daughter who were born at the time of the testator's death were lives in being at the time of his death, and, thus, the remainders to their heirs had to vest or not within the period of the rule and would be valid. The remainders to the heirs of the daughter's children born after the testator died would be invalid because of the possibility that vesting would take place beyond the period of the rule because the heirs could not be ascertained until the afterborn's death, and an interest cannot be vested until the interest holder is ascertained. (2) No. If the ultimate takers of an interest are not described as a single class but rather as a group of subclasses, and if the share to which each

subclass is entitled will be determined within the period of the rule, the gifts to the different subclasses are separable. In this case, the language of the will provided for a remainder to a subclass, and, thus, the fact that the remainders to the afterborn's heirs are invalid does not taint the other remainders.

EDITOR'S ANALYSIS: A class gift generally is subject to the all or nothing rule, which holds that the interest of all class members must vest before the interest of any of them is deemed to satisfy the rule. This case illustrates a situation where the all-or-nothing rule does not apply because of the existence of separate subclasses which are determined within the perpetuities period, thereby eliminating the possibility of afterborn children. The rule which applies is commonly known as the doctrine of severed shares.

QUICKNOTES

CLASS GIFT - A gift to a group of unspecified persons whose number, identity, and share of the gift will be determined sometime in the future.

RULE AGAINST PERPETUITIES - The doctrine that a future interest that is incapable of vesting within 21 years of lives in being at the time it is created is immediately void.

LIFE ESTATE - An interest in land measured by the life of the tenant or a third party.

REMAINDER - An interest in land that remains after the termination of the immediately preceding estate.

NOTES:

SECOND NATIONAL BANK OF NEW HAVEN v. HARRIS TRUST & SAVINGS BANK

Trustee (P) v. Executor (D)

29 Conn. Sup. 275 (1971).

NATURE OF CASE: Declaratory action and for the settlement of trust accounts.

FACT SUMMARY: Margaret Marsh exercised a general testamentary power of appointment by creating a second trust for her daughter, which was to last for thirty years.

CONCISE RULE OF LAW: The rule against perpetuities is computed from the date of death of the settlor of an inter vivos trust where the power to revoke, alter, or amend the trust was retained.

FACTS: Trowbridge established an inter vivos trust. Marsh, her daughter, was given a life estate with a general testamentary power of appointment over one-half the corpus. Upon default of appointment, the corpus was to go to her issue, if any, or the issue of her sister. Trowbridge retained the power to revoke, alter, or amend the trust as to income during her lifetime. Marsh attempted to exercise the power under her will. She established a trust for her daughter, which was to last for thirty years. At the end of the thirty year period, the trust was to end and the corpus be distributed to her. If the daughter died before the trust expired, it was to go to her issue. It was alleged that the attempted exercise violated the rule against perpetuities since the power related back to the date on which the trust was created.

ISSUE: Where the settlor retains the right to revoke, alter, or amend, is the perpetuities period computed from the date on which the trust was created?

HOLDING AND DECISION: (Shea, J.) No. A donee exercises the power as a mere conduit of the donor. The appointment is "read back" to the date of the instrument creating it. If it is created by will, this is the date of the testator's death. If created by an inter vivos instrument, the date is when the instrument was executed. Perpetuities periods are based on the date on which the power was created, not when it was exercised. However, an exception is made to the normal rule on inter vivos instruments where the settlor has retained the power to revoke, alter, or amend. Where such powers are retained, the instrument is ambulatory, and the power is not deemed to have vested in the donee until the settlor's death. This then becomes the measuring date for the perpetuities period. A vested interest is not subject to the rule. Therefore the gift to the daughter does not violate the rule. The remainder to the children is contingent on there being issue and that they survive their mother. The class cannot be ascertained until the daughter's death. Since the original trust instrument was executed before Marsh's birth, she could not be deemed a life in being for the perpetuities rule. Power to revoke, alter, or amend the income is not a sufficient retained interest to apply the exception to the general rule that the perpetuities period should be computed from the trustor's death. Therefore, the contingent remainder is too remote and violates the rule. We do not recognize cy pres in such situations, and the "second look" doctrine would not save the remainder. We find that the gift to the daughter is absolute, and the trust is valid. Only the remainder interest is invalid, and it will pass under the daughter's will if she dies before the trust terminates.

EDITOR'S ANALYSIS: The "second look" doctrine allows the court to look at the facts as they actually exist at the end of one or more life estates to determine if the rule has been violated. This is to avoid the unrealistic and overly technical assumptions for which the rule is famous, e.g., fertility for as long as a measuring life is in being. 6 American Law of Property, § 24.24.

QUICKNOTES

INTER VIVOS TRUST - Property that is held by one person for the benefit of another and which is created by an instrument that takes effect during the life of the grantor.

ISSUE PER STIRPES - Descendants who are entitled to the distribution of property by right of representation.

POWER OF APPOINTMENT - Power, created by another person in connection with a gratuitous transfer (often in trust), residing in a person (as trustee or otherwise) to affect the disposition or distribution of the property.

GUARDIAN AD LITEM - Person designated by the court to represent an infant or ward in a particular legal proceeding.

RULE AGAINST PERPETUITIES - The doctrine that a future interest that is incapable of vesting within twenty-one years of lives in being at the time it is created is immediately void.

NOTES:

MERCHANTS NATIONAL BANK v. CURTIS

Parties not identified

N.H. Sup. Ct., 98 N.H. 225, 97 A.2d 207 (1953).

NATURE OF CASE: Suit attacking the validity of a bequest.

FACT SUMMARY: Testatrix devised a remainder interest to her existing or afterborn grandchildren and their heirs, then to other relatives (D) should her grandchildren die without heirs.

CONCISE RULE OF LAW: When the preconditions to the vesting of a bequest have already occurred, its validity in terms of the rule against perpetuities should be evaluated according to what has actually come to pass rather than according to what could have transpired.

FACTS: Testatrix's will devised interests in realty to her son and daughter and granted a remainder interest to her granddaughter, Margaret May Curtis, and her heirs. The will further provided that any additional grandchildren who might be born should share equally with Margaret and that upon the death of testatrix's children, her entire estate should be distributed to her grandchildren and their heirs. By the sixth clause of her will, testatrix decreed that, should any of her grandchildren survive her children but then die without heirs of their body, then her property should pass to other designated relatives. Testatrix died in 1902. No additional grandchildren were born. Margaret survived both of testatrix's children but eventually died without leaving issue. The gift over to the relatives (D) designated in the sixth clause was then attacked by the Merchants National Bank (P) on the ground that the gift violated the rule against perpetuities. The relatives (D) argued that the Rule should not be applied since the preconditions to the vesting of the bequest had already occurred within a life in being plus twenty-one years.

ISSUE: In determining whether or not a bequest violates the rule against perpetuities, should the court take account of developments which have occurred since execution of the instrument by which the bequest was created?

HOLDING AND DECISION: (Kenison, C.J.) Yes. When the preconditions to the vesting of a bequest have already occurred, its validity in terms of the rule against perpetuities should be evaluated according to what has actually come to pass rather than according to what could have transpired. Most courts stubbornly adhere to the view that, for purposes of the Rule, the validity of a gift must be determined as of the moment of its creation. However, the rule against perpetuities is a harsh principle which often operates to defeat the intentions of a testator. Therefore, the courts of this state have long preferred to examine a gift in the light of subsequent developments and have consistently upheld gifts which actually vested within the perpetuities period, notwithstanding that there once existed a possibility of their vesting remotely. In this case, since Margaret's death without issue assures that the gift over to the other designated relatives (D) will not vest remotely, that gift should be upheld.

EDITOR'S ANALYSIS: The approach adopted by the court in this case has come to be known as the "wait-and-see" doctrine. Pennsylvania was the first state to enact a statute which incorporated the "wait-and-see" doctrine, and other jurisdictions have since followed suit. Commentators have complained that the adoption of an approach which neutralizes the force of the rule against perpetuities actually presages the demise of that Rule. More enlightened observers recognize that the "wait-and-see" doctrine preserves the intentions of the testator by upholding gifts which have already been relieved of the possibility of vesting remotely.

QUICKNOTES

LIFE ESTATE - An interest in land measured by the life of the tenant or a third party.

REMAINDER - An interest in land that remains after the termination of the immediately preceding estate.

RULE AGAINST PERPETUITIES - The doctrine that a future interest that is incapable of vesting within twenty-one years of lives in being at the time it is created is immediately void.

LIFE TENANT - An individual whose estate in real property is measured either by his own life or by that of another.

NOTES:

CHAPTER 12
TRUST ADMINISTRATION: THE FIDUCIARY OBLIGATION

QUICK REFERENCE RULES OF LAW

1. **Duties of the Trustee.** A trustee breaches his duty of loyalty to the beneficiaries when he engages in self-dealing. (Hartman v. Hartle)

   [For more information on self-dealing, see Casenote Law Outline on Wills, Trusts, and Estates, Chapter 12, § VIII, Self-Dealing.]

2. **Duties of the Trustee.** An executor will be personally liable where he has a conflict of interest and has not acted in good faith or his actions resulted in unfairness to the estate. (In re Rothko)

   [For more information on executors' conflicts of interest, see Casenote Law Outline on Wills, Trusts & Estates, Chapter 12, § VIII, Self-Dealing.]

3. **Duties of the Trustee.** While a corporate trustee should not retain its own stock to avoid a conflict of interest, the will may allow it to retain the shares without liability. (In re Heidenreich)

   [For more information on retention of investments, see Casenote Law Outline on Wills, Trusts & Estates, Chapter 12, § VII, Investments.]

4. **Duties of the Trustee.** A trustee is under a duty to the beneficiary not to delegate to others the doing of acts that the trustee can reasonably be required personally to perform. (Shriners Hospitals for Crippled Children v. Gardiner)

   [For more information on cofiduciaries, see Casenote Law Outline on Wills, Trusts and Estates, Chapter 12, § IX, Remedies Against Fiduciaries.]

5. **Duties of the Trustee.** A trustee who fails to unload trust assets that are declining in value may be liable to trust remaindermen. (Dennis v. Rhode Island Hospital Trust Co.)

6. **Duties of the Trustee.** Where the subject matter is one of fact in respect to which a person can have precise and accurate knowledge and he speaks as of his own knowledge and has no such knowledge, his affirmation constitutes constructive or technical fraud. (National Academy of Sciences v. Cambridge Trust Co.)

   [For more information on liability for improper distribution, see Casenote Law Outline on Wills, Trusts & Estates, Chapter 12, § XI, Distribution.]

7. **Powers of the Trustee.** The trustee is under a duty to the beneficiary to distribute the risk of loss by reasonable diversification of investments, unless under the circumstances it is prudent not to do so. (Estate of Collins)

   [For more information on diversification of investments, see Casenote Law Outline on Wills, Trusts & Estates, Chapter 12, § VII, Investments.]

8. **Liability of the Trustee to Third Parties.** Where a trustee has power to control the use of trust property and knowingly allows the property to be used for the disposal of hazardous wastes, the trustee is personally liable for response costs regardless of the trust's ability to indemnify him. (City of Phoenix v. Garbage Service Co.)

NOTES

HARTMAN v. HARTLE
Daughter of testatrix (P) v. Executor (D)
N..J., Ch. Ct. 95, N.J. Eq. 123, 122 A. 615 (1923).

NATURE OF CASE: Bill in equity to set aside the sale of property by executors for fraud and illegality.

FACT SUMMARY: After an executor (D) indirectly sold property to his wife, who resold the property at a substantial profit, Hartman (P), testatrix's daughter, filed a complaint to set aside the original sale.

CONCISE RULE OF LAW: A trustee breaches his duty of loyalty to the beneficiaries when he engages in self-dealing.

FACTS: Testatrix died leaving five children. She named her two sons-in-law (D) as executors. In her will, testatrix expressly directed the executors (D) to sell her real estate. The proceeds were to be divided equally among her children. However, part of the real estate was sold for $3,900 to Geick, a son of the testatrix. He bought it for his sister, Dieker, the wife of one of the executors (D). Dieker then resold the property for $5,500. Hartman (P), a second daughter of the testatrix, filed a complaint to set aside the first sale for fraud and illegality. She contended that the sale of the property by the executors (D) to Dieker, the wife of one of them, without previous authority from the court, was illegal and void.

ISSUE: Does a trustee breach his duty of loyalty to the beneficiaries when he engages in self-dealing?

HOLDING AND DECISION: (Foster, V.C.) Yes. A trustee breaches his duty of loyalty to the beneficiaries when he engages in self-dealing. It is the settled law of this state that a trustee cannot purchase from himself at his own sale and that his wife is under the same disability, unless leave to do so has been previously obtained under an order of the court. In view of the fact that the property is now owned by innocent purchasers, a resale cannot be ordered, but as an alternative, Dieker and the executors (D) will be held to pay one-fifth of their profit on the resale to Hartman (P). Decree so ordered.

EDITOR'S ANALYSIS: Once it is shown that a trustee has engaged in self-dealing, the no-further-inquiry rule is triggered; the trustee will be liable for any profit realized, without inquiry by the court as to the trustee's good faith or the transaction's reasonableness. The trustee may assert two defenses — either that the self-dealing was approved by the settlor or was fully disclosed to the beneficiaries, who then gave their consent. The strict no-further-inquiry rule is justified by the fiduciary relationship between the trustee and the beneficiaries, which is held to a higher standard than arm's-length transactions.

[For more information on self-dealing, see Casenote Law Outline on Wills, Trusts, and Estates, Chapter 12, § VIII, Self-Dealing.]

QUICKNOTES
DUTY OF LOYALTY - A director's duty to refrain from self-dealing or to take a position that is adverse to the corporation's best interests.

NOTES:

IN RE ROTHKO
Daughter of deceased (P) v. Executors (D)
43 N.Y.2d 305 (1977).

NATURE OF CASE: Action to remove executor and cancel contracts.

FACT SUMMARY: Rothko's executors (D) entered into a contract with a gallery to sell Rothko's paintings over a twelve-year period.

CONCISE RULE OF LAW: An executor will be personally liable where he has a conflict of interest and has not acted in good faith or his actions resulted in unfairness to the estate.

FACTS: Rothko died, leaving 798 paintings to his estate. Reis (D), Stamos (D), and Levine (D) were named executors. A contract was executed by the executors with The Marlborough Galleries (D) and their domestic corporation (D) selling them some paintings outright and giving them 50% commission on the remainder. The Gallery (D) was to pay for the paintings over a 12-year period and was to sell the other paintings over the same twelve-year period. At the time of his death, Rothko had a contract with Marlborough (D) to sell his paintings for a 10% commission. Moreover, Reis (D) was a director, secretary, and treasurer of Marlborough (D). Shortly after execution of the contract, Stamos (D) was given a lucrative contract by Marlborough (D). Rothko's daughter (P) brought an action to remove the executors, rescind the contracts with Marlborough (D), and for damages. A restraining order was issued, but Marlborough (D) subsequently sold fifty-seven of the paintings. The surrogate found that Reis (D) was in a position of having a conflict of interest; Stamos (D) had used his position to curry favors with Marlborough (D) and to obtain personal advantages; and Levine (D) was guilty of negligence in failing to ascertain and protect the estate against the conflict. All three executors (D) were ordered removed, the contract between Rothko and Marlborough (D) was deemed void. Marlborough (D) and the executors (D) appealed, alleging that there was no showing of unfairness or bad faith and that, in any event, they should not be liable for the appreciated value of the paintings but only their value on the date the contract was executed.

ISSUE: Where a conflict of interest exists, will the executors be liable for any bad faith or unfairness?

HOLDING AND DECISION: (Cooke, J.) Yes. An executor is not generally liable merely because he has a conflict of interest with respect to estate property which is sold. However, the executor is under the burden of establishing that he has acted in good faith and the plan was fair to the estate. The evidence herein is more than sufficient to establish a conflict and that the plan was unfair to the estate. Reis (D) was obviously in a position to personally benefit under the contract, and Stamos (D) accepted a beneficial

position with Marlborough (D). Levine (D) knew or should have known that his coexecutors were breaching their fiduciary duty, and this is sufficient to hold him liable for negligence for failing to act in a reasonable manner. Marlborough (D) is also liable since it had constructive notice of the breach of fiduciary duty. As for the measure of damages, an executor who is authorized to sell estate assets is not liable in damages for increases in value of the property if the executors were only guilty of selling at too low a price. An executor is only liable for appreciated value where he has a duty to retain the assets. To hold otherwise would place a burden on the executor's decision to sell the asset. However, where an executor is guilty of misfeasance rather than merely selling at too low a price, damages based on appreciated value may be imposed. Judgment is affirmed.

EDITOR'S ANALYSIS: In some jurisdictions, the courts or legislature have adopted the "no further inquiry" rule, i.e., if there is self-dealing or conflict, it is immaterial whether the transactions are fair or not; they are absolutely void. *Munson v. Syracuse, Geneva & Corning R.R. Co.*, 103 N.Y. 58 (1886). Most jurisdictions now follow the holding in *Rothko*, though few exceptions to the absolute prohibition are recognized. *Matter of Estate of Gaylord*, 552 P. 2d 392 (1976).

[For more information on executors' conflicts of interest, see Casenote Law Outline on Wills, Trusts & Estates, Chapter 12, § VIII, Self-Dealing.]

QUICKNOTES

FIDUCIARY DUTY - A legal obligation to act for the benefit of another, including subordinating one's personal interests to that of the other person.

DUTY OF LOYALTY - A director's duty to refrain from self-dealing or to take a position that is adverse to the corporation's best interests.

SELF-DEALING - Transaction in which a fiduciary uses property of another, held by virtue of the confidential relationship, for personal gain.

APPRECIATION - The increase in the fair market value of property over either an earlier value or the taxpayer's basis.

PUNITIVE DAMAGES - Damages exceeding the actual injury suffered for the purposes of punishment, deterrence and comfort to plaintiff.

NOTES:

IN RE HEIDENREICH
Beneficiaries (P) v. Successor trustee (D)
85 Misc. 2d 135, 378 N.Y.S.2d 982 (1976).

NATURE OF CASE: Action for an accounting.

FACT SUMMARY: The corporate trustee caused trust funds to be deposited in it and to retain its stock in the trust.

CONCISE RULE OF LAW: While a corporate trustee should not retain its own stock to avoid a conflict of interest, the will may allow it to retain the shares without liability.

FACTS: Heidenreich died owning 1,309 shares of Federation Bank and Trust Co. stock. The Bank was subsequently taken over by Franklin National Bank (D), which became the successor trustee of Heidenreich's trust. Franklin (D) retained its stock in the trust until trading in it was subsequently suspended. Beneficiaries (P) sought an accounting and to surcharge Franklin (D) for self-dealing in its stock, for depositing trust funds in its savings account, and for leaving trust funds in a checking account for more than one year. Franklin (D) alleged that it was authorized to retain the stock under the will and had exercised sound business judgment in retaining the stock. As for the savings account, it was being used for short-term deposits in order to have liquid assets available for investments. The checking account contained funds earmarked for Franklin (D) as commission on sales.

ISSUE: Will a trustee who is authorized by the trust instrument to retain its own stock in trust and who exercises sound business judgment as to its retention be surcharged for a decrease in its value?

HOLDING AND DECISION: (Benne, S.) No. As a general rule, a corporate trustee must refuse to be qualified or must sell its stock if it is an asset in a trust administered by it. Failure to do so constitutes a conflict of interest which will result in a surcharge if the stock declines in price. Mismanagement need not be shown. This automatic imposition of liability will not be imposed if the will directs or authorizes retention of the stock. In such cases, the corporate trustee will only be surcharged for an actual breach of fiduciary duty involving the stock. Here, it was established that the Bank (D) exercised reasonable business judgment in its decision to retain the stock, and it may not be surcharged for its sound discretion. There was no breach of its fiduciary duties with respect to either of the bank accounts. The savings account was necessary to have liquid funds for investments available immediately, and interest was paid on these funds. The checking account represented funds earmarked for commissions and involved no breach of duty.

EDITOR'S ANALYSIS: Testator may waive the individual loyalty rule and authorize the corporate trustee to retain stock or use trust funds to purchase such stock. Matter of Ryan, 186 Misc. 688 (1945). Stock dividends may also be retained in such cases as well as new stock in the event of a merger. Scott, Trusts, § 231.2. The conflict is allowed so long as it remains substantially the same, i.e., it does not increase markedly in scope.

[For more information on retention of investments, see Casenote Law Outline on Wills, Trusts & Estates, Chapter 12, § VII, Investments.]

QUICKNOTES

SUCCESSOR TRUSTEE - A trustee who succeeds a previous trustee.

GUARDIAN AD LITEM - Person designated by the court to represent an infant or ward in a particular legal proceeding.

FIDUCIARY - Person holding a legal obligation to act for the benefit of another.

NOTES:

SHRINERS HOSPITALS FOR CRIPPLED CHILDREN v. GARDINER

Beneficiary (P) v. Trustee (D)

Ariz. Sup. Ct., 152 Ariz. 527, 733 P.2d 1110 (1987).

NATURE OF CASE: Appeal from the reversal of a denial of a petition to surcharge a trustee for the full amount of a loss to the trust.

FACT SUMMARY: After Mary Jane Gardiner (D), as trustee for the trust established by her mother, delegated the investment duties to her nephew Charles, a stockbroker, Charles embezzled a large sum of money from the trust, and Shriners Hospitals (P), the remainderman, petitioned the court to surcharge Mary Jane (D) for the full amount of the embezzlement.

CONCISE RULE OF LAW: A trustee is under a duty to the beneficiary not to delegate to others the doing of acts that the trustee can reasonably be required personally to perform.

FACTS: Laurabel Gardiner established a trust to provide income to her daughter, Mary Jane Gardiner (D), her two grandchildren, Charles and Robert, and a now-deceased daughter-in-law. The remainder of the estate was to pass to Shriners Hospitals (P) upon the death of the life income beneficiaries. Laurabel appointed Mary Jane (D) as trustee, and Charles and Robert as alternate trustees. Because Mary Jane (D) was not an experienced investor, she placed the trust assets with a brokerage house, allowing Charles, an investment counselor and stockbroker, to make all the trust's investment decisions. After Charles embezzled a large sum from the trust, Shriners Hospitals (P) brought a petition to surcharge Mary Jane (D) for the full amount of the embezzlement. The trial court denied the petition. The court of appeals reversed. Mary Jane (D) appealed.

ISSUE: Is a trustee under a duty to the beneficiary not to delegate to others the doing of acts that the trustee can reasonably be required personally to perform?

HOLDING AND DECISION: (Hays, J.) Yes. A trustee is under a duty to the beneficiary not to delegate to others the doing of acts that the trustee can reasonably be required personally to perform. Although an inexperienced trustee must seek expert advice, he is not ordinarily justified in relying on such advice but must exercise his own judgment. Here, Charles was functioning as a surrogate trustee. Because Mary Jane (D) was not exercising any control over the selection of investments, she clearly breached her duties to act prudently and to personally perform her duties as a trustee. However, the nature of the loss indicates that her breach was not causally connected to Charles' diversion of funds. Because the record is inadequate, the relative culpability of Charles, Mary Jane (D), and Dean Witter Reynolds is unclear. Vacated and remanded for a determination of those culpabilities.

EDITOR'S ANALYSIS: At the time of this decision, the court was applying the nondelegation rule then found in the Restatement (Second) of Trusts, §§ 171 and 227. However, those sections have been revised and the rule has been repealed by the Restatement (Third) of Trusts (1992). Section 171 now provides that a trustee has a duty to personally perform the responsibilities of the trusteeship except as a prudent person might delegate those responsibilities to others.

[For more information on cofiduciaries, see Casenote Law Outline on Wills, Trusts and Estates, Chapter 12, § IX, Remedies Against Fiduciaries.]

QUICKNOTES

BENEFICIARY - A third party who is the recipient of the benefit of a transaction undertaken by another.

TRUSTEE - A person who is entrusted to keep or administer something.

TESTATOR - One who executes a will.

EQUAL PROTECTION - A constitutional guarantee that no person shall be denied the same protection of the laws enjoyed by other persons in life circumstances.

NOTES:

DENNIS v. RHODE ISLAND HOSPITAL
TRUST NATIONAL BANK
Beneficiaries (P) v. Trustee (D)
744 F.2d 893 (1st Cir. 1984).

NATURE OF CASE: Appeal of certain orders in an action based on breach of fiduciary duty.

FACT SUMMARY: The Bank (D) held onto certain real estate in a declining market, leaving a relatively small corpus for the remaindermen.

CONCISE RULE OF LAW: A trustee who fails to unload trust assets that are declining in value may be liable to trust remaindermen.

FACTS: A testamentary trust created in 1920 was due to terminate in 1991. During the life of the trust, its income was to go to the testator's living issue; upon its termination, the principal was to go to the testators then-living issue. The principal trust assets were three commercial buildings in downtown Providence, R.I. From 1920 on, apart from a brief renaissance after World War II, the buildings' values decreased, although rents remained fairly high. The three buildings were sold in 1945, 1970, and 1979, respectively. Eventually, the two remaindermen brought an action against Rhode Island Hospital Trust National Bank (D), alleging breach of fiduciary duty. The district court found the Bank (D) to have improperly favored the income beneficiaries over the remaindermen by failing to unload income-producing but depreciating assets, and awarded a $365,781.67 surcharge. The Bank (D) appealed.

ISSUE: May a trustee who fails to unload trust assets that are declining in value be liable to the trust remaindermen?

HOLDING AND DECISION: (Breyer, C.J.) Yes. A trustee who fails to unload trust assets that are declining in value may be liable to the trust remaindermen. A trustee is obligated to treat all beneficiaries impartially; he may not favor one class over another. A failure to abide by the principle may give rise to the aggrieved class. Here, the district court held that the Bank (D) should have realized that the buildings, although generating good income, were declining in value to the detriment of the remaindermen. From this, the court was free to conclude that the Bank (D) improperly favored the income beneficiaries over the remaindermen, and its holding was therefore appropriate. [The court modified the damages to $345,246.56.] Affirmed as modified.

EDITOR'S ANALYSIS: As this case shows, all beneficiaries are not created equally. Sometimes, there can be actual adversity between beneficiary classes. A trustee, to discharge his fiduciary duties, must sometimes walk a tightrope between the classes.

QUICKNOTES

FIDUCIARY DUTY - A legal obligation to act for the benefit of another, including subordinating one's personal interests to that of the other person.

REMAINDERMAN - A person who has an interest in property to commence upon the termination of a present possessory interest.

LIFE TENANT - An individual whose estate in real property is measured either by his own life or by that of another.

INCOME BENEFICIARY - A person who is the recipient of income generated by certain property.

NOTES:

NATIONAL ACADEMY OF SCIENCES v. CAMBRIDGE TRUST COMPANY

Remainderman (P) v. Trustees (D)

346 N.E.2d 879 (1976).

NATURE OF CASE: Appeal from a petition seeking revocation of seven decrees allowing the trustee's accounting.

FACT SUMMARY: The National Academy of Sciences (P), a remainderman under a trust, brought an action seeking revocation of seven court decrees allowing accounts of the Cambridge Trust Company (D), the trustees.

CONCISE RULE OF LAW: Where the subject matter is one of fact in respect to which a person can have precise and accurate knowledge and he speaks as of his own knowledge and has no such knowledge, his affirmation constitutes constructive or technical fraud.

FACTS: The will of Troland left all of his real and personal property to be held in trust by the Cambridge Trust Company (D), with the net income to be paid to his wife, provided she did not remarry. On his wife's remarriage or death, the Bank (D) was to transfer the trust and trusteeship to the National Academy of Sciences (P). The Bank (D) paid income from the trust to the widow until her death in 1967. In 1945, the widow remarried without the Bank's (D) knowledge. In 1968, the Bank (D) brought a suit for recovery of amounts paid to the widow subsequent to the date of her marriage. In this litigation, the Bank (D) recovered $41,000, from which it paid legal fees of $14,000. The total amount collected by the widow after her marriage was $106,000. The Bank (D) presented this account, and it was allowed. Thereafter, the Academy (P) brought an action seeking revocation of the Bank's (D) account. The judge revoked the accounting and ordered restoration to the trusts of those amounts erroneously delivered to the decedent's widow. The court of appeals affirmed. An appeal was taken to the Supreme Court of Massachusetts.

ISSUE: Where the subject matter is one of fact in respect to which a person can have knowledge and he speaks as of his own knowledge and has no such knowledge, does his affirmation constitute fraud?

HOLDING AND DECISION: (Reardon, J.) Yes. The principle is well settled that if a person makes a representation of fact as of his own knowledge and such representation is not true as to a subject matter susceptible of knowledge, if the party to whom it is made relies and acts upon it as true and sustains damage by it, it is fraud, for which the party making it is responsible. In this case, the marital status of Mrs. Troland/Flynn was a fact susceptible of precise knowledge. The Bank (D) made representations concerning this fact of its own knowledge when it had no such knowledge, and the Academy (P) to whom the representations were made relied on them to its detriment. The Bank (D) exerted no effort at all to ascertain if Mrs. Troland had remarried even to the extent of annually requesting a statement or certificate from her to that effect. It follows that the decree of the probate court is affirmed

EDITOR'S ANALYSIS: In order to avoid expensive accountings, provisions are often inserted in a trust instrument providing that judicial accountings should be dispensed with and accounts rendered periodically to the adult income beneficiaries of the trust. In the case of testamentary trusts, a few courts have indicated that a testator will not be permitted to dispense with statutorily required accountings. (Bogert & Bogert, Trusts & Trustees, § 973, 2d ed. 1962). In the case of inter vivos trusts, which are not placed under judicial supervision by statutes, it would appear that a "no judicial accounting" provision does not contravene public policy.

[For more information on liability for improper distribution, see Casenote Law Outline on Wills, Trusts & Estates, Chapter 12, § XI, Distribution.]

QUICKNOTES

FIDUCIARY DUTY - A legal obligation to act for the benefit of another, including subordinating one's personal interests to that of the other person.

CONSTRUCTIVE FRAUD - Breach of a duty at law or in equity that tends to deceive another to whom the duty is owed, resulting in damages.

NOTES:

ESTATE OF COLLINS

Beneficiaries (P) v. Trustees (D)

Cal. Sup. Ct., 72 Cal. A.P. 3d 663 (1977).

NATURE OF CASE: Appeal from an action for damages for breach of a trust.

FACT SUMMARY: Plaintiffs, beneficiaries under a testamentary trust, brought suit against Lamb (D) and Millikan (D), the trustees, alleging that they had improperly invested $50,000.

CONCISE RULE OF LAW: The trustee is under a duty to the beneficiary to distribute the risk of loss by reasonable diversification of investments, unless under the circumstances it is prudent not to do so.

FACTS: The primary beneficiaries under the Collins testamentary trust were his wife and children. The will authorized the trustees, Lamb (D) and Millikan (D), to purchase every kind of property or investment. It also provided that the trustees had absolute discretion in exercising the provisions of the trust. After probate, Lamb (D) and Millikan (D) had about $50,000 available for investment. Millikan's (D) clients included two real property developers, Downing and Ward. The trustees (D) learned that the developers wanted to borrow $50,000, which would be secured by a second trust deed to 9.38 acres of unimproved real property. This property was subject to a $90,000 first trust deed. The trustees (D) knew the property had been sold earlier for $107,000. However, they did not have the property appraised, relying instead on the word of the two real estate brokers in the area. In fact, when the trustees (D) made the loan, there were six notices of default and three lawsuits pending against the developers. After the developers declared bankruptcy, the trustees (D) became the owners of the property. Later, the holder of the first trust deed foreclosed, and the trust fund lost about $60,000. Several years later, the trustees (D) had improperly invested $50,000 and requested that the trustees (D) be surcharged. The trial court ruled in favor of the trustees (D) and terminated the trust. The beneficiaries (P) appealed.

ISSUE: Are trustees under a duty to the beneficiary to diversify the trust investments?

HOLDING AND DECISION: (Kavs, J.) Yes. California relies on the prudent investor rule, which encompasses the following guidelines. First, the trustee is under a duty to the beneficiary to distribute the risk of loss by reasonable diversification of investments, unless under the circumstances it is prudent not to do so. Second, ordinarily, second or other junior mortgages are not proper trust investments, unless taking a second mortgage is a reasonable method of settling a claim or making possible the sale of property. Third, in buying a mortgage for trust investment, the trust should give careful attention to the valuation of the property in order to make certain that his margin of security is adequate. This court thinks that the trustees, Lamb (D) and Millikan (D), violated every applicable rule. First, they failed totally to diversify the investments. Second, the trustees (D) invested in junior mortgages on unimproved real property and left an inadequate margin of security. As noted, the land had recently been sold for $107,000 and was subject to a first trust deed of $90,000. Thus, unless the land was worth more than $140,000, there was no margin of security at all. The trustees (D) did not have the land appraised. Thus, any assumption that there was a margin of security would have been little more than a guess. Third, the backup security obtained by the trustees (D) was no security at all. The builders pledged 20 percent of their stock, but the trustees (D) never obtained possession of the stock, placed it in escrow, or even had it legended. In conclusion, the evidence does not support the trial court's conclusion that the trustees (D) acted properly.

EDITOR'S ANALYSIS: "Running throughout the disparate legal approaches to the regulation of risk is a consistent concern with one particular type of risk: the risk of loss. In addition to focusing solely on risk of loss, current regulation is limited to minimizing that risk on each particular security, rather than on the portfolio as a whole. In evaluating the investment of trust funds, the prudent man rule treats each investment separately. Losses in one investment cannot be set off against other investments, and each investment must stand or fall by itself." (The Regulation of Risky Investments, 83 Harv. L. Rev. 603, 616-621, 1970.)

[For more information on diversification of investments, see Casenote Law Outline on Wills, Trusts & Estates, Chapter 12, § VII, Investments.]

QUICKNOTES

TESTAMENTARY TRUST - A trust created by will and only effective after the grantor's death, since the assets that comprise the corpus of the trust are assumed to vest at that time.

FORECLOSURE - An action to recover the amount due on a mortgage of real property where the owner has failed to pay their debt, terminating the owner's interest in the property which must then be sold to satisfy the debt.

DUTY TO DIVERSIFY - Duty of a trustee, in the administration of the trust, to diversify the investments made with the trust's funds or property.

FIDUCIARY DUTY - A legal obligation to act for the benefit of another, including subordinating one's personal interests to that of the other person.

CITY OF PHOENIX v. GARBAGE SERVICE CO.
City (P) v. Trustee (D)
827 F. Supp. 600 (D. Ariz. 1993).

NATURE OF CASE: Motion for partial summary judgment to limit liability in action to recover cleanup costs.

FACT SUMMARY: The City of Phoenix (P) filed this action to recover response costs incurred in cleaning up hazardous substances deposited in a landfill while the property was an asset in a trust estate for which Valley National Bank (VNB) (D) was the trustee.

CONCISE RULE OF LAW: Where a trustee has power to control the use of trust property and knowingly allows the property to be used for the disposal of hazardous wastes, the trustee is personally liable for response costs regardless of the trust's ability to indemnify him.

FACTS: Estes conveyed a landfill, retaining an option to purchase the property. After his death, Valley National Bank (VNB) (D), as trustee of the estate, exercised that option. All the stock of Garbage Services Co. (GSC) (D), manager of the property, was also a trust asset. The City of Phoenix (P) acquired the entire landfill through condemnation proceedings, then filed an action to recover response costs incurred in cleaning up hazardous substances allegedly deposited while VNB (D) was trustee. VNB (D) asserted that, as a trustee, it was not personally liable for response costs and that its liability should be limited to the amount of the assets held in trust. VNB (D) then moved for partial summary judgment to limit its liability.

ISSUE: Where a trustee has power to control the use of trust property and knowingly allows the property to be used for the disposal of hazardous wastes, is the trustee personally liable for response costs regardless of the trust's ability to indemnify him?

HOLDING AND DECISION: (Conti, J.) Yes. Where a trustee has power to control the use of trust property and knowingly allows the property to be used for the disposal of hazardous wastes, the trustee is personally liable for response costs regardless of the trust's ability to indemnify him. The trust instrument provided VNB (D) with full power to hold, manage, operate, and control trust property, also vesting VNB (D) with all the powers held by an absolute owner of property. Thus, VNB (D) had authority to control the use of trust property as a matter of law. VNB (D) made the decision to purchase a waste disposal site as a trust asset and to continue leasing the landfill to GSC (D) for disposal of hazardous substances. Thus, VNB's (D) motion for partial summary judgment limiting its liability must be denied.

EDITOR'S ANALYSIS: Liability for response costs for cleanup of hazardous materials is provided for by the Comprehensive Environmental Response, Compensation, and Liability Act (CERCLA), 42 U.S.C. § 9607. The court also referred to the rules of liability of trustees for tort provided in §§ 264 and 265 of the Restatement (Second) of Torts. Since nothing in CERCLA or its legislative history indicated congressional intent with regard to the problems at issue here, the court concluded that Congress expected the courts to develop a federal common law to supplement the statute.

QUICKNOTES

TESTAMENTARY TRUST - A trust created by will and only effective after the grantor's death, since the assets that comprise the corpus of the trust are assumed to vest at that time.

PERSONAL LIABILITY - An obligation pursuant to which the personal assets of an individual may be required for payment.

INDEMNIFICATION - The payment by a corporation of expenses incurred by its officers or directors as a result of litigation involving the corporation.

REVOCABLE TRUST - The holding of property by one party for the benefit of another pursuant to an instrument in which the creator reserves the right to revoke the trust.

NOTES:

CHAPTER 13
WEALTH TRANSFER TAXATION: TAX PLANNING

QUICK REFERENCE RULES OF LAW

1. **The Federal Gift Tax.** If a trustee is free to exercise his unfettered discretion and there is nothing to impel or compel him to invade the corpus, the settlor retains a mere expectancy which does not make the gift of corpus incomplete, thus indicating that the settlor has abandoned dominion and control over the property. (Holtz's Estate v. Commissioner)

   [For more information on estate taxes, see Casenote Law Outline on Wills, Trusts & Estates, Chapter 10, § III, Tax Advantages of Irrevocable Trusts.]

2. **The Federal Gift Tax.** When a trust instrument gives a beneficiary the legal power to demand immediate possession of corpus, that power constitutes a present interest in property sufficient to qualify for a gift tax exclusion. (Estate of Cristofani v. Commissioner)

   [For more information on annual exemption, see Casenote Law Outline on Wills, Trusts and Estates, Chapter 10, § III, Tax Advantages of Irrevocable Trusts.]

3. **The Federal Estate Tax.** The value of property disposed of during a decedent's lifetime shall be included in the gross estate where she has retained possession or enjoyment of it until her death and the transfer was not a bona fide sale for adequate and full consideration. (Estate of Maxwell v. Commissioner)

4. **The Federal Gift Tax.** The corpus of a trust included in an estate will not be fixed solely because the settlor named himself as trustee. (Old Country Trust Co. v. United States)

   [For more information on taxable estates, see Casenote Law Outline on Wills, Trusts & Estates, Chapter 10, § III, Tax Advantages of Irrevocable Trusts.]

5. **The Federal Gift Tax.** A power vested in a trustee to invade the principal of the trust for his own benefit is sufficient to find the decedent trustee to have a general power of appointment, unless the power is limited by an ascertainable standard related to health, education, support, or maintenance. (Estate of Vissering v. Commissioner)

   [For more information on estate tax consequences, see Casenote Law Outline on Wills, Trusts and Estates, Chapter 10, § V, Discretionary Trusts.]

6. **The Federal Gift Tax.** A trust provision making the beneficiary the trustee and designating the proceeds to be used for the beneficiary's "benefit" render the corpus part of the beneficiary's taxable estate. (De Oliveira v. United States)

   [For more information on bypass trusts, see Casenote Law Outline on Wills, Trusts & Estates, Chapter 10, § III, Tax Advantages of Irrevocable Trusts.]

7. **Insert Section Heading.** Where a settlor's executors elect to take a marital deduction in the estate of the settlor for qualifying terminable interest property, the trust property must then be included in the estate of the surviving spouse for federal estate tax purposes. (Loeser v. Talbot)

   [For more information on marital deduction, see Casenote Law Outline on Wills, Trusts and Estates, Chapter 10, § III, Tax Advantages of Irrevocable Trusts.]

HOLTZ'S ESTATE v. COMMISSIONER
Trustee (P) v. Commissioner (D)
U.S. Tax Ct., 38 T.C. 37 (1962).

NATURE OF CASE: Appeal from imposition of gift tax.

FACT SUMMARY: Holtz's estate (P) disputed a determination by the Commissioner (D) that taxable gifts resulted from transfers to a trust that he established.

CONCISE RULE OF LAW: If a trustee is free to exercise his unfettered discretion and there is nothing to impel or compel him to invade the corpus, the settlor retains a mere expectancy which does not make the gift of corpus incomplete, thus indicating that the settlor has abandoned dominion and control over the property.

FACTS: Holtz transferred funds to a trust by deed of trust in 1953, wherein Holtz was the settlor and the Land Title Bank was the trustee. The trust instrument provided that during the lifetime of the settlor the income should be paid to him and as much principal as the trustee "may from time to time think is desirable for the welfare, comfort and support of the Settlor, or for his hospitalization or other emergency needs." At the settlor's death, the income of the trust would go to his wife if she survived him, as well as any of the principal that she might need in accordance with the trustee's discretion. The trust was to terminate at the death of the survivor of the settlor and his wife, and the remaining principal was payable to the survivor's estate. Holtz transferred property worth $384,117 to the trust in 1953, and in 1955, he transferred an additional $50,000 in cash. The Commissioner (D) subsequently determined that as a result of these transfers, Holtz made taxable gifts which were subject to the appropriate gift tax. Holtz's estate (P) contested and claimed that the transfers were not completed gifts and not subject to a gift tax.

ISSUE: If a trustee is free to exercise his unfettered discretion and there is nothing to impel or compel him to invade the corpus, does the settlor retain a mere expectancy which does not make the gift of corpus incomplete?

HOLDING AND DECISION: (Drennan, J.) Yes. The rule generally is that if the trustee is free to exercise his unfettered discretion and there is nothing to impel or compel him to invade the corpus, the settlor retains a mere expectancy which establishes a completed gift to the corpus. However, where, as here, the trustee's discretion is governed by some external standard which a court may apply in compelling compliance with the conditions of the trust agreement and the trustee's power to invade is unlimited, then the gift of corpus in unlimited. Since the trustee had the unfettered power to use all of the corpus for the benefit of the settlor, it was entirely possible that the entire corpus might be distributed to the settlor during his lifetime with the result that no one other than the settlor would receive any portion

thereof. As long as that possibility was present pursuant to the terms of the trust agreement, then the settlor had not abandoned sufficient control and dominion over the property to make the gift complete. Reversed.

EDITOR'S ANALYSIS: The donor has the primary liability for paying the gift tax, and if the donor does not pay, then the donee is liable for the unpaid gift tax. The executor or administrator of a decedent's estate has personal liability for payment of the estate tax but is only limited for reimbursement out of the decedent's estate. Persons in possession of the decedents property are liable for the tax due if there is no administration of the estate.

[For more information on estate taxes, see Casenote Law Outline on Wills, Trusts & Estates, Chapter 10, § III, Tax Advantages of Irrevocable Trusts.]

QUICKNOTES
GIFT TAX - A tax levied on the transfer of property that is made as a gift.

SETTLOR - The grantor or donor of property that is to be held in trust for the benefit of another.

NOTES:

ESTATE OF CRISTOFANI v. COMMISSIONER
Trustee (P) v. Commissioner (D)
T.C., 97 T.C. 74 (1991).

NATURE OF CASE: Appeal from a disallowance of an annual gift exclusion.

FACT SUMMARY: After establishing an irrevocable trust for her two children and five grandchildren, Maria Cristofani claimed two $70,000 annual transfers to the trust qualified as annual exclusions under federal tax law.

CONCISE RULE OF LAW: When a trust instrument gives a beneficiary the legal power to demand immediate possession of corpus, that power constitutes a present interest in property sufficient to qualify for a gift tax exclusion.

FACTS: Decedent Maria Cristofani established an irrevocable trust for her two children and five grandchildren. The parents were named as trustees for the children's trust. All seven beneficiaries of the trust had the right to withdraw an annual amount not to exceed the amount specified for the federal gift tax exclusion, that is, up to $10,000. There was no agreement or understanding between Maria, the trustees, and the beneficiaries that the grandchildren would not immediately exercise their withdrawal rights. Thus, Maria did not report two $70,000 transfers to the trust, claiming them as seven annual exclusions for each of the applicable periods. The Commissioner (D) allowed the annual exclusions with respect to Maria's two children but disallowed the exclusions for the five grandchildren after determining that they were not transfers of present interests in property. Maria's estate (P) appealed.

ISSUE: When a trust instrument gives a beneficiary the legal power to demand immediate possession of corpus, does that power constitute a present interest in property?

HOLDING AND DECISION: (Ruwe, J.) Yes. When a trust instrument gives a beneficiary the legal power to demand immediate possession of corpus, that power constitutes a present interest in property sufficient to qualify for a gift tax exclusion. The likelihood that a beneficiary will actually receive present enjoyment of the property is not the test for determining whether a present interest has been received. In this case, each grandchild possessed the legal right to withdraw trust corpus, and the trustees would be unable to legally resist a grandchild's withdrawal demand. Moreover, based upon the provisions of the children's trust, Cristofani intended to benefit her grandchildren, contrary to the contention of the Commissioner (D). Although the grandchildren never exercised their respective withdrawal rights, this does not vitiate the fact that they had the legal right to do so. Accordingly, the exclusions are allowed.

EDITOR'S ANALYSIS: The court here relied on Crummey v. Commissioner, 397 F.2d 82 (9th Cir. 1968), which originally granted the gift tax shelter to beneficiaries with withdrawal powers. This case is important because it extends the annual exclusion to so-called Crummey power holders who are only contingent beneficiaries, like Maria's grandchildren. It is a victory for taxpayers because it supports an increased number of $10,000 tax-free gifts available to trustors.

[For more information on annual exemption, see Casenote Law Outline on Wills, Trusts and Estates, Chapter 10, § III, Tax Advantages of Irrevocable Trusts.]

QUICKNOTES
DURABLE POWER OF ATTORNEY - A written document pursuant to which one party confers the authority to act as an agent on his behalf to another party and which is to become effective if the grantor should later become incapacitated.

GIFT TAX - A tax levied on the transfer of property that is made as a gift.

DONEE - A person to whom a gift is made.

FUTURE INTEREST - An interest in property the right to possession or enjoyment of which is to take place at some time in the future.

REMAINDER INTEREST - An interest in land that remains after the termination of the immediately preceding estate.

CORPUS - The principal property comprising a trust, not including interest or income.

NOTES:

ESTATE OF MAXWELL v. COMMISSIONER
Estate (P) v. Tax commissioner (D)
3 F.3d 591 (2nd Cir. 1993).

NATURE OF CASE: Appeal from assessment of estate tax deficiency.

FACT SUMMARY: When decedent transferred property to her son and his wife at the end of her life with the intention of remaining in possession so that he would not have to pay off a mortgage note executed in her favor, the Commissioner of the IRS (D) assessed a deficiency against her estate (P) when it reported only the unpaid balance on the note rather than the fair market value of the residence, which was twice as much.

CONCISE RULE OF LAW: The value of property disposed of during a decedent's lifetime shall be included in the gross estate where she has retained possession or enjoyment of it until her death and the transfer was not a bona fide sale for adequate and full consideration.

FACTS: Decedent, an eighty-two-year-old suffering from cancer, conveyed her personal residence of twenty-seven years to her son and only heir and his wife, the Maxwells, for $270,000. Decedent forgave $20,000 of the purchase price at the time of the transfer, and a note for $250,000 was executed in her favor. Simultaneously, the home was leased back to her for five years. Two days later, decedent executed a will with a provision forgiving the balance owing on the note at her death. After the transfer, she continued to live alone in the house until her death two years later. During that time, the rent payments by decedent functionally canceled out interest payments on the note paid by the Maxwells, and she forgave $20,000 on the note each year. Less than two months after her death, the house was sold for $550,000. On the decedent's estate tax return, the estate (P) reported only the $210,000 remaining on the debt. The IRS Commissioner (D) found that the transaction was a transfer with retained life estate and assessed an estate tax deficiency to adjust for the difference between the reported $210,000 and the fair market value of $550,000. The estate (P) appealed to the Tax Court. At oral argument, the estate (P) admitted that there was an intention among the parties that the mortgage note not be paid. The Tax Court affirmed the Commissioner's (D) ruling, and the estate (P) appealed.

ISSUE: Shall the value of property disposed of during a decedent's lifetime be included in the gross estate where she has retained possession or enjoyment of the property until her death and the transfer was not a bona fide sale for adequate and full consideration?

HOLDING AND DECISION: (Lasker, J.) Yes. The value of property disposed of during a decedent's lifetime shall be included in the gross estate where she has retained possession or enjoyment of it until her death, unless the transfer was a bona fide sale for adequate and full consideration. Possession or enjoyment of property is retained by the transferor when there is an express or implied understanding to that effect among the parties at the time of the transfer. The burden is on the decedent's estate to disprove the existence of any adverse implied agreement or understanding. The estate (P) has not met its burden in this case. Similarly, intent is a relevant inquiry in determining whether a transaction is bona fide. Where, as here, there is an implied agreement between the parties that the grantee would never be called upon to make any payments to the grantor, the note given by the grantee has no value at all. Therefore, the conveyance to the Maxwells was not a bona fide sale for an adequate and full consideration. Affirmed.

EDITOR'S ANALYSIS: The case above involved the application of § 2036(a) of the Internal Revenue Code. Section 2036(a) provides: "The value of the gross estate shall include the value of all property to the extent of any interest therein of which the decedent has at any time made a transfer (except in case of a bona fide sale for an adequate and full consideration in money or money's worth), by trust or otherwise, under which he has retained for his life or for any period which does not in fact end before his death — (1) The possession or enjoyment of, or the right to the income from, the property, or (2) The right, either alone or in conjunction with any person, to designate the persons who shall possess or enjoy the property or the income therefrom."

QUICKNOTES
LIFE ESTATE - An interest in land measured by the life of the tenant or a third party.

DECEDENT - A person who is deceased.

CONSIDERATION - Value given by one party in exchange for performance, or a promise to perform, by another party.

BONA FIDE - In good faith.

OLD COLONY TRUST CO. v. UNITED STATES
Estate Administrator (D) v. U.S. (P)
423 F.2d 601 (1st Cir. 1970).

NATURE OF CASE: Appeal from finding of estate tax deficiency.

FACT SUMMARY: Old Colony (D), the administrator of the estate of the unnamed decedent, contended that the estate should not be taxed on a trust established by the settlor which gave the trustee power to stop payments to the settlor's son at any time.

CONCISE RULE OF LAW: The corpus of a trust included in an estate will not be fixed solely because the settlor named himself as trustee.

FACTS: The decedent, unnamed in the case, established an inter vivos trust prior to his death in which the initial life beneficiary of the trust was the settlor's adult son. Eighty percent of the income was normally to be payable to him and the balance added to the principal. Article 4 of the trust agreement permitted the trustees to increase the percentage of income payable to the son beyond the 80% "in their absolute discretion . . . when in their opinion such increase is needed in case of sickness, or desirable in view of changed circumstances." In addition, under Article 4 the trustees were given the discretion to cease paying income to the son and add it all to principal "during such period as the Trustees may decide that the stoppage of such payments is for his best interests." Article 7 gave the trustees broad administrative and management powers over the trust corpus. After the death of the settlor, who also had acted as the sole trustee of the trust, the Government (P) sought to include the corpus of the trust in the estate of the settlor, contending that the settlor had possessed the ownership of the corpus because he could designate the persons who could enjoy its income and that until the date of his death he had an absolute right to alter, amend, or terminate the trust. After the trial court ruled for the Government (P), the executor of the Estate (D) appealed.

ISSUE: Will the corpus of a trust included in an estate not be taxed solely because the settlor named himself as trustee?

HOLDING AND DECISION: (Aldrich, J.) Yes. A settlor will not find the corpus of the trust included in his estate merely because he named himself a trustee. He must have reserved a power to himself that is inconsistent with the full termination of ownership. Trustee powers given for the administration or management of the trust must be equitably exercised for the benefit of the trust as a whole. It is difficult to see how a power can be subject to control by the probate court and exercisable only in what the trustee fairly concludes is in the interests of the trust and its beneficiaries as a whole and at the same time be an ownership power. However, under Article 4 of the trust, the trustees could increase the life tenant's income "in case of sickness, or in view of changed circumstances." Alternatively, they could reduce it "for his best interests." Additional payments to a beneficiary whenever in his best interests is a broad standard, showing the plain indicia of ownership. With the present settlor-trustee free to determine the standard himself, a finding of ownership was warranted. To put it another way, the cost of holding onto the strings may prove to be a rope burn. Affirmed.

EDITOR'S ANALYSIS: In this case, the court held that the mere grant of administrative control to the trustees did not equate to indicia of ownership. In its decision, the court held that no aggregation of purely administrative powers can meet the government's amorphous test of "sufficient dominion and control" so as to be equated with ownership. The court also noted that trustee powers were not to be construed more broadly for tax purposes than a probate court would construe them for administrative purposes.

[For more information on taxable estates, see Casenote Law Outline on Wills, Trusts & Estates, Chapter 10, § III, Tax Advantages of Irrevocable Trusts.]

QUICKNOTES

INTER VIVOS TRUST - Property that is held by one person for the benefit of another and which is created by an instrument that takes effect during the life of the grantor.

TRUST CORPUS - The aggregate body of assets placed into a trust.

NOTES:

ESTATE OF VISSERING v. COMMISSIONER
Trustees (P) v. Commissioner (D)
990 F.2d 578 (10th Cir. 1993).

NATURE OF CASE: Appeal from a judgment including the assets of a trust in the gross estate of a cotrustee.

FACT SUMMARY: Because the tax court determined that Vissering, at the time of his death, held a general power of appointment over the assets of a trust of which he was a cotrustee, the court included the assets of the trust in Vissering's gross estate (P) for federal estate tax purposes.

CONCISE RULE OF LAW: A power vested in a trustee to invade the principal of the trust for his own benefit is sufficient to find the decedent trustee to have a general power of appointment, unless the power is limited by an ascertainable standard related to health, education, support, or maintenance.

FACTS: Vissering and a bank were cotrustees of a trust created by his mother. The trust agreement authorized the trustees to pay over, use, or expend, for the direct or indirect benefit of any of the beneficiaries, whatever amount or amounts of the principal of the trust as may, in the discretion of the trustees, be required for the continued comfort, support, maintenance, or education of said beneficiary. The tax court found that Vissering held a general power of appointment at the time of his death, and therefore, the assets of the trust were to be included in his gross estate for federal estate tax purposes. The Estate (P) appealed.

ISSUE: Is a power vested in a trustee to invade the principal of the trust for his own benefit sufficient to find the decedent trustee to have a general power of appointment, unless the power is limited by an ascertainable standard related to health, education, support, or maintenance?

HOLDING AND DECISION: (Logan, C.J.) Yes. A power vested in a trustee to invade the principal of the trust for his own benefit is sufficient to find the decedent trustee to have a general power of appointment, unless the power is limited by an ascertainable standard related to health, education, support, or maintenance. A trust document permitting invasion of principal for comfort, without further qualifying language, creates a general power of appointment. However, there is modifying language in the trust at issue. "Comfort," in context, does not permit an unlimited power of invasion. Moreover, invasion of the corpus is permitted only to the extent "required," not to the extent "determined" or "desired." Thus, the tax court erred in finding that Vissering had a general power of appointment includable in his estate (P). Reversed and remanded.

EDITOR'S ANALYSIS: The court of appeals undertook a de novo review. Since the trust was created in Florida, specifying that Florida law controlled, the court of appeals looked to what it believed the Florida courts would hold. The estate (P) argued unsuccessfully that Vissering (P) was not a trustee at the time of death since he had been judged incapacitated by a New Mexico court.

[For more information on estate tax consequences, see Casenote Law Outline on Wills, Trusts and Estates, Chapter 10, § V, Discretionary Trusts.]

QUICKNOTES

POWER OF APPOINTMENT - Power, created by another person in connection with a gratuitous transfer (often in trust), residing in a person (as trustee or otherwise) to affect the disposition or distribution of the property.

CONTINGENT BENEFICIARY - A third party who is the recipient of the benefit of a transaction undertaken by another, the receipt of which is based on the uncertain happening of another event.

REMAINDER BENEFICIARY - A person who is to receive property that is held in trust after the termination of a preceding income interest.

NOTES:

DE OLIVEIRA v. UNITED STATES

Executor (P) v. IRS (D)

767 F.2d 1344 (9th Cir. 1985).

NATURE OF CASE: Appeal of order dismissing action seeking estate tax refund.

FACT SUMMARY: The IRS (D) contended that a trust provision making the beneficiary the trustee and designating the proceeds to be used for her "benefit" rendered the corpus part of the beneficiary's taxable estate.

CONCISE RULE OF LAW: A trust provision making the beneficiary the trustee and designating the proceeds to be used for the beneficiary's "benefit" render the corpus part of the beneficiary's taxable estate.

FACTS: Jose de Oliveira created a testamentary trust. His wife, Serafina, was designated trustee. During her life, she was sole beneficiary. The trust instructed that the proceeds were to be used for her benefit. Upon her death, the corpus was to be distributed to Jose's children. When Serafina died, the IRS (D) ruled that the trust corpus was part of Serafina's estate. Her executor (P) paid the assessment and sued for a refund. The district court granted summary judgment in favor of the IRS (D), and the executor (P) appealed.

ISSUE: Will a trust provision making the beneficiary the trustee and designating the proceeds to be used for the beneficiary's "benefit" render the corpus part of the beneficiary's taxable estate?

HOLDING AND DECISION: (Sneed, J.) Yes. A trust provision making the beneficiary the trustee and designating the proceeds to be used for the beneficiary's benefit will render the corpus part of the beneficiary's taxable estate. Under 26 U.S.C. § 2041, trust corpus shall be considered part of a decedent taxpayer's estate if the taxpayer had a general power of appointment over the corpus. When a taxpayer is both trustee and beneficiary, the taxpayer necessarily has such power. The powers of the taxpayer as trustee may be limited by trust language. However, the mere recitation that the proceeds shall be used for the taxpayer's "benefit" is sufficient to limit the taxpayer's appointment power so as to render § 2041 inoperative, as the taxpayer retains full discretion. This being so, the refund claim was properly denied. Affirmed.

EDITOR'S ANALYSIS: The executor (P) argued that certain extrinsic evidence demonstrated that Jose had not intended to give Serafina a general power to alienate the proceeds. The court refused to consider this. The court took the position that it had to construe the will as it was written and not rewrite it to satisfy the testator's purposes.

_____

[For more information on bypass trusts, see Casenote Law Outline on Wills, Trusts & Estates, Chapter 10, § III, Tax Advantages of Irrevocable Trusts.]

QUICKNOTES

TESTAMENTARY TRUST - A trust created by will and only effective after the grantor's death, since the assets that comprise the corpus of the trust are assumed to vest at that time.

ESTATE TAX - A tax levied on the right to dispose of property upon death.

CORPUS - The principal property comprising a trust, not including interest or income.

EXTRINSIC EVIDENCE - Evidence that is not contained within the text of a document or contract but which is derived from the parties' statements or the circumstances under which the agreement was made.

POWER OF ATTORNEY - A written instrument which allows a person to appoint an agent and confer authority to perform certain specified acts on his behalf.

NOTES:

LOESER v. TALBOT
Trustees (P) v. Beneficiaries (D)
Mass. Sup. Ct., 412 Mass. 361, 589 N.E.2d 301 (1992).

NATURE OF CASE: Grant of direct appellate review of a complaint for reformation of a trust.

FACT SUMMARY: The trustees (P) and beneficiaries (D) of a trust sought reformation due to a scrivener's error, since the error would defeat the settlor's attempt to qualify the trust property for the marital deduction allowed under federal estate tax law.

CONCISE RULE OF LAW: Where a settlor's executors elect to take a marital deduction in the estate of the settlor for qualifying terminable interest property, the trust property must then be included in the estate of the surviving spouse for federal estate tax purposes.

FACTS: A trust established by Talbot created a terminable interest trust to Mrs. Talbot which would pay her an income during her lifetime. Talbot intended that the trust was to terminate upon her death, whereupon any unpaid trust income would be subject to her general testamentary power of appointment, and any remaining principal would be subject to her special testamentary power of appointment. The trustees and beneficiaries contended, however, that the above powers of appointment were reversed in the trust instrument due to a scrivener's error. Such error defeated Talbot's attempt to qualify the trust property for the marital deduction allowed under federal estate tax law. Thus, the trustees (P) and beneficiaries (D) sought reformation of the instrument. The probate court reserved and reported the case without decision to the appeals court. The supreme court granted the parties' application for direct appellate review.

ISSUE: Where a settlor's executors elect to take a marital deduction in the estate of the settlor for qualifying terminable interest property, must the trust property then be included in the estate of the surviving spouse for federal estate tax purposes?

HOLDING AND DECISION: (Liacos, C.J.) Yes. Where a settlor's executors elect to take a marital deduction in the estate of the settlor for qualifying terminable interest property, the trust property must then be included in the estate of the surviving spouse for federal estate tax purposes. Here, the trust document shows on its face that the powers of appointment granted to Mrs. Talbot were an integral part of Talbot's plan to qualify the trust for the marital deduction. If the powers of appointment as stated in the trust are simply reversed, the trust instrument implements a complex estate plan. Absent reformation, the powers of appointment thwart an otherwise coherent plan. Thus, reformation is necessary to effectuate Talbot's actual intent. The case is remanded to the probate court for entry of a judgment of reformation.

EDITOR'S ANALYSIS: The marital deduction provision is found in § 2056(7) of the Internal Revenue Code. The court noted that a mistake or inadvertence of a scrivener would be reformed upon full, clear, and decisive proof of such a mistake. If the requested reformation had not been granted here, the trust property would have been subject to nearly $400,000 in otherwise avoidable taxes.

[For more information on marital deduction, see Casenote Law Outline on Wills, Trusts and Estates, Chapter 10, § III, Tax Advantages of Irrevocable Trusts.]

QUICKNOTES
MARITAL DEDUCTION - A tax deduction under federal law for transfers of property made between spouses.

POWER OF APPOINTMENT - Power, created by another person in connection with a gratuitous transfer (often in trust), residing in a person (as trustee or otherwise) to affect the disposition or distribution of the property.

GENERAL POWER OF APPOINTMENT - Authority granted to an individual, pursuant to a will or deed, to make decisions regarding the selection of persons to receive the income or property of an estate following the death of the grantor, and which is exercisable in favor of any person.

SPECIAL POWER OF APPOINTMENT - Authority granted to an individual, pursuant to a will or deed, to make decisions regarding the selection of persons to receive the income or property of an estate following the death of the grantor; the donee may only exercise the power in favor of specified persons.

NOTES:

NOTES

ABBREVIATIONS FOR BRIEFING

The following list of abbreviations will assist you in the process of briefing and provide an illustration of the technique of formulating functional personal abbreviations for commonly encountered words, phrases, and concepts.

acceptance	acp	offer	O
affirmed	aff	offeree	OE
answer	ans	offeror	OR
assumption of risk	a/r	ordinance	ord
attorney	atty	pain and suffering	p/s
beyond a reasonable doubt	b/r/d	parol evidence	p/e
bona fide purchaser	BFP	plaintiff	P
breach of contract	br/k	prima facie	p/f
cause of action	c/a	probable cause	p/c
common law	c/l	proximate cause	px/c
Constitution	Con	real property	r/p
constitutional	con	reasonable doubt	r/d
contract	K	reasonable man	r/m
contributory negligence	c/n	rebuttable presumption	rb/p
cross	x	remanded	rem
cross-complaint	x/c	res ipsa loquitur	RIL
cross-examination	x/ex	respondent superior	r/s
cruel and unusual punishment	c/u/p	Restatement	RS
defendant	D	reversed	rev
dismissed	dis	Rule Against Perpetuities	RAP
double jeopardy	d/j	search and seizure	s/s
due process	d/p	search warrant	s/w
equal protection	e/p	self-defense	s/d
equity	eq	specific performance	s/p
evidence	ev	statute of limitations	S/L
exclude	exc	statute of frauds	S/F
exclusionary rule	exc/r	statute	S
felony	f/m	summary judgment	s/j
freedom of speech	f/s	tenancy in common	t/c
good faith	g/f	tenancy at will	t/w
habeas corpus	h/c	tenant	t
hearsay	hr	third party	TP
husband	H	third party beneficiary	TPB
in loco parentis	ILP	transferred intent	TI
injunction	inj	unconscionable	uncon
inter vivos	I/v	unconstitutional	unconst
joint tenancy	j/t	undue influence	u/e
judgment	judgt	Uniform Commercial Code	UCC
jurisdiction	jur	unilateral	uni
last clear chance	LCC	vendee	VE
long-arm statute	LAS	vendor	VR
majority view	maj	versus	v
meeting of minds	MOM	void for vagueness	VFV
minority view	min	weight of the evidence	w/e
Miranda warnings	Mir/w	weight of authority	w/a
Miranda rule	Mir/r	wife	W
negligence	neg	with	w/
notice	mtc	within	w/I
nuisance	nus	without prejudice	w/o/p
obligation	ob	without	w/o
obscene	obs	wrongful death	wr/d